ORIENTAL COOKING

ORIENTAL COOKING

Khalid Aziz,   Deh-Ta Hsiung
Emi Kazuko,   Sallie Morris

Edited by Jeni Wright

WHSMITH

EXCLUSIVE
·BOOKS·

Acknowledgements

Cookery Editor: Eve Dowling
General Editor: Jeni Wright

Art Editor/Design: Alyson Kyles
Designer: Sue Storey

Photography: Martin Brigdale
Stylist: Liz Hippisley

Home Economists: Sarah Bush
                    Dolly Meers
                    Sallie Morris

Illustration: Lorraine Harrison

Notes

For all recipes, quantities are given in both metric and imperial measures. Follow either set but *not* a mixture of both, as they are not interchangeable.

All spoon measures are level.
I tablespoon = 15ml
I teaspoon   = 5ml
All eggs are sizes 3 or 4 (standard).

Details of specialist ingredients can be found in the glossary on pages 184–187

The publishers would like to thank the following for providing the photographs in this book: Biofotos 1, 7; Sally & Richard Greenhill 8 left; Susan Griggs Agency (Robert Holmes) 9 above, (Keith MacGregor) 6, (Joseph F. Viesti) 8 right; Zefa Picture Library 9 below.

This edition published
exclusively for W H Smith
by Octopus Books Limited
59, Grosvenor Street
LONDON WIX 9DA

© Octopus Books Limited 1986

ISBN 0 7064 2578 2

Printed In Italy

CONTENTS

INTRODUCTION

The subject of oriental cookery is immensely rich and varied. In this volume four specialist authors have come together to bring you their own individual interpretations, making this a valuable and unique collection of authentic recipes from the Orient.

The four chapters of this book will take you on an exciting culinary journey: through the sub-continent of **India** where you will find that 'fiery' curries are only a small part of the diverse cuisine based on religious beliefs, geography, climate and availability of ingredients; around **China**, where for centuries simple ingredients of differing colours, textures and flavours have been combined with infinite care to create a harmonious dish; into **Japan & Korea**, where you will discover Japan's culinary secrets – for centuries hidden from Western eyes – and sample the taste and visual delights of their sophisticated cooking. Finally, island-hop around **South-East Asia**, an area that comprises a variety of races, landscapes and cultures and has many culinary experiences to offer.

Every recipe in this book will interest and inspire you; each has an informative introduction charting fascinating facts about its history, traditions and customs, as well as interesting information regarding the cooking styles and techniques that are involved A glossary of foods has also been included to help identify the more obscure ingredients! For the more ambitious, each chapter includes a section on **Menu Planning & Customs** and provides a comprehensive guide to cooking, serving and eating a meal in the traditional style of each country.

Oriental Cooking captures the essence of the Far East in words, pictures and, above all, in the taste of the recipes you can create at home.

In the chapter on **Indian & Pakistan** the recipes are separated into sections according to types of dishes, rather than the different regional styles. Regional differences can be seen through the various culinary techniques used. These range from the barbecue-style tandoori food of northern India and Pakistan, where meat is marinated before cooking, to the rich, slow-cooked curries of the Mughal-influenced Delhi school. Central India has created drier vegetable dishes that cook in a matter of minutes, whereas further south the dishes become hotter and coconut is frequently added. At the southern tip of the sub-continent there are the fiery concoctions of Madras, while the coastal and delta regions have developed spicy masalas for coating fish prior to baking or charcoal grilling.

Cooking Inidan food is far more straightforward than many other styles of cooking; there are no heart-stopping soufflé-type dishes, for example! Indian food is forgiving, especially when it comes to the curries, where the technique is simple, based on making a spicy sauce in which the main ingredient is cooked. There are no special utensils required with Indian cookery – most recipes require no more than a heavy-based saucepan. Even the tandoori dishes, which get their name from the clay oven, or *tandoor*, in which they are traditionally cooked, can be made using the combination of a conventional Western oven and a charcoal barbecue.

China is a vast country with many distinct regional cooking styles, but for the purpose of this book the Chinese chapter is divided into sections according to different cooking methods. These sections also follow one another according to their order in a Chinese meal, making it easier for the Western reader to select an authentic Chinese menu. The vast expanse of China means that the climate ranges from sub-arctic conditions in the north to tropical temperatures in the south, thus giving China tremendous regional differences and making Chinese food immensely varied. However, the fundamental character of Chinese cooking is the same throughout the whole country – whether the Peking cuisine of the north, the diverse Cantonese-style of cooking in the south, or the piquant and spicy Sichuan food of the west, all Chinese food is prepared, cooked and served according to the *fan-cai* principle. Chinese meals should always have two parts: *fan* and *cai*. The *fan* is the staple grain part: in the north of China it is likely to be based on wheat flour, whereas in the south it is almost always rice. The *cai* are all the other dishes, in other words the meat, poultry, fish and vegetables. *Cai* dishes are chosen to harmonize with one another, not only in flavour but also in colour, aroma and texture, so that all the senses are satisfied in one meal.

Remember, too, that the Chinese cooking tradition of harmony extends beyond the food itself to those who are eating it, an aspect which is often overlooked. There is a great feeling of togetherness in the way Chinese people eat; everyone gathers around the table and partakes of all the dishes in communal style.

Japan & Korea are combined in one chapter. Although the cooking styles of these two countries are quite distinct, there are many similarities due to geographical, historical and cultural links. Quality and freshness of ingredients are of prime importance when preparing both Japanese and Korean food, and no self-respecting cook from either country would consider preparing a meal with inferior raw materials. Although perhaps less well-known in the West than other oriental cuisines, both Japanese and Korean foods are surprisingly simple to prepare and cook.

Japanese food in particular is appreciated as much for its aesthetic beauty as for its flavour, and if the Western cook has patience and is willing to spend time on careful preparation and presentation, the effort will be well rewarded. Some of the garnishes and decorations which

ABOVE *Indonesia: bananas grow prolifically throughout South-East Asia and are incorporated in many of the traditional dishes.* RIGHT *Thailand: Bangkok's famous floating vegetable market.*

are seen in Japanese restaurants require a considerable amount of skill and are best left to the professionals, but all of the garnishes used in this book are quite simple to prepare at home. Grated daikon (Japanese radish) is the easiest of all the garnishes for savoury foods, and yet it is authentic and is a great favourite with the Japanese themselves. Carrots can be easily shaped into pretty flowers, fans and triangles, tomatoes into roses and the rind of citrus fruits into fans.

The geographical area known as **South-East Asia** has, for the purposes of this volume, been divided into six separate sections — Indonesia, Malaysia & Singapore, Thailand, Indo-China (Cambodia, Laos and Vietnam), Burma and the Philippines. Many similarities exist between these countries in that geography and climate produce common raw materials and ingredients. However, this vast area embraces so many different peoples, religions, cultures and creeds, and has been subject to so much foreign invasion and influence from the West, that there is a great diversity in cooking styles and techniques. The recipes in this chapter have been chosen to illustrate this, and to show how each country has retained its own individuality, character and charm. Take a closer look at Indonesia and Malaysia; these cuisines reveal that the Indonesians have been strongly influenced by Dutch settlers and so have a more sophisticated, Western-style of eating, whereas the Malaysians have evolved a rich combination of three separate cuisines — Malay, Chinese and Indian. There are many specialist ingredients in South-East Asian cooking, most of which can be found in good oriental stores and supermarkets. Although many of these ingredients may have strange-sounding names, you will be surprised how soon you become familiar with them. Take the ubiquitous dried shrimp paste for example, which goes by the various names of *blachan*, *terasi*, *ngapi* and *kapi* according to the country in which it is used. It may seem unusually exotic at first, but you will quickly become adept at dry-frying and pounding it before use. Almost without exception, such specialist ingredients are inexpensive to buy and have good keeping qualities. This goes for cooking equipment too; a wok, steamer, mortar and pestle, blender or food processor are the most commonly used pieces of equipment, together with good sharp knives and heavy chopping boards or blocks, which are essential items in any well-equipped Western kitchen.

Confucius said, 'To eat is heaven', and discovering the delights of *Oriental Cooking* is sure to open-up a whole new world.

Selamat Makan — Good Eating.   JENI WRIGHT

ABOVE RIGHT *Japan: the magnificent Mount Fuji whose majestic stature dominates the Japanese landscape.*
BELOW RIGHT *Philippines: rice terraces. Without exception, rice is the staple food through the Orient.*

— INDIA & PAKISTAN —

The Indian sub-continent was one of the earliest regions of the developing world to be criss-crossed by a network of railway lines. Transportation across vast areas of land has meant that the various cooking styles of India are now to be found virtually throughout the country. Distinct cooking styles do still exist, but they owe their survival to a combination of different religions, as well as
wealth, geography and climate.

Hinduism is the predominant religion. Most Hindus are vegetarians, and those who are not *never* eat beef, for the cow is a sacred animal. Muslims and Sikhs are meat eaters, although Muslims regard the pig as unclean and therefore do not eat pork. When it comes to wealth, vegetables are cheap and meat is expensive. Therefore the poorer classes of all religions eat mostly vegetarian food, reserving meat for high days and holidays. Even the more humble Indian food is imaginative – over the centuries the poorer people have learnt to make use of the basic foods, such as the numerous varieties of pulses, turning them into tasty dishes simply by the addition of a few spices. In the areas where food can be gathered from the sea or
the waters of the great river deltas, fish and crustacean
dishes form a valuable part of the diet.

Geography and climate have made their mark on the cuisine of India in that the further south one goes, the hotter the climate and the spicier the food. Also, due to the vast acreage of wheat grown in areas such as the Punjab, a wide selection of breads are popular in the north, whereas rice predominates in the south.

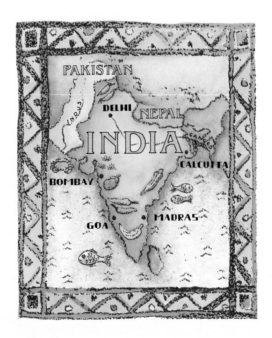

INDIA & PAKISTAN

SNACKS

There is a great tradition of snacks in the Indian sub-continent, and it would be unthinkable for you to be invited to take tea, either in the morning or in the afternoon, without some kind of snack being offered. Whereas in the West this tends to be limited to a few biscuits, in India snacks accompanying tea can range from tit-bits made with flour or semolina to quite substantial and filling meat kebabs and small vegetable fritters called Pakoras.

Snacks are also very popular on shopping expeditions to bazaars, where row upon row of vendors can be seen selling their wares. The Indians were making and eating fast food long before anyone in the West even heard of fish and chip shops and hamburger bars!

Indian snacks are in the main fairly easy to make; to be served at their best many have to be eaten freshly cooked, although some can be cooked in batches and stored in airtight containers.

Suji Karkarias

Fried Semolina Cakes

Semolina, made from hard durum wheat, gives these cakes their characteristic crisp texture. The combination of sweetness and crispness makes these cakes a good accompaniment to lemon tea. They will keep fresh for up to 1 week in an airtight container.

MAKES 20

225 g (8 oz) semolina
750 ml (1¼ pints) milk
175 g (6 oz) soft brown sugar
75 g (3 oz) ghee, melted
20 green cardamoms
10 cloves
25 g (1 oz) shelled pistachios, chopped
3 eggs
vegetable oil, for deep-frying

Put the semolina in a bowl and slowly add the milk, mixing well with a spoon to avoid lumps forming. Sprinkle in the brown sugar, add the ghee and mix again until evenly incorporated.

Transfer the mixture to a heavy-based saucepan and bring slowly to the boil, stirring constantly. Continue to boil gently until the mixture has the consistency of very thick custard, then remove the pan from the heat and set aside to cool.

Meanwhile, remove the outer pods from the cardamoms and place the seeds in a mortar and pestle with the cloves. Grind together until both are reduced to a fairly coarse powder, then mix in the chopped pistachios, but do not grind any further.

Break the eggs one by one into the cold semolina and whisk them into the mixture. Sprinkle in the cardamoms, cloves and pistachios.

Heat the oil in a deep, heavy-based frying pan until a small spoonful of the mixture immediately starts to sizzle and float to the surface when dropped into the pan. Test several times to ensure that the oil is the right temperature. Drop dessertspoonfuls of the mixture into the hot oil and fry in batches until golden brown. Remove with a perforated spoon and place on paper towels to drain while frying the remainder. Serve while slightly warm or leave to cool completely.

Pakoras | Shami Kebab

Chick Pea Flour Fritters

Chick pea flour is far more absorbent than ordinary wheat flour, which means that very small amounts can be mixed with quite a considerable amount of liquid to form a very thick batter. Feel free to experiment with other fillings than aubergine and spinach. Both savoury and sweet fillings can be used – try mushrooms, or apple and banana. Pakoras will keep for up to 1 hour in a warm oven.

MAKES ABOUT 12

175 g (6 oz) natural yogurt
75 g (3 oz) besan (chick pea flour)
2 teaspoons salt
1 teaspoon chilli powder
1 teaspoon garam masala
½ teaspoon turmeric
½ teaspoon freshly ground black pepper
1 long aubergine, weighing about 450 g (1 lb), or about 12 large spinach leaves
600 ml (1 pint) vegetable oil, for deep-frying

Put the yogurt in a medium bowl and sift in the besan, whisking it in well. (The flour tends to form quite hard lumps; these need to be pressed through the sieve with the back of a spoon.) Add the salt, chilli powder, garam masala, turmeric and black pepper and mix in well. Place the bowl in a cool place for at least 1 hour; during this time the flour will absorb the moisture from the yogurt and the mixture will become quite stiff.

Trim the aubergine, but do not peel. Cut the aubergine into 2.5 cm (1 inch) cubes. Heat the oil in a deep, heavy-based frying pan until a small drop of the batter immediately starts to sizzle and float to the surface when dropped into the pan. Coat the pieces of aubergine with the batter; it does not matter if the aubergine is not totally coated. Deep-fry the pakoras in batches in the hot oil until they are golden brown, remove with a perforated spoon and drain on paper towels.

If you are using spinach leaves, remove the hard central rib from any of the larger leaves, then cut the leaves into 5 cm (2 inch) squares. Coat with the batter and fry in the same way as the aubergine slices. Serve hot, as soon as possible after cooking.

Ground Meat Patties

Shami Kebabs can form quite a substantial snack – often a meal in themselves. They are a little time-consuming to prepare, but worth the effort.

MAKES ABOUT 10

50 g (2 oz) ghee
2 medium onions, peeled and thinly sliced
2 garlic cloves, peeled and thinly sliced
4 fresh green chillies, trimmed and chopped
2 teaspoons freshly ground black pepper
2 teaspoons chilli powder
2 teaspoons garam masala
1 teaspoon ground cumin
½ teaspoon ground cinnamon
2 teaspoons salt
100 g (4 oz) channa dal (chick peas), soaked in 1 litre (1¾ pints) cold water overnight
750 g (1½ lb) minced lamb or beef
2 tablespoons chopped fresh coriander leaves
1 egg, beaten
vegetable oil, for shallow-frying
Garnish:
1 large onion, peeled and sliced into thin rings
fresh coriander leaves
2 tomatoes, cut into wedges
1 lemon, cut into wedges

Heat the ghee in a heavy-based saucepan, add the onions, garlic, chillies, spices and salt and fry gently. Drain the channa dal, then add the dal to the pan and cover with fresh cold water. Bring to the boil, then cover the pan and simmer for 1 hour or until tender. Increase the heat and add the minced meat, stirring constantly until the meat is thoroughly cooked and the liquid has been absorbed. Allow to cool.

Grind the mixture to a fine paste with a hand grinder or in a food processor. Mix in the chopped coriander, then chill in the refrigerator for 30 minutes. Form into about 10 patties and coat in the beaten egg. Heat the oil in a deep, heavy-based frying pan, then shallow fry the patties in batches until golden brown, turning once, Garnish and serve.

Dosas

Thin Spiced Pancakes

This snack is traditionally eaten freshly cooked at breakfast. It makes use of the two most freely available ingredients in India: rice and lentils. Traditionally, Dosas are cooked on a heated flat stone, but an ordinary shallow frying pan will serve the same purpose. If liked, 50–100 g (2–4 oz) chopped coriander or spinach leaves may be whisked into the batter, or 1 teaspoon caraway seeds or aniseed.

MAKES 10–15

175 g (6 oz) basmati rice
100 g (4 oz) lentils
2 teaspoons salt
½ teaspoon turmeric
300 ml (½ pint) milk
about 100 g (4 oz) ghee, for frying

Mix the rice and lentils together and wash thoroughly, using at least 3 changes of water. Drain, place in a large bowl and add 2 litres (3½ pints) fresh cold water. Leave to soak for 24 hours.

Drain off the water and grind the rice and lentils finely in a blender or food processor. Sprinkle in the salt and turmeric, then pour in the milk to make a batter, whisking well. Heat a little of the ghee in a shallow, heavy-based frying pan, then pour a little of the batter into the centre of the pan, allowing it to spread to the edges. Cook on one side only until the centre becomes solid, then slide out of the pan on to a warmed serving plate. Repeat with the remaining batter, adding more ghee as necessary. Serve hot, with a selection of chutneys, or eat dosas with Shami Kebab/Ground Meat Patties (page 13) or Ekoori/Indian-style Scrambled Egg, (page 16).

Saag Roti

Chick Pea Flour Bread with Spinach
The nearest Western equivalent to this particular snack would be a slice of pizza. This Eastern recipe is every bit as tasty.

MAKES 6

450 g (1 lb) besan (chick pea flour)
2 teaspoons freshly ground black pepper
1½ teaspoons salt
4 tablespoons chopped fresh coriander leaves
300 ml (½ pint) milk
4 fresh green chillies, cut into
5 mm (¼ inch) pieces
2 teaspoons caraway seeds
12 fresh young spinach leaves, hard central stems removed
50 g (2 oz) ghee
melted butter, to serve

Sift the besan into a bowl together with the black pepper and salt. (The flour tends to form quite hard lumps; these need to be pressed through the sieve with the back of a spoon.) Mix in the chopped coriander. Gradually add the milk, kneading the flour into a hard dough. Knead for at least 10 minutes, then leave the dough to rest in a cool place for 4 hours.

Knead the dough once again, sprinkling in the chillies and caraway seeds. Form the dough into 6 balls then roll each ball into a circle, about 1 cm (½ inch) thick. Take 2 spinach leaves and lay them on top of 1 circle of dough. Fold the dough in half, form into a ball and roll out again into a circle about 1 cm (½ inch) thick. Repeat this process with the remaining spinach leaves and circles of dough. Melt the ghee in a deep, heavy-based frying pan and shallow-fry the bread until brown on each side. Cut each circle of bread into wedges and serve piping hot, covered with melted butter.

Namak Pare

Savoury Unleavened Bread
This is a simple recipe for a very tasty snack. Part of its attraction comes from the inclusion of lovage or caraway seeds. The bread may be stored in an airtight container for up to 1 week.

MAKES ABOUT 25

50 g (2 oz) ghee
100 g (4 oz) strong plain flour
½ teaspoon salt
1 teaspoon lovage or caraway seeds
25 g (1 oz) natural yogurt
vegetable oil, for shallow frying

Heat the ghee in a small saucepan until almost smoking. Sift the flour and salt into a bowl, stir in the lovage or caraway seeds, then pour on the hot ghee and mix well. Add the yogurt and 2 tablespoons cold water and mix to a moist dough.

Knead the dough in the bowl for 5–10 minutes, then set aside to rest for 20 minutes or so. Turn the dough on to a work surface and roll out to a square, about 2 cm (¾ inch) thick. Cut into about 25 cubes. Heat a little oil in a heavy-based frying pan, then shallow-fry the cubes in batches for about 3 minutes until golden brown. Drain on paper towels and leave to cool before serving.

LEFT: *Clockwise from top; Chick Pea Flour Fritters (page 13), Spiced Chick Peas (page 17), Ground Meat Patties (page 13), Chick Pea Flour Bread with Spinach, Thin Spiced Pancakes.*

Gol Guppas

Tamarind Wafers

This is one of the strangest snacks in the world!
As with so many snacks in hot countries, the
idea behind it is to replace some of the loss of
body fluid and salts in a tasty and palatable way.
The tamarind, which gives the main flavouring
to the liquid, is in itself very bitter, and the
addition of salt makes for a juice which is very
much an acquired taste. However, once you do
acquire a taste for Gol Guppas, the chances are
you will want to try them again and again.

MAKES ABOUT 30

100 g (4 oz) strong plain flour
pinch of salt
600 ml (1 pint) vegetable oil, for deep-frying
Tamarind juice:
50 g (2 oz) tamarind
juice of ½ lemon
2 teaspoons salt
1 teaspoon chilli powder
1 teaspoon garam masala
½ teaspoon ground ginger
½ teaspoon freshly ground black pepper

First make the juice: place the tamarind in a bowl, pour
on 600 ml (1 pint) boiling water and leave to soak for at
least 30 minutes.

Meanwhile, make the wafers: sift the flour and salt into
a bowl and gradually add 150 ml (¼ pint) cold water to
form a very stiff, hard dough. Turn the dough on to a
floured surface and knead for at least 10 minutes, then
roll out very thinly, until no more than 1.5 mm (1/16 inch)
thick. Using a plain 2.5 cm (1 inch) pastry cutter, cut the
dough into about 30 circles.

Heat the oil in a deep, heavy-based frying pan until a
small piece of pastry immediately starts to sizzle and float
to the surface when dropped into the pan. Drop a few of
the wafers into the hot oil – they should puff up
immediately. Turn the wafers constantly until they are
uniformly golden brown, then remove from the oil with
a perforated spoon. Leave to drain and cool on paper
towels while frying the remaining wafers.

Meanwhile, strain the liquid from the tamarind
through a wire sieve into a clean bowl, rubbing the
tamarind pulp and seed against the mesh. Add the lemon
juice, sprinkle in the salt, chilli powder, garam masala,
ginger and black pepper and stir well to mix. Chill in the
refrigerator until ready to serve.

To serve Gol Guppas: put 4 or 5 wafers in individual
bowls, then spoon in the chilled juice. To eat the gol
guppas, a small hole should be made in each one and the
juice spooned in.

Ekoori

Indian-style Scrambled Egg

This is a breakfast-time favourite, although it is
equally tasty served in the afternoon. The
technique is very similar to scrambling eggs
Western style, and, no doubt, the now
traditional way of serving it on toast is very
much a Western import. As an alternative, try
serving Ekoori on freshly made Dosas/Thin
Spiced Pancakes (page 14). Or make it a more
substantial dish by adding 225 g (8 oz) peeled
prawns with the onion and garlic. Cooked
mussels or clams could also be used, so too
could flaked crabmeat.

SERVES 4

6 eggs
50 g (2 oz) ghee
1 medium onion, peeled and thinly sliced
1 garlic clove, peeled and thinly sliced
10 cm (4 inch) piece fresh root ginger, peeled
and cut into thin strips
1 teaspoon turmeric
1 teaspoon garam masala
½ teaspoon chilli powder
1 teaspoon salt
4 fresh green chillies, chopped into
5 mm (¼ inch) pieces
hot toast, to serve
chopped fresh coriander leaves, to garnish

Whisk the eggs in a bowl and set aside. Heat the ghee in a
heavy-based saucepan, add the onion and garlic and fry
gently for 4–5 minutes until soft. Add the strips of fresh
ginger and fry gently for a further 2 minutes until
softened, stirring constantly. Add the turmeric, garam
masala, chilli powder and salt and cook for a further
minute, stirring constantly.

Whisk the eggs once again and add to the saucepan.
Cook over gentle heat as for scrambled eggs, scraping
the coagulated egg from the side of the pan until the
mixture is soft and creamy. Remove from the heat
immediately, as the eggs will continue cooking in the
heat of the pan and it is important not to overcook them.

Sprinkle the chopped chillies into the egg, then fold
gently to mix. Pile the scrambled egg on to slices of hot
toast and sprinkle with chopped coriander leaves. Serve
immediately.

Bhalli | Channa Dal

Steamed Lentil Cakes

This is a very popular dish to eat in the heat of the afternoon. Although quite complicated to make, it is well worth the effort.

MAKES 6–8

350 g (12 oz) red lentils
1 teaspoon ground cumin
1 teaspoon chilli powder
1 teaspoon salt
½ teaspoon freshly ground black pepper
25 g (1 oz) fresh coriander leaves, chopped
juice of 1 lemon
225 g (8 oz) natural yogurt

Wash the lentils thoroughly, using at least 3 changes of water. Drain, place in a large bowl and add 1.75 litres (3 pints) fresh cold water. Leave to soak for 36 hours.

Drain off the water and grind the lentils to a fine paste in a blender or food processor. Using cheesecloth or a strong tea towel, squeeze the excess water from the lentils. Transfer the paste to a bowl and mix in the remaining ingredients, except the lemon juice and yogurt. Shape into cakes, 5 cm (2 inches) in diameter and 1 cm (½ inch) thick. Pat dry with paper towels.

Place the cakes in the top of a steamer, cover and steam for 1 hour. If you do not have a steamer, place the cakes in a shallow dish, stand the dish in a roasting tin filled with enough hot water to come halfway up the sides of the dish. Cover the dish and tin with foil, then place the tin in a preheated moderately hot oven (190°C/375°F, Gas Mark 5) and steam for 1 hour. Remove the cakes when they are cooked and allow them to cool completely.

Mix the lemon juice into the yogurt. Put the lentil cakes in a shallow dish and cover with the yogurt mixture. Marinate in the refrigerator for at least 2 hours before serving.

Spiced Chick Peas

These are particularly popular amongst cinema-goers in India. Whereas in the West popcorn is the great cinema snack, in India it is Channa Dal. As the process of making Channa Dal involves quite a lot of time by way of soaking the split peas, it is worth cooking a reasonable amount at one time. Although best eaten within 1 day of making, they will keep for up to 2 weeks in an airtight container.

MAKES ABOUT 450 g (1 lb)

450 g (1 lb) channa dal (chick peas)
1 teaspoon salt
2 teaspoons bicarbonate of soda
vegetable oil, for deep-frying
1 tablespoon garam masala
2 teaspoons chilli powder
1 teaspoon freshly ground black pepper
2 teaspoons salt
2 teaspoons raw cane or soft brown sugar

Wash the channa dal thoroughly. Put the salt and bicarbonate of soda in a large bowl, pour in 2 litres (3½ pints) cold water and stir until dissolved. Add the channa dal and leave to soak for 48 hours.

Drain the channa dal and wash thoroughly in fresh cold water. Drain once more, then spread out on a baking tray and allow to dry in a preheated cool oven (150°C/300°F, Gas Mark 2) for about 30 minutes. Heat the oil in a deep-fat frier until one of the chick peas immediately starts to sizzle and float to the surface when dropped into the pan. Deep-fry the channa dal a few at a time until they start to change colour, then remove with a perforated spoon and drain on paper towels while frying the remainder.

Put the warm channa dal in a large jar with the spices, salt and sugar. Shake until all the channa dal are evenly coated.

17

INDIA & PAKISTAN
THE CURRIES

The word curry comes from the Tamil word, *kari*, which translates literally as 'sauce'. For the mass population of India, 'sauce' is quite important, as it is the only means by which otherwise boring or substandard main ingredients are given flavour and interest. It is for this reason that Indian food tastes so rich to the Western palate, for when these flavoursome sauces are combined with high-quality ingredients, the result is a truly magnificent dish.

Today, the word curry has come to mean virtually any Indian main dish. The recipes which follow include a fair number of vegetarian dishes, which are becoming increasingly popular in the West, as a result of the growing trend towards eating less meat. Any one of the following curries can be cooked and eaten on its own, with perhaps just rice or bread as an accompaniment, but combining one or two, or even more, dishes together will make for the beginnings of a truly majestic Indian feast.

This selection of curries includes many of the traditional favourites such as Roghan Gosht/Lamb with Yogurt and Tomatoes (page 21) as well as more unusual curries.

Calcutta Gosht

Calcutta Beef Curry

This recipe really comes into its own when you have the good-quality meat that is available in the West. In Calcutta, where the recipe originated, it is most frequently made with lamb or goat meat. Using beef brings out the richness of the sauce.

SERVES 4–6

1 kg (2–2¼ lb) braising steak
1 teaspoon salt
1 tablespoon chilli powder
2 teaspoons ground coriander
2 teaspoons freshly ground black pepper
1½ teaspoons turmeric
1 teaspoon ground cumin
1 litre (1¾ pints) milk
100 g (4 oz) ghee
2 large onions, peeled and thinly sliced
5 garlic cloves, peeled and thinly sliced
7.5 cm (3 inch) piece fresh root ginger, peeled and thinly sliced
2 teaspoons garam masala

Cut the beef into 4 cm (1½ inch) cubes, being careful to trim away excess fat and gristle. Put the salt and ground spices, except the garam masala, in a large bowl. Mix in a little of the milk to make a paste, then continue stirring in the milk until it is all used up. Put the cubes of beef in the bowl and turn in the milk and spice mixture until evenly coated.

Heat the ghee in a large, heavy-based saucepan, add the onions, garlic and ginger and fry gently for 4–5 minutes until soft. Remove the beef from the milk and spice mixture with a perforated spoon, add to the pan and fry over moderate heat, turning the cubes constantly until they are sealed on all sides.

Increase the heat, add the milk and spice mixture and bring to the boil. Cover the pan, reduce the heat and cook gently for 1½–2 hours, or until the beef is tender and the sauce reduced.

Just before serving, sprinkle in the garam masala, increase the heat and boil off any excess liquid so that you are left with a thick sauce coating the cubes of beef. Transfer the hot curry to a warmed serving dish and serve immediately.

Keema Karela

Minced Beef with Bitter Gourd

Karela is a curious-looking vegetable, long and rather gnarled and bright green in colour. It is easy to obtain from Asian and Caribbean greengrocers in large cities, but if you cannot find it, fresh courgettes may be substituted. Canned karela can also be used.

SERVES 4–6

450 g (1 lb) fresh karela (bitter gourd), or
225 g (8 oz) can karela
juice of 1 lemon
100 g (4 oz) ghee
2 medium onions, peeled and thinly sliced
2 garlic cloves, peeled and thinly sliced
7.5 cm (3 inch) piece fresh root ginger, peeled and sliced
1 teaspoon salt
1½ teaspoons freshly ground black pepper
1 teaspoon chilli powder
1 teaspoon ground cumin
750 g (1½ lb) minced beef
2 teaspoons garam masala

Wash the fresh karela, top and tail, then cut into 1 cm (½ inch) slices. Place the slices in a bowl and sprinkle with the lemon juice. (If using canned karela, drain the brine from the can, wash the karela once with clean cold water and drain again, making sure not to lose any of the seeds. Place in a bowl and sprinkle with the lemon juice.)

Heat the ghee in a heavy-based saucepan. Add the onions, garlic and ginger and fry gently for 2–3 minutes, making sure that they do not brown. Add the salt and spices, except the garam masala. Stir well, then add the minced beef. At this stage it may be necessary to add a little water to prevent the mixture sticking to the bottom of the pan – the quantity of water depends on the water content of the onions and the fat content of the beef. Turn the minced beef continuously until it starts to change colour.

Add the slices of karela together with the lemon juice in which they have been soaking. Reduce the heat and continue to cook gently for about 5–7 minutes until the karela is soft. Sprinkle in the garam masala, stir the mixture well to ensure it is well distributed, then cook for a further 2 minutes. Serve hot.

BELOW: *Left, Calcutta Beef Curry. Right, Lamb with Extra Onions (page 21).*

Nargisi Kofta

Indian 'Scotch Egg' Curry

The use of eggs in India is, to a certain extent, still regarded as a sign of affluence. This dish, combining minced beef and hard-boiled eggs in a rich tomato-based sauce, makes a good centrepiece for any curry-based meal.

SERVES 6

7 eggs
450 g (1 lb) minced beef
1½ teaspoons freshly ground black pepper
1 teaspoon salt
2 garlic cloves, peeled and roughly chopped
1 teaspoon ground cumin
1 bunch fresh coriander
vegetable oil, for shallow-frying
Sauce:
150 g (5 oz) ghee
4 large onions, peeled and thinly sliced
3 garlic cloves, peeled and thinly sliced
15 cm (6 inch) piece fresh root ginger, peeled
and thinly sliced
1 teaspoon salt,
2 teaspoons freshly ground black pepper
1½ teaspoons chilli powder
1½ teaspoons turmeric
150 g (5 oz) tomato purée
600 ml (1 pint) rich beef stock
2 teaspoons garam masala

Hard-boil 6 of the eggs and allow to cool. Mix the minced beef with the black pepper, salt, garlic, cumin and most of the leaves from the bunch of coriander (reserving a few for the garnish). Put through the finest blade of a mincer or work in a food processor, then bind with the remaining egg. Knead well and divide into 6 portions.

Shell the hard-boiled eggs and shape each portion of minced meat around each one to form a ball. Pour about 1 cm (½ inch) oil into a heavy-based frying pan. Heat the oil until hot, then add the covered eggs and fry gently until golden brown on all sides. Drain, place on paper towels and keep hot in a warm oven.

Make the sauce: heat the ghee in a large, heavy-based saucepan, add the onions, garlic and ginger and fry gently for 4–5 minutes until soft. Add the salt and spices, except the garam masala, stir well and cook for 2 minutes. Stir in the tomato purée and stock and bring to the boil. Boil vigorously for 5 minutes, or until the sauce is reduced to three-quarters of its original volume.

Add the covered eggs to the sauce and cook very gently for a further 15 minutes. Sprinkle in the garam masala, stirring it evenly into the sauce. Transfer to a warmed serving dish, garnish with the reserved coriander leaves and serve hot.

Jhinge ka Pathia

Prawn Curry with Coconut

This dish comes from the south-west coast of India, where prawns are caught using an ingenious method involving the letting down of counterbalanced nets, which trap fish and shellfish as they swim in and out with the tide. As the tide turns the nets are lifted out of the water to harvest the catch. In the West it is possible to pay quite considerable sums for large prawns, but there is little point in using them in this recipe as the result is very much the same with the smaller prawns.

SERVES 4–6

450 g (1 lb) frozen peeled prawns
75 g (3 oz) ghee
1 large onion, peeled and thinly sliced
2 garlic cloves, peeled and thinly sliced
7.5 cm (3 inch) piece fresh root ginger, peeled
and thinly sliced
5 cm (2 inch) cinnamon stick
1 bay leaf
2 teaspoons chilli powder
2 teaspoons garam masala
1 teaspoon fenugreek seeds
1½ teaspoons salt
1 teaspoon freshly ground black pepper
225 g (8 oz) natural yogurt
175 g (6 oz) tomato purée
50 g (2 oz) desiccated coconut
chopped fresh coriander leaves, to garnish

Remove the prawns from their packet and spread out on a plate to defrost. Heat the ghee in a heavy-based saucepan, add the onion, garlic and ginger and fry gently for 4–5 minutes until soft. Add the cinnamon and bay leaf, stir for 1 minute, then add the chilli powder, garam masala, fenugreek, salt and black pepper. Stir well and fry for a further 2 minutes.

Stir in the yogurt and tomato purée. Increase the heat, add the prawns and their liquid and stir to make a fairly thick sauce. (You may have to add a little water to prevent the mixture from becoming too dry.) Simmer for 2 minutes, then add the desiccated coconut and cook for a further 5 minutes, stirring carefully to ensure that the prawns do not break up. Serve hot, garnished with a sprinkling of chopped coriander leaves.

Roghan Gosht

Lamb with Yogurt and Tomatoes

Roghan Gosht is typical of the lamb cookery in northern India and Pakistan, and this dish has become very well known in the West, thanks mainly to the advent of Tandoori restaurants. This particular recipe marinates the meat in yogurt and contains a substantial quantity of tomato purée, which gives the dish a very deep red sauce.

SERVES 4–6

I kg (2–2¼ lb) boneless shoulder of lamb
juice of 2 lemons
450 g (1 lb) natural yogurt
½–1 teaspoon salt
2 medium onions
4 garlic cloves
5–7.5 cm (2–3 inch) piece fresh root ginger
75 g (3 oz) ghee
2 teaspoons chilli powder
2 teaspoons ground coriander
2 teaspoons ground cumin
1 teaspoon freshly ground black pepper
10 green cardamoms
225 g (8 oz) tomato purée

Cut the lamb into 2.5 cm (1 inch) cubes, being careful to trim away all fat and gristle. Put the cubes in a large bowl and sprinkle in the lemon juice. Add the yogurt and salt and stir well to mix. Cover the bowl and leave to marinate in a cool place for at least 24 hours, or in the bottom of the refrigerator for up to 3 days. Turn the cubes of meat from time to time to ensure they are all coated in the marinade.

When ready to cook the marinated meat, peel and thinly slice the onions, garlic and ginger. Heat the ghee in a heavy-based saucepan, add the onions, garlic and ginger and fry gently for 4–5 minutes until soft. Add the ground spices, stir well and cook for a further 2 minutes, then add the cardamoms and stir in the tomato purée, meat and marinade. Bring to the boil, stirring constantly. Add 300 ml (½ pint) boiling water, then cover the saucepan and cook for 1–1½ hours, until the meat is tender. Serve hot.

Gosht Dopiaza

Lamb with Extra Onions

The Hindi word for onion is *piaz* and the word for two is *do* (pronounced as dough), therefore Gosht Dopiaza means 'meat with double onions'. Onions form a crucial part of virtually all Indian curry dishes and, in fact, many Indians regard onions as vegetables in themselves.

SERVES 4–6

750 g (1½ lb) boneless shoulder of lamb
5 large onions, peeled
100 g (4 oz) ghee
6 garlic cloves, peeled
7.5 cm (3 inch) piece fresh root ginger, peeled
1 tablespoon chilli powder
2 teaspoons ground coriander
2 teaspoons ground cumin
2 teaspoons freshly ground black pepper
1½ teaspoons turmeric
2 teaspoons salt
350 g (12 oz) natural yogurt
300 ml (½ pint) beef stock
6 fresh green chillies, cut into 5 mm (¼ inch) pieces
1 tablespoon fenugreek seeds
2 tablespoons chopped fresh mint leaves

Cut the lamb into 4 cm (1½ inch) cubes, being careful to trim away excess fat and gristle. Work 1 onion to a paste in a blender or food processor, then transfer to a bowl. Add the cubes of lamb and mix well together.

Heat the ghee in a heavy-based saucepan, add the cubes of lamb and fry until sealed on all sides. Meanwhile, thinly slice the remaining onions, the garlic and ginger. Remove the cubes of lamb from the pan with a perforated spoon and set aside.

Add the onions, garlic and ginger to the pan and fry gently for 4–5 minutes until soft. Meanwhile, mix the ground spices and salt with the yogurt. Add the yogurt and spice mixture to the pan, increase the heat and add the lamb, stirring constantly. Add the stock, stir well and bring to the boil. Cover the pan, reduce the heat and cook gently for 40 minutes. Add the fresh chillies with the fenugreek seeds and mint, simmer for a further 5–10 minutes, or until the meat is cooked through. Serve hot.

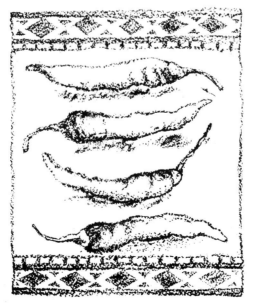

Shikar ka Vindaloo

Hot Pork Curry with Vinegar

Pork is not very widely eaten in India, for reasons of religion and hygiene. The word *shikar* can mean any animal which has been hunted, but in general it is taken to mean the wild boar traditionally hunted by men on horseback armed with lances. Wild boar is not essential for this recipe – ordinary pork from the butcher will do.

SERVES 4–6

750 g (1½ lb) boneless pork shoulder
200 ml (7fl oz) malt vinegar
2 teaspoons salt
4 teaspoons coriander seeds
4 teaspoons cumin seeds
seeds of 20 green cardamoms
2 teaspoons black peppercorns
10 cloves
2 teaspoons turmeric
75 g (3 oz) ghee
2 large onions, peeled and thinly sliced
6 garlic cloves, peeled and thinly sliced
7.5 cm (3 inch) piece fresh root ginger, peeled
and thinly sliced
5 bay leaves
2 teaspoons chilli powder
2 teaspoons garam masala

Cut the pork into 4 cm (1½ inch) cubes, being careful to trim away excess fat and gristle. Put the cubes in a bowl, pour in the vinegar and sprinkle in the salt. Mix well together, then cover and leave to marinate in a cool place for 2 hours.

Meanwhile, put the coriander, cumin and cardamom seeds in a mortar and pestle with the peppercorns, cloves and turmeric. Grind to a powder, then spoon a little of the vinegar from the pork into the mixture to make a thick paste. Remove the pork from the marinade with a perforated spoon and place in a clean bowl. Reserve the vinegar marinade. Stir the spiced paste into the pork, cover and leave to marinate in a cool place overnight.

Heat the ghee in a heavy-based saucepan, add the onions, garlic and ginger and fry gently for 4–5 minutes until soft. Add the bay leaves and chilli powder and stir well to mix. Add the pork cubes, turning continuously to seal them. Increase the heat and add the reserved vinegar marinade. Cover the pan, reduce the heat and cook the pork gently for 1¼ hours, or until thoroughly cooked. Sprinkle in the garam masala just before serving. Serve hot or chilled.

BELOW: *Whole Spiced Baked Chicken.* OPPOSITE: *Fish Ball Curry (page 24), served with Leavened Bread with Poppy Seeds (page 34).*

Murgh Mussalum

Whole Spiced Baked Chicken

Three separate techniques are used to create this fascinating recipe, which is one of the tastiest of hot Indian chicken dishes. First the chicken is marinated in a hot sauce, then it is steamed, and finally it is roasted. As with virtually all chicken recipes from India, it makes use of poultry that has been skinned rather than plucked. It seems the simple reason for this is that Indian butchers have always regarded plucking far too time-consuming, and prefer to remove the skin and feathers together when they draw the bird. Skinning a chicken is fairly straightforward, but if you are not sure how to set about it, your butcher should help you.

SERVES 4

1 tablespoon coriander seeds
1 tablespoon cumin seeds
2 bay leaves
1.5 kg (3½ lb) roasting chicken
100 g (4 oz) thick natural yogurt
1 medium onion, peeled and roughly chopped
3 garlic cloves, peeled and roughly chopped
3 fresh green chillies, roughly chopped
Roasting mixture:
100 g (4 oz) ghee
1 large onion, peeled and thinly sliced
2 garlic cloves, peeled and thinly sliced
7.5 cm (3 inch) piece fresh root ginger, peeled and thinly sliced
5 cm (2 inch) cinnamon stick
10 cloves
10 cardamoms
2 teaspoons black peppercorns
2 teaspoons salt
150 ml (¼ pint) chicken stock
2 teaspoons garam masala
Garnish:
fresh coriander leaves
lemon wedges

Spread the coriander, cumin seeds and bay leaves on a baking tray. Roast in a preheated moderately hot oven (200°C/400°F, Gas Mark 6) for 10–15 minutes, until the bay leaves are crisp. Meanwhile, skin the chicken and wash well. Pat the chicken dry with paper towels, then make deep slashes in the leg and breast meat with a sharp knife.

Put the yogurt, onion, garlic and fresh chillies in a blender or food processor and work until liquidized. Grind the roasted seeds and bay leaves together in a mortar and pestle and add to the yogurt mixture. Rub this mixture over the bird, then leave to marinate in a cool place for 24 hours, basting the chicken from time to time with the yogurt mixture.

When ready to cook the chicken, make the roasting mixture: heat the ghee in a casserole with a close-fitting lid. Add the onion, garlic and ginger and fry gently for 4–5 minutes until soft. Gently pound the cinnamon, cloves, cardamoms and peppercorns in a mortar and pestle and add to the casserole. Sprinkle in the salt, then add the chicken stock and bring to the boil. Add the garam masala, stirring well, then add the chicken together with the marinade. Cover tightly, increase the heat and shake the casserole continuously for 2 minutes.

Transfer the casserole to a preheated moderately hot oven (190°C/375°F, Gas Mark 5) and cook for 1 hour. Remove the casserole from the oven and increase the oven temperature to hot (230°C/450°F, Gas Mark 8). Remove the bird from the casserole and place in a roasting tin. Baste with some of the sauce from the casserole, then roast in the oven for about 30 minutes, or until the outside of the chicken is crisp and the juices run clear when the thickest part of a thigh is pierced with the point of a sharp knife. Liquidize the remaining juices from the casserole in a blender or food processor, then reheat. Serve the chicken hot, garnished with coriander and lemon wedges. Serve the juices in a separate bowl.

Muchli Kari

Fish Ball Curry

By and large, the coasts of India are still remarkably free of pollution and teeming with seafood. In the main, fish is grilled or baked whole. Some of the fish are so odd-looking – often covered with spines – that they need to be disguised in some way to make them appear palatable. Hence this recipe for fish ball curry.

SERVES 4–6

750 g (1½ lb) white fish fillets (haddock or cod)
juice of ½ lemon
1 egg
salt
freshly ground black pepper
50 g (2 oz) besan (chick pea flour)
4 fresh green chillies, topped, tailed and finely chopped
1 medium onion, peeled and finely chopped
2 tablespoons breadcrumbs
vegetable oil or ghee, for shallow-frying
Sauce:
100 g (4 oz) ghee
1 large onion, peeled and thinly sliced
2 garlic cloves, peeled and thinly sliced
7.5 cm (3 inch) cinnamon stick
2 bay leaves
2 teaspoons ground cumin
2 teaspoons ground coriander
1½ teaspoons turmeric
1 teaspoon chilli powder
150 g (5 oz) tomato purée
600 ml (1 pint) chicken stock
juice of ½ lemon
50 g (2 oz) desiccated coconut
seeds of 10 cardamoms
2 teaspoons fenugreek seeds
fresh coriander leaves, to garnish

Arrange the fish fillets in an ovenproof dish and sprinkle with the lemon juice. Cover the dish with foil and stand in a roasting tin. Pour in enough hot water to come halfway up the sides of the dish, then poach in a preheated moderate oven (160°C/325°F, Gas Mark 3) for 15 minutes, or until the fish is fully cooked. Remove the dish from the roasting tin and allow the fish to cool.

Whisk the egg in a medium bowl with 1½ teaspoons salt and pepper to taste. Sift in the besan, whisking all the time to make a smooth batter. (The flour tends to form quite hard lumps; these need to be pressed through the sieve with the back of a spoon.)

Flake the fish into the bowl, discarding the skin and any bones. Add the chillies, onion and breadcrumbs, to the batter to form a stiff paste. Break off lumps about the size of an apricot and form into balls – there should be about 20 altogether. Heat the oil or ghee in a deep, heavy-based frying pan and shallow fry the balls in batches until they are uniformly brown. Remove from the frying pan with a perforated spoon, drain on paper towels and keep hot in a warm oven.

Make the sauce: heat the ghee in a heavy-based saucepan, add the onion and garlic and fry gently for 4–5 minutes until soft. Add the cinnamon, bay leaves, cumin, coriander, turmeric and chilli, stir well and cook for a further 2 minutes. Stir in the tomato purée, increase the heat and bring to the boil, slowly stirring in the chicken stock and lemon juice. Sprinkle in 1 teaspoon salt and the coconut, then boil the sauce gently for 10 minutes.

Grind the cardamom seeds in a mortar and pestle with the fenugreek. Sprinkle into the sauce, reduce the heat and add the fish balls. Simmer for 5 minutes. Transfer to a warmed serving dish, garnish and serve hot.

Dum Aloo

Steamed Potatoes

The *dum* method of cooking is quite popular in India. Traditionally it is done on a charcoal fire, in a saucepan with a concave lid. Red hot coals are heaped up around the saucepan and a few coals are actually put into the lid to provide heat from above. In this way, steam is maintained above the surface of the cooking curry, which keeps beautifully moist.

SERVES 4–6

750 g (1½ lb) potatoes
50 g (2 oz) ghee
2 medium onions, peeled and finely chopped
1 teaspoon chilli powder
1 teaspoon garam masala
1 teaspoon turmeric
1 teaspoon freshly ground black pepper
½ teaspoon ground ginger
1 teaspoon salt
150 g (5 oz) natural yogurt
100 g (4 oz) tomato purée

Scrub the potatoes but do not peel them, then cut into halves, or quarters if they are very large. Heat the ghee in a small frying pan, add the onions and fry gently, until just beginning to soften. Add the spices and salt, stir well and fry for a further minute. Stir in the yogurt and tomato purée and cook for another minute.

Arrange the potatoes in a casserole with a tight-fitting lid. Pour the spice mixture over the potatoes and cover the casserole. Bake in a preheated moderate oven (180°C/350°F, Gas Mark 4) for about 45 minutes, or until the potatoes are cooked. Serve hot.

Baigan Tamatar

Aubergines with Tomatoes

If you have never tried an Indian vegetable dish, then this one is a must. The rich flavour imparted by the combination of whole tomatoes and concentrated tomato purée greatly enhances that of the aubergines themselves. When choosing aubergines for this dish, try to select only those which are firm, unwrinkled and deep purple in hue.

SERVES 4–6

750 g (1½ lb) aubergines
juice of 1 lemon
175 g (6 oz) ghee
2 medium onions, peeled and thinly sliced
4 garlic cloves, peeled and thinly sliced
7.5 cm (3 inch) piece fresh root ginger, peeled and thinly sliced
2 teaspoons kalonji (onion seeds)
7.5 cm (3 inch) cinnamon stick
2 teaspoons coriander seeds
2 teaspoons cumin seeds
2 teaspoons freshly ground black pepper
2 teaspoons salt
2 teaspoons garam masala
1½ teaspoons turmeric
1 teaspoon chilli powder
400 g (14 oz) can tomatoes
100 g (4 oz) tomato purée
dried red chillies, to garnish

Using a sharp knife cut the aubergines in half lengthways, then cut again lengthways into quarters. Cut the aubergine crossways at 4 cm (1½ inch) intervals to form chunks. Place in a bowl and mix in the lemon juice.

Heat the ghee in a heavy-based saucepan, add the onions, garlic and ginger and fry gently for 4–5 minutes until soft. Add the kalonji, cinnamon, coriander and cumin; stir well. Fry for 2 minutes, then stir in the pepper, salt, garam masala, turmeric and chilli powder.

Add the tomatoes with their juice and the tomato purée, stir well and bring to the boil. Add 600 ml (1 pint) boiling water, the aubergine pieces and lemon juice. Bring to the boil and simmer gently for 15–20 minutes, until soft. Garnish and serve hot.

Saag Tamatar

Spinach with Tomatoes

Spinach is a very popular vegetable throughout the Indian sub-continent and is noted for its nutritional qualities, as in the West. The strain of spinach grown in India tends to be much stronger in flavour than that grown in the West; some of it can taste quite bitter, and so the addition of sweeter tomatoes is intended to counteract this. If fresh spinach is not available, frozen spinach can be used, in which case use only half the weight specified for fresh.

SERVES 4–6

1 kg (2–2¼ lb) fresh spinach
175 g (6 oz) ghee
2 large onions, peeled and thinly sliced
2 garlic cloves, peeled and thinly sliced
150 g (5 oz) fresh root ginger
2 teaspoons chilli powder
2 teaspoons turmeric
2 teaspoons garam masala
2 teaspoons coriander seeds
1 teaspoon ground coriander
1 teaspoon cumin seeds
1½ teaspoons salt
2 teaspoons freshly ground black pepper
400 g (14 oz) can tomatoes

Wash the spinach and shake it dry. Cut it into strips about 2.5 cm (1 inch) wide, removing any of the thicker stalks. Heat the ghee in a heavy-based saucepan, add the onions and garlic and fry gently for 4–5 minutes.

Meanwhile, peel the ginger and cut into strips about 3 mm (⅛ inch) thick. Add the ginger to the pan and continue cooking gently for a further 5–6 minutes. Add the chilli powder, turmeric, garam masala, coriander, cumin, salt and black pepper, stir well and cook for 1 minute.

Add the spinach and toss to coat in the spice mixture. Add the tomatoes with their juice and bring to the boil, stirring; then add enough boiling water to prevent the spinach sticking to the bottom of the pan. Stir well and simmer for 5–10 minutes, until both the spinach and tomatoes are cooked through. Serve hot.

Aviyal

Mixed Vegetable Curry with Coconut

This recipe originates from the south of India. It makes use of fresh coconut as one of the main ingredients, which adds both texture and flavour to any vegetable dish. This dish reheats well and also freezes successfully, therefore it is the ideal curry to make in large quantities.

SERVES 6–8

225 g (8 oz) runner beans
225 g (8 oz) fresh coconut 'meat'
225 g (8 oz) green leafy cabbage, eg Savoy
225 g (8 oz) karela (bitter gourd)
225 g (8 oz) carrots
225 g (8 oz) green mango (optional)
225 g (8 oz) green bananas (optional)
juice of 2 lemons
100 g (4 oz) ghee
2 large onions, peeled and thinly sliced
6 garlic cloves, peeled and thinly sliced
two 7.5 cm (3 inch) pieces fresh root ginger,
peeled and thinly sliced
10 bay leaves
1 tablespoon kalonji (onion seeds)
1 tablespoon turmeric
2 teaspoons ground coriander
2 teaspoons ground cumin
10 cardamoms
1 teaspoon salt
1 teaspoon freshly ground black pepper
4 teaspoons garam masala
5 fresh green chillies, finely chopped

String the runner beans and cut them into 2.5 cm (1 inch) pieces. Thinly slice the coconut. Remove the stalk from the cabbage and cut the leaves into 1 cm (½ inch) strips. Top and tail the karela and cut into 1 cm (½ inch) slices. Scrub, top and tail the carrots and cut into 1 cm (½ inch) slices. Remove the peel from the green mango, if using, and cut into 2.5 cm (1 inch) pieces. If using green bananas, peel them and cut the flesh into 1 cm (½ inch) slices. Mix the vegetables in a large bowl with the lemon juice.

Heat the ghee in a large, heavy-based saucepan, add the onions, garlic and ginger and fry gently for 4–5 minutes until soft. Add the bay leaves and kalonji, stir-fry for 1 minute, then add the turmeric, coriander, cumin, cardamoms, salt and pepper. Stir for 1 further minute, then add the vegetables and stir thoroughly.

Add 1 litre (1¾ pints) boiling water and bring to the boil, stirring constantly. Reduce the heat to a very gentle simmer, cover the pan with a tight-fitting lid and simmer very gently for 20–25 minutes, or until the vegetables are cooked through. Sprinkle in the garam masala and stir in the chillies. Cook for a further 2 minutes. Serve hot.

Bhindi Bhajji

Curried Okra

This vegetable is well known throughout the tropical world, and is found in recipes from the Caribbean right across through India to China. As with most green vegetables, bhindi (also known as okra or ladies' fingers) are best cooked fresh. It is possible to buy them in cans, but both the flavour and texture are sadly lacking. Fresh bhindi can be recognized by their bright green appearance, the absence of too many black patches on the outside of the vegetable, and the fact that they break cleanly when snapped, with an audible 'pop'. One warning when handling fresh bhindi: the outer surface is covered with tiny, almost invisible, needle-like spines, which soften on cooking, and can be very painful if they get in your eyes.

SERVES 4–6

450 g (1 lb) bhindi (okra)
75 g (3 oz) ghee
1 large onion, peeled and thinly sliced
2 garlic cloves, peeled and thinly sliced
7.5 cm (3 inch) piece fresh root ginger, peeled
and thinly sliced
1½ teaspoons ground cumin
1½ teaspoons turmeric
1 teaspoon ground coriander
1 teaspoon freshly ground black pepper
1 teaspoon salt
100 g (4 oz) canned tomatoes
1 tablespoon garam masala

Pick over bhindi, and discard any that are blemished. Wash them in cold water, then top and tail them and cut into 1 cm (½ inch) pieces. Heat the ghee in a heavy-based saucepan, add the onion, garlic and ginger and fry gently for 4–5 minutes until soft. Add the spices and salt, stir well and fry for a further 3 minutes. Add the bhindi and turn carefully with a wooden spoon so that they become evenly coated with the spice mixture.

Add the tomatoes with their juice, increase the heat and add 150 ml (¼ pint) boiling water. Bring to the boil and simmer for about 10 minutes until the bhindi are cooked but still crunchy – test by biting into a piece. Sprinkle in the garam masala and stir for a further minute. Serve hot.

OPPOSITE: *Clockwise from top; Mixed Vegetable Curry with Coconut, Curried Okra, Steamed Potatoes (page 24), Aubergines with Tomatoes (page 25).*

INDIA & PAKISTAN
TANDOORI DISHES

Tandoori food gets its name from the clay oven, or *tandoor*, in which the food is cooked. Tandoor ovens can vary in size from 1 metre (3 feet) in height and ½ metre (18 inches) in diameter, to far larger commercial ones, which can be 2–3 metres (6–9 feet) deep and 1½–2 metres (4–6 feet) in diameter. The smaller tandoors are invariably used indoors and set in brick to protect them from damage; larger tandoors are usually outside and set into the ground.

When a tandoor is new, the clay is first rubbed with fresh spinach leaves. This has a two-fold action of removing any surface clay dust and sealing the existing surface. A charcoal fire is then lit and allowed to burn slowly in the base of the tandoor for at least 2 hours. Very high temperatures are reached inside the oven so that when a piece of meat is lowered into the tandoor the outside of the meat is completely sealed and the meat cooks very quickly, thus preventing the escape of too much moisture. This quick-cooking process does not allow enough time for spices and other flavourings to penetrate the meat as in normal cooking methods, and for this reason all tandoori food is marinated before cooking.

A tandoor is not a normal piece of equipment in a Western kitchen, but quite acceptable results can be achieved using a combination of a conventional oven for the main cooking and a charcoal barbecue to finish.

Husseini Kebab

Marinated Cubes of Lamb
The key ingredients to this dish are the aromatic spices: roasted coriander, cumin and aniseed. It is best to bone the lamb yourself, as most butchers do not remove sufficient fat when boning meat.

SERVES 4–6

1 kg (2–2¼ lb) shoulder of lamb
juice of 1 lemon
2 teaspoons salt
1½ teaspoons freshly ground black pepper
1 medium onion
2 garlic cloves
7.5 cm (3 inch) piece fresh root ginger
1½ teaspoons chilli powder
225 g (8 oz) natural yogurt
2 teaspoons coriander seeds
2 teaspoons cumin seeds
1 teaspoon aniseed

Bone the meat and trim off all excess fat. Cut the meat into 2.5 cm (1 inch) cubes, place in a bowl and sprinkle with the lemon juice, salt and freshly ground black pepper. Rub this mixture well into the cubes of meat, then set the bowl aside.

Peel the onion, garlic and ginger and mince finely in a blender or food processor with the chilli powder and yogurt, then strain in the juice from the lamb. Blend well, then pour over the lamb.

Cover the bowl and leave the lamb to marinate in a cool place for at least 24 hours, turning the cubes over from time to time to ensure that they are all evenly coated in the yogurt marinade.

Meanwhile, spread the coriander, cumin and aniseed out on a baking tray and roast in a preheated moderately hot oven (200°C/400°F, Gas Mark 6) for 10–15 minutes. Remove the spices from the oven and leave until cold, then transfer to a mortar and pestle and grind to a fine powder.

Thread the cubes of lamb on to oiled metal kebab skewers and sprinkle over the ground roasted spices. Place the skewers on the preheated grid of the barbecue and cook gently over charcoal until the lamb is tender, turning the skewers frequently so that the meat browns on all sides. Serve hot.

Murgh Masala

Double Spiced Chicken
Strips of chicken are first marinated, then barbecued over charcoal and finally cooked in a spicy sauce.

SERVES 4–6

4 chicken breasts, skinned and boned
juice of 1 lemon
1½ teaspoons salt
2 teaspoons freshly ground black pepper
1 medium onion
2 garlic cloves
5 cm (2 inch) piece fresh root ginger
350 g (12 oz) natural yogurt
Masala:
75 g (3 oz) ghee
1 medium onion, peeled and thinly sliced
1 garlic clove, peeled and thinly sliced
1½ teaspoons turmeric
1½ teaspoons chilli powder
1 teaspoon ground cinnamon
seeds of 20 cardamoms
2 teaspoons coriander seeds
2 teaspoons aniseed

Cut the chicken meat into strips about 2.5 cm (1 inch) wide, place in a bowl and sprinkle with the lemon juice, salt and pepper. Rub in well, then set aside.

Peel the onion, garlic and ginger and mince finely in a blender or food processor. Add the yogurt and strain in the juice from the chicken. Work until blended, then pour over the chicken. Cover and marinate in the refrigerator for at least 24 hours.

Thread the chicken on to kebab skewers. Reserve the marinade. Barbecue as slowly as possible until just cooked through (it is important not to overcook the chicken). Remove the skewers.

Meanwhile, make the masala: heat the ghee in a large, heavy-based frying pan, add the onion and garlic and fry gently for 4–5 minutes until soft. Sprinkle in the turmeric, chilli and cinnamon, stir well and fry for 1 minute, then add the cardamom and coriander seeds and the aniseed. Stir for 2 minutes, then add the reserved yogurt marinade. Mix well and bring to the boil. Add the chicken pieces and cook for 2–3 minutes. Serve hot.

Tandoori Muchli

Charcoal-grilled Fish
Traditionally, freshly caught fish is rubbed with a spicy mixture known as a masala, wrapped in a banana leaf and cooked in the ashes of a fire. The effect of the cooking process that combines baking and steaming in the banana leaf traps the juices given off by the fish and gives a beautifully moist and piquant result. Using foil is equally successful.

SERVES 4

1–1.5 kg (2–3½ lb) halibut, cleaned and washed
juice of 1 lemon
2 teaspoons salt
1½ teaspoons freshly ground black pepper
Masala:
1 large onion
1 garlic clove
1 tablespoon chopped fresh coriander leaves
4 teaspoons natural yogurt
2 teaspoons garam masala
1 teaspoon chilli powder
1 teaspoon ground coriander
1 teaspoon ground cumin
1 teaspoon ground fenugreek

Select a baking dish which is large enough to take the whole fish, then line with a sheet of foil 2½ times the size of the fish itself. Make 4 or 5 deep cuts in both sides of the fish. Rub the lemon juice on the fish and sprinkle with the salt and pepper. Place the fish on the foil and set aside.

Make the masala: peel and finely mince the onion and garlic, then place in a bowl with the chopped coriander leaves, yogurt, garam masala, chilli powder, coriander, cumin and fenugreek. Mix well, then smear over the fish and inside the cuts and the cavity. Draw up the sides of the foil to make a tent shape, fold over and seal. Leave to marinate in a cool place for at least 4 hours.

Bake the fish in a preheated moderate oven (160°C/325°F, Gas Mark 3) for 20 minutes. Carefully remove the fish from the foil, place on a wire mesh and finish cooking over a charcoal barbecue. Care is obviously needed at this stage; if the fish is already over-cooked, there is a risk that it will break up when it is transferred to the barbecue. If preferred, finish cooking by the oven method.

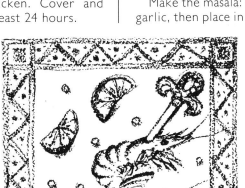

Murgh Tandoori

Tandoori Chicken

Although whole baby chickens or poussins are traditionally used for Murgh Tandoori, chicken quarters are used here as they lend themselves more readily to being finished off on a barbecue. The beauty of this method is that the chicken can be roasted in the oven several hours in advance, kept in the refrigerator, then finished off on the barbecue.

SERVES 8

8 chicken pieces
juice of 2 lemons
2 teaspoons salt
Marinade:
10 cloves
2 teaspoons coriander seeds
2 teaspoons cumin seeds
seeds of 10 cardamoms
2 medium onions
4 garlic cloves
7.5 cm (3 inch) piece fresh root ginger
2 teaspoons chilli powder
2 teaspoons freshly ground black pepper
1½ teaspoons turmeric
350 g (12 oz) natural yogurt
orange or red food colouring (optional)

Remove the skin from the chicken pieces and discard. Wash the chicken and pat dry with paper towels. Make deep slashes in each piece with a sharp knife. Put the pieces in a bowl and sprinkle with the lemon juice and salt. Rub this mixture in well, then cover the bowl and leave in a cool place for 1 hour.

Meanwhile, prepare the marinade: spread the cloves, coriander, cumin and cardamom seeds out on a baking tray and roast in a preheated moderately hot oven (200°C/400°F, Gas Mark 6) for 10–15 minutes. Remove from the oven and allow to cool, then grind coarsely in a mortar and pestle. Peel and finely mince the onions, garlic and ginger, then place in a blender or food processor and sprinkle with the chilli powder, black pepper and turmeric. Add the yogurt and ground roasted spices, strain in the lemon juice from the chicken and blend well. Add sufficient food colouring to give a bright colour, if liked.

Arrange the chicken pieces in a single layer in a roasting tin and pour over the marinade. Cover the tin and leave the chicken to marinate in the refrigerator for at least 24 hours, turning the pieces over occasionally.

Transfer the roasting tin to a preheated moderately hot oven (200°C/400°F, Gas Mark 6) and roast for 20 minutes. Transfer the chicken to a barbecue and cook until the outside is crisp. Serve hot or cold.

BELOW: *Left, Barbecued King Prawns. Centre, Minced Beef on Skewers. Right, Tandoori Chicken.*

Tandoori Jhinghe

Barbecued King Prawns

The prawns may be peeled first and then marinated, or split and marinated in their shells. If you choose to remove the shells before marinating, then the marinating time need only be for 3–4 hours; marinate overnight if leaving the prawns in their shells.

SERVES 4–6

1 kg (2–2¼ lb) king prawns
juice of 2 lemons
1½ teaspoons salt
1½ teaspoons freshly ground black pepper
Marinade:
2 teaspoons coriander seeds
2 teaspoons fenugreek seeds
seeds of 20 green cardamoms
1½ teaspoons kalonji (onion seeds)
4 bay leaves
1 large onion
3 garlic cloves
7.5 cm (3 inch) piece fresh root ginger
350 g (12 oz) natural yogurt
1½ teaspoons turmeric
100 g (4 oz) ghee, melted
few drops of red food colouring
1 teaspoon aniseed

Wash the prawns and peel them if wished. Alternatively, split the undersides with a sharp knife and slightly flatten them. Put the prawns in a bowl and sprinkle with the lemon juice, salt and pepper. Mix well, then set aside.

Make the marinade: spread the coriander, fenugreek, cardamom and kalonji out on a baking tray. Add the bay leaves and roast in a preheated moderately hot oven (200°C/400°F, Gas Mark 6) for 10–15 minutes. Cool, then grind in a mortar and pestle. Peel and mince the onion, garlic and ginger and place in a blender or food processor with the yogurt and turmeric. Work until blended, add the ground roasted spices and ghee and work again for 30 seconds. Add the food colouring.

Pour the marinade over the prawns, then cover and marinate in the refrigerator for 3–4 hours if the prawns are peeled, otherwise overnight. Remove the prawns from the marinade, thread on to skewers and sprinkle over the aniseed. Barbecue gently until cooked, turning frequently and brushing with the marinade. Serve hot.

Seekh Kebab

Minced Beef on Skewers

These kebabs are best cooked on thick skewers, to enable the meat to be cooked from the inside as well as the outside.

SERVES 4–6

750 g (1½ lb) minced beef
2 large onions, peeled and roughly chopped
4 garlic cloves, peeled and roughly chopped
75 g (3 oz) breadcrumbs
3 tablespoons chopped fresh coriander leaves
2 teaspoons garam masala
2 teaspoons freshly ground black pepper
1½ teaspoons poppy seeds
1½ teaspoons sesame seeds
½ teaspoon chilli powder
1½ teaspoons salt
2 eggs, beaten
Garnish:
lettuce leaves
lime slices
chopped raw onion

Pass the beef, onions and garlic through the finest blade of a mincer, or work in a food processor. Transfer to a bowl, knead well, then mix in the remaining ingredients. Knead again for 1 minute, then chill in the refrigerator for 30 minutes.

Press the mixture on to 6 skewers, in sausage shapes about 10 cm (4 inches) long. (There should be enough mixture to make 12 shapes, 2 on each skewer.) Barbecue gently until cooked, turning frequently. Serve hot, garnished with lettuce, lime and onion.

INDIA & PAKISTAN
ACCOMPANIMENTS

Accompaniments to Indian food range from carbohydrates such as bread and rice, which add bulk to the meal, to various yogurt and lentil-based sauces. Some of the sauces can be extremely hot, in some cases red chillies themselves form the main ingredient, or they can be rather cooler, such as the mild-flavoured Tandoori Chatni/Mint-flavoured sauce (below), which serves to add piquancy to the range of tandoori dishes.

Raeta/Yogurt with Cucumber or Tomato (below) is another popular accompaniment, especially if you are cooking for someone new to Indian food. With yogurt as its base, Raeta serves as the most effective 'fire extinguisher'!

Tandoori Chatni

Mint-flavoured Sauce

'Chatni' is the general name given to any sauce or pickle-like accompaniment. Chatnis can range from very hot and fiery concoctions such as chilli chatni, which is made entirely from green and red chillies, to rather milder chatnis made from sweetened aubergine or, as in this case, mint and yogurt. This chatni is good with tandoori dishes, particularly the drier ones such as Seekh Kebab/Minced Beef on Skewers (page 31).

MAKES ABOUT 300 ML ($\frac{1}{2}$ PINT)

225 g (8 oz) natural yogurt
2 tablespoons vinegar
2 teaspoons honey
juice of $\frac{1}{2}$ lemon
$\frac{1}{2}$ teaspoon salt
$\frac{1}{2}$ teaspoon freshly ground black pepper
$\frac{1}{2}$ teaspoon chilli powder
green food colouring (optional)
1 tablespoon chopped fresh mint

Put the yogurt in a serving bowl. Heat the vinegar and honey in a small saucepan until the honey has melted. Leave to cool, then mix into the yogurt. Add the lemon juice, sprinkle in the salt, pepper and chilli powder and stir well. If liked, add food colouring to give the chatni a very pale green colour, then mix in the chopped mint. Cover the bowl and chill for 1 hour before serving.

Raeta

Yogurt with Cucumber or Tomato

Raeta is one of the most important accompaniments to Indian food, as it counteracts any hotness. Although this recipe calls for either cucumber or tomato, try experimenting with cold cooked potato, cut into cubes, or serve with Pakoras/Chick Pea Flour Fritters (page 13) made by frying the batter in small lumps.

It is important to make sure that the yogurt is thin; ideally it should be the consistency of warm pouring custard. If the yogurt is too thick, thin it down with a little milk.

MAKES ABOUT 300 ML ($\frac{1}{2}$ PINT)

225 g (8 oz) natural yogurt
7.5 cm (3 inch) piece cucumber, or
2 medium tomatoes
pinch of salt
$\frac{1}{2}$ teaspoon freshly ground black pepper
pinch of chilli powder, to garnish

Put the yogurt in a serving bowl, thinning it down with a little milk if necessary. Cut the cucumber lengthways into thin strips. (If using tomatoes, quarter them, then cut each quarter in half.) Mix the cucumber or tomatoes into the yogurt, sprinkling with the salt and black pepper. Cover the bowl and chill the yogurt in the refrigerator for $1\frac{1}{2}$ hours. Garnish with the chilli powder just before serving.

Tarka Dal | Poppadoms

Lentil Sauce with Hot Topping

Dal, or lentil sauce, is one of the most commonly found staple dishes throughout the whole of the Indian sub-continent. There are many different types of pulse from which sauces such as this are made, but the secret of this particular recipe is the topping, which is poured over the dal prior to serving. The combination of garlic and lovage seeds gives a real piquancy to the dish and it is certainly a flavour worth trying.

SERVES 4–6

450 g (1 lb) red lentils
50 g (2 oz) ghee
1 medium onion, peeled and thinly sliced
1 garlic clove, peeled and thinly sliced
1½ teaspoons turmeric
½ teaspoon salt
1 teaspoon freshly ground black pepper
4 fresh green chillies, topped and tailed
Tarka:
2 tablespoons sesame seed oil
4 garlic cloves, peeled and thinly sliced
1 small onion, peeled and thinly sliced
1 teaspoon lovage seeds

Wash the lentils well in at least 3 complete changes of cold water. Drain and pick out any stones or discoloured lentils. Heat the ghee in a heavy-based saucepan, add the onion and garlic and fry gently for 4–5 minutes until soft. Sprinkle in the turmeric, salt and pepper, then add the lentils, stirring well so that they become well coated.

Pour in 1 litre (1¾ pints) water, bring to the boil, then add the whole chillies. Boil for about 20 minutes, stirring from time to time until the lentils have turned into a yellow sauce, the consistency of a thick custard. (It may be necessary to add more water during cooking, depending on the absorbency of the lentils.) Pour the dal into a warmed serving dish, cover and keep hot in a preheated moderate oven (180°C/350°F, Gas Mark 4).

Make the tarka: heat the oil in a frying pan until smoking. Add the garlic and onion, fry quickly until the garlic blackens, then throw in the lovage seeds. Fry for a further 10 seconds, then pour over the dal. Serve hot.

Lentil Flour Crisps

Virtually all the Poppadoms that are eaten in the West are imported from India; this is because they are notoriously very difficult to make, and imported ones are inexpensive to buy. However, if you do wish to have a go at making them yourself, the following recipe is quick and straightforward.

MAKES ABOUT 20

450 g (1 lb) red lentils or urhad (lentil) flour
4½ teaspoons salt
1 tablespoon baking powder
about 50 g (2 oz) ghee
2 teaspoons black peppercorns
vegetable oil, for frying

If using lentils, grind them into a fine flour in a blender or food processor. Sift the lentil flour, salt and baking powder into a bowl and gradually add 250 ml (8 fl oz) tepid water to form a very hard dough.

Warm the ghee until melted. Knead the dough for at least 20 minutes, sprinkling it with enough melted ghee to prevent it sticking to the bowl. Crush the peppercorns, sprinkle them over the dough, then knead them in until evenly distributed.

Break the dough into about 20 pieces the size of golf balls. Roll out each piece very thinly, until about 15 cm (6 inches) in diameter. Stack them on top of each other, separating each one with a sheet of greaseproof paper, then dry them out in a preheated moderate oven (180°C/350°F, Gas Mark 4) for about 2–2½ hours. Store in an airtight tin; they will keep for several weeks.

To cook the poppadoms: pour oil into a deep, heavy frying pan to a depth of 2.5 cm (1 inch). Heat the oil until very hot (a small piece of poppadom will immediately start to sizzle and float to the surface when dropped into the pan). Fry the poppadoms two at a time in the hot oil, rotating them for 5–10 seconds as they cook, using a combination of slotted spoon and fish slice. Turn them over and fry for a further 5–10 seconds. Lift them out of the frying pan, allowing excess oil to drain back, then stack them on end (as in a toast rack) in a warm place until well drained. Ideally, poppadoms should be served within 1 hour of frying, but they can be kept crisp, or be re-crisped, in a hot oven.

Chawal | Naan

Rice

Rice is the Indian equivalent to potatoes in most Western countries. There are a number of varieties of rice, but the best ones to use are good-quality Basmati and Patna. Both of these are long grain varieties, and in India they are savoured for their intrinsic flavour alone. For this reason, rice served with most Indian meals is simply boiled. However, by using various flavourings such as saffron, turmeric and lovage, and substituting chicken or beef stock for plain water, it is possible to produce a variety of interesting flavours.

The amount of rice given here is only a general guide, for the simple reason that it is very hard to gauge the exact quantity of rice which will be eaten at a particular sitting. Much will depend on what else is on offer and, of course, the size of individual appetites. As long as the same cup is used to measure both the rice and water, the cooking method is the same, no matter what the quantity

FOR 1 PERSON

½ cup long grain rice
1½ cups water
pinch of salt

Wash the rice well in at least 3 complete changes of cold water (it may need to be washed more if the water continues to be clouded by rice dust particles). Drain the rice, then pick over to remove any stones or other 'undesirable' objects.

Place the rice in a large saucepan and pour in the measured water, which should cover the rice well. Add the salt, bring to the boil and simmer, uncovered, until cooked. The secret of good rice cookery is not to simmer for a specified time, but check the rice constantly during cooking by removing a few grains and biting them, and to stop the cooking process before it has gone too far. The rice is just right when there is just a hint of a hard centre to the rice grains. If you find that too much water has been absorbed before this point is reached, then add a little more, which should preferably be boiling, so as not to hold up the cooking. Drain the rice when cooked.

To colour and flavour rice: place a pinch of saffron threads in a large cup, pour on boiling water to cover and leave to infuse for 20 minutes. Strain the saffron-coloured water into the rice as it simmers. As saffron is expensive, an alternative and more economical way of colouring rice (and to a certain extent flavouring it) is to use turmeric. Use ¼ teaspoon for each ½ cup rice, adding it to the water during the cooking process.

Leavened Bread with Poppy Seeds

Naan is traditionally cooked on the walls of a clay oven (*tandoor*). Rolled-out dough is slapped on the inside of the oven wall, near the top where it cooks very quickly in the fierce heat. Special irons are used, one has a flat end to scrape the Naan from the wall, the other a hook to remove it from the oven. Watching Naan cooked in this traditional way is fascinating, as the baker has to know exactly when to remove the Naan from the oven and how to hook it without it dropping into the hot coals.

MAKES 6

450 g (1 lb) strong plain white flour
1 teaspoon baking powder
1 teaspoon salt
2 eggs, beaten
300 ml (½ pint) milk
1 tablespoon honey
50 g (2 oz) ghee
2 tablespoons poppy seeds

Sift the flour, baking powder and salt into a bowl. Add the eggs and mix well. Warm the milk and honey gently in a saucepan until the honey has melted, then add gradually to the flour and egg mixture to form a dough. Knead well for 5–10 minutes.

Warm the ghee until melted. Divide the dough into 6 equal pieces, brush one with a little of the ghee and knead again. Form into an oval shape, about 1 cm (½ inch) thick. Pick up some of the poppy seeds with moistened hands and press them into the dough. Repeat with the remaining pieces and melted ghee to make 6 naan altogether.

Arrange the naan on baking sheets and bake in a preheated hot oven (220°C/425°F, Gas Mark 7) for about 10 minutes, until the bread is puffed, golden and slightly scorched. Alternatively, cook under an extremely hot grill for 1½ minutes on each side. Serve hot, straight from the oven or grill.

Paratha

Fried Unleavened Bread

Paratha is perhaps the best Indian bread to try if you are a newcomer to Indian cooking. It is easy to make and requires no special skills – in fact it is very hard to get a Paratha wrong! Plain Parathas can be eaten as an accompaniment. Stuff the breads with a mixture such as potatoes and peas or spinach and potato to make them a more filling meal.

MAKES 4–6

450 g (1 lb) chapatti or wholemeal flour
1 teaspoon salt
225 g (8 oz) ghee

Sift the flour and salt into a bowl, gradually add 600 ml (1 pint) water and mix to a hard dough. Knead the dough for at least 10 minutes, until it glistens and does not stick to the bowl. Cover the bowl with a wet cloth and leave in a cool place for 4 hours.

Warm the ghee until melted. Divide dough into 4–6 balls and roll each one out on a floured board to a circle about 5 mm ($\frac{1}{4}$ inch) thick. With a pastry brush, generously brush some of the melted ghee over the surface of a circle of dough. Starting at one side, roll the dough up to form a sausage shape. Take one end of the sausage and wrap round and round to form a spiral. Roll this spiral out to a circle 5 mm ($\frac{1}{4}$ inch) thick. Brush with more melted ghee and repeat the process four times. Finally, roll out the dough until slightly less than 5 mm ($\frac{1}{4}$ inch) thick. Repeat with the remaining dough to make 4–6 parathas altogether. Heat the remaining ghee in a heavy-based frying pan until fairly hot. Fry the parathas until golden brown and crisp on both sides, turning once. Drain and serve immediately.

BELOW: *Clockwise from top; Lentil Flour Crisps (page 33), Lentil Sauce with Hot Topping (page 33), Fried Unleavened Bread, Leavened Bread with Poppy Seeds (page 34), Rice (page 34).*

INDIA & PAKISTAN
PUDDINGS

Puddings, desserts and sweetmeats are very popular in India, and are not restricted to traditional mealtimes. Many sweets are designed to be eaten at any time, often in the afternoon with tea.

Apart from the various flour-based confections, which have similarities to Western cakes, Indian cooks have perfected many exotic recipes which make use of concentrated milk, or *khoa*, as a principal ingredient. Traditionally, this milk was produced by boiling several pints of milk over a long period of time so that the water content evaporated and the milk became concentrated. These days few people are likely to have time for such a laborious procedure, and recipes have developed which make use of full fat milk powder (baby milk formula). The flavour of the finished sweet is just as good. The recipe for Barfi/Fudge (page 39) makes use of this type of milk.

Ras-O-Malai

Cream Cheese in a Sweet Cream Sauce

This is one of the most delicious of all the Indian puddings. It is rich beyond belief; a mixture of semolina and the traditional Indian cream cheese known as *panir*, flavoured with almonds and poached in a light syrup. The resulting confection is then immersed in a thick cream sauce flavoured with rose water. When making *panir*, use a full cream milk.

SERVES 6–8

Ras:
1.2 litres (2 pints) full cream milk
juice of 2 lemons
100 g (4 oz) semolina
1 tablespoon chopped blanched almonds
1 tablespoon honey
Syrup:
6 cardamoms
6 cloves
7.5 cm (3 inch) cinnamon stick
175 g (6 oz) clear honey
Malai:
150 ml ($\frac{1}{4}$ pint) milk
300 ml ($\frac{1}{2}$ pint) double cream
1 teaspoon rose water
1 tablespoon chopped pistachios

Make the ras: heat the milk in a heavy-based saucepan, add the lemon juice and bring to the boil. (The milk will curdle.) Continue to boil for a further 5–10 minutes. Leave to cool, then drain off the whey, leaving the curds behind. Place the curds in a double thickness of cheesecloth, tie up and place in a sieve. Top with a weight to help remove the moisture. Leave overnight.

The next day, mix the resulting cheese (*panir*) with the semolina to form a dough, then break into 12–16 pieces the size of golf balls. Roll to a smooth shape, make a small indentation in the top of each ball and add a pinch of chopped almonds and a little honey. Reform the balls to seal this mixture inside. Set aside in a cool place.

Make the syrup: bring 1 litre (1$\frac{3}{4}$ pints) water to the boil in a heavy-based saucepan together with the cardamoms, cloves and cinnamon stick. Lower the heat, add the honey and stir until melted. Increase the heat and boil rapidly, without stirring, until reduced to a syrup, three-quarters of the original volume. Gently add the cream cheese balls to the syrup and poach lightly for 1 hour 20 minutes. Remove the balls carefully with a perforated spoon, leave to cool, then chill in the refrigerator for about 2 hours.

Make the malai: boil the milk in a heavy-based saucepan until reduced to two-thirds of its original volume. Leave to cool, then stir in the double cream and sprinkle in the rose water and pistachios. Leave to cool, then chill in the refrigerator before pouring over the cream cheese balls. Allow to soak for several hours before serving.

Meeta Samosa

Sweet Indian Pastries with Potato Filling
Samosas are most often filled with a savoury
mixture; here is a sweet version. In India, sweet
Samosas are a classic teatime snack.

MAKES 16–20

100 g (4 oz) plain flour
pinch of salt
25 g (1 oz) ghee
Filling:
450 g (1 lb) potatoes
1 tablespoon chopped blanched almonds
seeds of 20 cardamoms
2 tablespoons clear honey
2 teaspoons sultanas
1 tablespoon chopped pistachios
vegetable oil, for deep-frying

Sift the flour and salt into a bowl. Rub in the ghee, then
add a little warm water to make a very hard, stiff dough.
Roll into a large ball and set aside.

Make the filling: scrub the potatoes, then cook them in
boiling water until just soft. It is important not to
overcook the potatoes at this stage. Remove the skins
from the potatoes, cut the flesh into 1 cm ($\frac{1}{2}$ inch) cubes
and place in a bowl. Add the almonds and mix together.

Pound the cardamom seeds in a mortar and pestle.
Warm the honey in a small saucepan so that it becomes
very runny, sprinkle in the cardamom seeds, then pour
over the potato and almond mixture. Finally, sprinkle
over the sultanas and pistachios.

Make the samosas: break the dough into 8–10 pieces
the size of walnuts. Form into smooth balls. Roll out each
ball on a floured surface to a very
thin circle, about 1 mm ($\frac{1}{16}$ inch)
thick. Place the circles of dough
one on top of the other, with a
light dusting of flour between
each one. With a sharp knife, cut
into 16–20 semi-circles.

Place 2 teaspoons of filling on to
one side of each semi-circle, then
fold the dough in a cone shape.
Seal all the edges by moistening
the dough with water. Heat the
oil in a deep-fat frier until hot,
then deep-fry the samosas in
batches until they are crisp and
light brown on all sides. Remove
from the oil with a perforated
spoon and drain on paper towels.
Serve hot or cold.

Gulab Jamun

Deep-fried Milk Pastry in Thick Syrup
A very sticky, but flavoursome, Indian
sweetmeat, which uses a very thick syrup to add
an aromatic flavour to deep-fried pastry balls.
Gulab Jamun should be eaten fresh to be
enjoyed at their best, although they will keep in
their syrup for several days if chilled in the
refrigerator.

SERVES 4–6

1 litre (1$\frac{3}{4}$ pints) milk
juice of 2 lemons
100 g (4 oz) semolina
vegetable oil, for deep-frying
Syrup:
5 cardamoms
5 cloves
225 g (8 oz) sugar
2 teaspoons rose water

Heat the milk in a heavy-based saucepan, add the lemon
juice and bring to the boil. (The milk will curdle.)
Continue to boil for a further 5–10 minutes. Leave to
cool, then drain off the whey, leaving the curds behind.
Place the curds in a double thickness of cheesecloth, tie
up and place in a sieve. Top with a weight to help remove
the moisture. Leave overnight.

The next day, mix the resulting cheese (*panir*) with
the semolina to form a dough, then break into about 15
pieces the size of unshelled hazelnuts. Form into smooth
balls. Heat the oil in a deep-fat frier until a ball of dough
immediately starts to sizzle and float to the surface when
dropped into the pan. Deep-fry the balls in batches until
golden brown, then remove with
a perforated spoon and drain on
paper towels. Keep warm.

Make the syrup: bring 300 ml ($\frac{1}{2}$
pint) water to the boil in a heavy-
based saucepan together with the
cardamoms and cloves. Lower the
heat, add the sugar and stir until
dissolved. Increase the heat and
boil rapidly, without stirring, until the syrup starts to thicken.
Allow to cool slightly, then sprinkle in the rose water. Put the
pastry balls in a serving bowl and
pour over the syrup. Serve warm.

Jallebi

Deep-fried Pretzels

In India, Jallebi are sold in restaurants, and at wayside stalls which specialize solely in Jallebi cooking. At these stalls, men sit cross-legged in front of huge vats of hot oil, spooning or piping whirls of Jallebi batter into the oil, cooking them until crisp, then dunking the fried Jallebi into a warm aromatic syrup. This is the best way of serving Jallebis, although they can be eaten some time after they have been cooked, in which case they will have absorbed much more of the spicy sugar syrup.

MAKES 15–20 PRETZELS

450 g (1 lb) plain flour
½ teaspoon salt
225 g (8 oz) natural yogurt, at room temperature
1 tablespoon brown sugar
25 g (1 oz) 'easy blend' dried yeast
vegetable oil, for deep-frying
Syrup:
10 cardamoms
10 cloves
7.5 cm (3 inch) cinnamon stick
450 g (1 lb) brown sugar

Sift the flour and salt into a warmed large bowl, then gradually add the yogurt and a little warm water to form a batter that is the consistency of double cream. Add the sugar, stir in well, then sprinkle in the dried yeast. Cover with a clean teatowel and place in a warm place for 6 hours to allow the yeast to work.

Make the syrup: bring 1 litre (1¾ pints) water to the boil in a heavy-based saucepan together with the cardamoms, cloves and cinnamon stick. Lower the heat, add the sugar and stir until dissolved. Increase the heat and boil rapidly, without stirring, until the volume has reduced by half to a heavy syrup. Keep warm.

To fry the jallebi: heat the oil in a deep-fat frier until a small spoonful of batter immediately starts to sizzle and float to the surface when dropped into the pan. Spoon the batter into the oil, creating whirls by moving the spoon in a circular fashion. An easier way of doing this is to put the batter into a piping bag with a very small opening, about 3 mm (⅛ inch) and to squeeze whirls of batter about 10 cm (4 inches) in diameter into the hot oil. Cook until the jallebi are golden brown in colour, then remove immediately with a perforated spoon and drain. Immerse the freshly cooked jallebis in the warm syrup for 5 minutes or so. Remove, drain and serve.

BELOW: *Left, Deep-fried Milk Pastry in Thick Syrup (page 37). Centre, Indian Ice Cream with Pistachios (page 39). Right, Cream Cheese in a Sweet Cream Sauce (page 36).* OPPOSITE: *Top, Fudge (page 39). Bottom, Deep-fried Pretzels.*

Barfi

Fudge

There are many different types of Indian sweets – all very rich and consisting mostly of sugar, milk and flavourings such as nuts, fruit and spices. Barfi is the general name given to a whole range of fudge-like sweetmeats. Such was the laborious traditional method of making it, involving hours spent boiling down litres of milk, that Barfi was seldom prepared at home, but usually bought from professional confectioners. Resourceful Indian cooks have learnt how to make use of milk powder, and this has greatly simplified the making of Barfi.

MAKES ABOUT 750 g (1½ lb)

350 g (12 oz) thick honey
10 cloves
7.5 cm (3 inch) cinnamon stick
seeds of 20 cardamoms
175 g (6 oz) full fat milk powder, or
baby milk formula
1 tablespoon chopped pistachios

Heat the honey gently in a heavy-based saucepan with 150 ml (¼ pint) water until melted. Bring to the boil and add the cloves and cinnamon stick. Boil for 10–15 minutes, without stirring, to make a very thick syrup. If the syrup is not thick enough, boil it for a little longer. While the syrup is thickening, pound the cardamom seeds in a mortar and pestle, then transfer to a bowl, add the milk powder and stir well to mix.

Remove the syrup from the heat and sprinkle in the milk powder and cardamom seed mixture, stirring it into a thick paste. Spread the mixture evenly in an ungreased fudge tin, about 20 cm (8 inches) square and 4 cm (1½ inches) deep.

Sprinkle the chopped pistachios over the top of the mixture and press them in lightly with the palm of your hand. With a sharp knife, make cuts in the mixture. Traditionally, a diamond shape is used, but the barfi can be cut into any shape. Leave in a cool place until solidified, then remove from the tin before serving.

Pista Kulfi

Indian Ice Cream with Pistachios

This recipe calls for the inclusion of condensed milk, and to make it even richer, double cream. Traditionally, Kulfi is served from conical moulds.

SERVES 6-8

300 ml (½ pint) double cream
300 ml (½ pint) milk
400 g (14 oz) can condensed milk
1 tablespoon clear honey
2 tablespoons chopped pistachios
2 teaspoons rose water
green food colouring (optional)

Heat the cream, milk, condensed milk and honey together in a heavy-based saucepan. Bring gently to the boil, stirring constantly, then simmer for 45 minutes over very low heat.

Remove the pan from the heat and sprinkle in the pistachios and rose water, then add a little food colouring, if using. Allow the mixture to cool.

Pour the mixture into a shallow 900 ml (1½ pint) freezer container or 6–8 kulfi moulds and freeze for 3–4 hours. Remove from the freezer and leave to stand at room temperature for 20–30 minutes to soften. To serve, turn out of the kulfi moulds or cut into squares.

INDIA & PAKISTAN
MENUS & CUSTOMS

The Hindu people of India and Pakistan are by and large vegetarians. Sikhs and Muslims, however, enjoy meat as an essential part of their everyday diet. Despite these and other basic differences, such as the fact that Muslims do not eat pork and Hindus do not eat beef, the same basic rules of balanced diet apply all over India. From a humble meal of rice, vegetables and pulses, to a magnificent banquet, the emphasis with all Indian food is very much on balance.

The Traditional Indian Meal

As a general rule, an Indian meal usually consists of several different dishes which are placed on the table together. Everyone helps themselves to as little or as much as they want, in whatever order they fancy. There is usually a choice of one meat or fish dish or sometimes both, depending on the wealth of the family and the type of occasion, several different vegetable dishes, some kind of bread or rice, yogurt, a salad, and a selection of chutneys, relishes and similar accompaniments. In the case of a vegetarian meal, the number of vegetable dishes is increased, lentils and/or another pulse dish are included, and yogurt is always served. Cooking styles, techniques and ingredients obviously vary from one region and religion to another, but it is true to say that Indian meals are always balanced in terms of colour, flavour and, above all, texture. If meat or fish is cooked in a 'wet' sauce, for example, the cook will ensure that

there is at least one 'dry' vegetable dish to provide contrast. This is a simple, commonsense rule to apply when you are making up an Indian menu at home.

How Many Courses? There are no hard and fast rules when it comes to deciding which dishes to serve. Indian custom is to offer a selection of different dishes from which guests may choose, as they will not all like, or even want to try, the same dish. Indians do not traditionally eat one course after another, but if you prefer to follow a Western-style pattern of eating with Indian food, then by all means do so – Indian food is extremely adaptable. Foods such as *samosas*, *pakoras* and *dosas*, for example, which are normally eaten throughout the day as snacks in India, make the most appetizing starters for a dinner party, and are now traditionally served as such in Indian restaurants in the West. The 'main course' can then follow with a selection of different curries, tandoori dishes and vegetables, served together with accompaniments such as rice or bread, salad, yogurt-based dishes, chutneys and relishes. Due to the scarcity of meat and fish and the large number of vegetarians in India, vegetables are always regarded as dishes in their own right. When planning an Indian meal, they should not be served as accompaniments as they usually are in the West, but should be given equal importance with the meat and fish dishes. Desserts are normally reserved for celebrations and feasts in India, and sweetmeats are

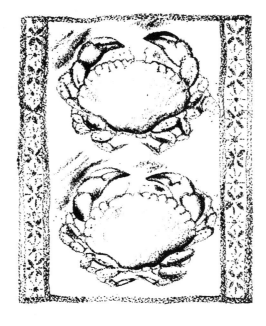

eaten throughout the day as snacks rather than to mark the end of a meal, but this is no reason why Indian sweet dishes cannot be offered as Western-style desserts.

Rice or Bread? Carbohydrate in the form of rice or bread is a central part of every Indian meal, no matter what the occasion, as it forms the staple diet for the vast majority of Indians. Quite apart from this, however, rice and bread are essential for providing contrast to hot and spicy foods – something that most Westerners will appreciate.

In India, the eating of both rice and bread together is frowned upon, although the choice does not normally arise – bread is eaten more in the north where vast acres of wheat are grown, whereas rice is eaten in the paddy growing areas of southern India.

When planning an Indian meal at home, rice is certainly the easier choice. Most Indian breads must be freshly cooked to be enjoyed at their best, and this can be tricky if you are entertaining guests and do not want to be confined to the kitchen before the meal. If you are serving rice, observe the Indian rule of spooning only a small amount on to individual plates, then grouping portions of the other dishes around it so that guests can take a little rice with each mouthful of meat, fish or vegetables, etc. Never mound rice up in the centre of the plate and pour curry over it.

How to Serve and Eat Indian Food
It is the Hindu tradition to serve food on a *thali*, a circular metal tray or plate, although in some parts of southern India, food is eaten off banana leaves. The *thali* is rather like an artist's palette in that small portions of each dish are arranged around the edge, either in small bowls or directly on the tray, then the diner uses the centre of the tray to eat off, mixing and blending different flavours, colours and textures according to individual choice. Obviously it would be impractical to serve food in this way in a Western home, but to give an Indian meal a touch of authenticity, encourage your guests to use their plates in the same way as a *thali*, grouping helpings of different dishes around a central portion of rice.

Throughout the Indian sub-continent, it is traditional to eat with the right hand. The left hand is never used to touch food because it is considered unclean. Nowadays, however, many Indians use cutlery to eat their food, and when serving Indian food by all means provide dessertspoons and forks, at least for the main course. If you are serving bread, encourage your guests to break it with their fingers and then use it to scoop up their food – they will be surprised how easy it is and how much more enjoyable the food tastes.

What to Drink with Indian Food Tea is the universal drink in India, served sweet and milky, although many drink sweet drinks based on essences such as sandalwood and mint, or a yogurt drink called *lassi*. With an Indian meal at home, you will probably find the most suitable drinks are ice-cold water, chilled lager or a light beer; fine wines are not appropriate.

—— Sample Menus ——

CURRY SUPPER
Ground Meat Patties
Lamb with Yogurt and Tomatoes
Curried Okra
Rice
Deep-fried Milk Pastry in Thick Syrup

TANDOORI LUNCH
Chick Pea Flour Fritters
Tandoori Chicken
Aubergines with Tomatoes
Steamed Potatoes
Charcoal-grilled Fish
Leavened Bread with Poppy Seeds
Mint-flavoured Sauce
Indian Ice Cream with Pistachios

VEGETARIAN FEAST
Spiced Chick Peas
Rice with Vegetables
Mixed Vegetable Curry with Coconut
Curried Okra
Lentil Sauce with Hot Topping
Vermicelli Pudding

SEAFOOD CELEBRATION MEAL
Lentil Flour Crisps
Steamed Lentil Cakes
Fish Ball Curry
Prawn Curry with Coconut
Spinach with Tomatoes
Steamed Potatoes
Fried Unleavened Bread
Cream Cheese in a Sweet Cream Sauce

KEBAB PARTY
Chick Pea Flour Bread with Spinach
Marinated Cubes of Lamb
Minced Beef on Skewers
Barbecued King Prawns
Lentil Sauce with Hot Topping
Mint-flavoured Sauce
Yogurt with Cucumber or Tomato
Rice
Indian Salad

NOTE: Adjust quantities of individual dishes according to the number of people being served

ID-UL-FITR CELEBRATION

Id-Ul-Fitr is a Muslim festival celebrating the end of Ramadan, the thirty days of fasting. In Islam, this involves abstinence from eating and drinking between sunrise and sunset. Bearing in mind the hot desert climates in which most Muslims live, fasting can be particularly trying. Nonetheless, it is practised by millions of Muslims, and so there is much rejoicing at the end of Ramadan. Everyone celebrates in fine style – with new clothes, prayers, visits to friends and relations and, of course, good food.

FOR 8–10 PEOPLE

Ground Meat Patties (page 13)
Minced Beef on Skewers (page 31)

Spiced Leg of Lamb
Royal Lamb Curry
Potato and Cauliflower Curry
Spinach with Tomatoes (page 25)
Indian Salad
Rice with Stock and Spices
Yogurt with Cucumber or Tomato (page 32)
Unleavened Bread

Fried Bread in Saffron and Pistachio Sauce
Vermicelli Pudding

Salat

Indian Salad

Indian salads are invariably chopped and mixed with various spices, some of them quite hot. This recipe is not too hot, although it does call for the inclusion of chopped green chillies. Their use is optional. Almost any combination of vegetables can be used in this salad. Try Chinese leaves instead of lettuce and celery in place of the cucumber

SERVES 4 as an individual dish

1 lettuce
1 teaspoon salt
1 teaspoon freshly ground black pepper
1 teaspoon chilli powder
4 tomatoes
½ cucumber
1 large onion
2 teaspoons coriander seeds
juice of 1 lemon
4 fresh green chillies (optional)
½ teaspoon paprika, to finish

Separate the lettuce leaves, then wash and pat dry with paper towels or a clean teatowel. Mix together the salt, pepper and chilli powder. Pile one lettuce leaf on top of another, sprinkling each one with a little of the spice mixture. When you have 5 or 6 leaves together, cut them crossways into 2.5 cm (1 inch) shreds.

Put the shredded spiced lettuce leaves in a large salad bowl. Chop the tomatoes and cucumber, add to the lettuce and toss gently to mix. Peel the onion. Slice half of the onion into thin rings and coarsely chop the other half. Mix the chopped onion with the lettuce, tomatoes and cucumber.

Dry-fry the coriander seeds in a heavy-based frying pan, then crush coarsely in a mortar and pestle. Mix into the salad and sprinkle with the lemon juice. Arrange the onion rings over the top of the salad. Top and tail the chillies (if using), then chop into 5 mm ($\frac{1}{4}$ inch) pieces and sprinkle on top of the onions. Chill in the refrigerator and sprinkle with the paprika before serving.

RIGHT: *Clockwise from top; Spiced Leg of Lamb (page 44), Indian Salad, Rice with Stock and Spices (page 44), Potato and Cauliflower Curry (page 45), Unleavened Bread (page 45).*

Raan | Palao

Spiced Leg of Lamb

Raan is very typical of the northern areas of India, especially the more temperate climates where livestock eats well on good grass, producing excellent meat. Ideally, use a large leg of lamb, weighing about 3 kg (7 lb)

SERVES 8 as an individual dish

3 kg (7 lb) leg of lamb, trimmed of fat
3 lemons
2 teaspoons salt
10 garlic cloves, peeled
two 7.5 cm (3 inch) pieces fresh root ginger, peeled
1 teaspoon freshly ground black pepper
1 teaspoon saffron threads (optional)
5 cm (2 inch) cinnamon stick
10 cloves
seeds of 20 cardamoms
2 tablespoons clear honey
450 g (1 lb) natural yogurt
50 g (2 oz) shelled pistachios
100 g (4 oz) blanched almonds
2 teaspoons chilli powder
1 teaspoon turmeric

Make deep slashes in the lamb with a sharp knife. Place in an ovenproof dish or casserole with a tight-fitting lid. Cut 2 of the lemons in half, then rub the cut surfaces over the lamb, squeezing the juice into the slashes in the meat. Sprinkle with the salt and set aside.

Work the garlic and ginger to a paste in a blender or food processor. Add the pepper, then rub the mixture into the meat. Cover and marinate for 8 hours.

If using saffron threads, put them in a cup and pour over boiling water to cover, then leave to infuse for 20 minutes. Meanwhile, crush the cinnamon, cloves and cardamom seeds in a mortar and pestle. Put the honey in a blender or food processor with the yogurt, pistachios, almonds, chilli powder and turmeric. Work until well mixed together, then sprinkle in the crushed cinnamon, cloves and cardamoms. Strain in the saffron liquid (if used) and work for 30 seconds. Pour this mixture over the lamb, making sure to cover as much of the meat as possible. Cover and marinate for a further 8 hours.

Place the covered dish in a preheated hot oven (230°C/450°F, Gas Mark 8) and cook for 10 minutes. Reduce the temperature to moderate (180°C/350°F, Gas Mark 4) and cook for a further 2 hours, basting the meat every 15 minutes or so. Remove the lid of the dish, increase the oven temperature to hot (220°C/425°F, Gas Mark 7) and cook for a further 10 minutes. Raan can be served hot, straight from the oven, but it is more traditional to serve it after it has cooled for an hour or so.

Rice with Stock and Spices

For many people, rice is a very difficult dish to get right. The method of cooking rice on page 34 should cause few problems, and the following recipe is safe for beginners and newcomers to rice cooking, as the addition of ghee tends to prevent the grains of rice sticking together. If wished, garnish with slices of tomato and hard-boiled egg just before serving.

SERVES 6–8 as an individual dish

750g (1½ lb) long grain rice, preferably Basmati or Patna
100 g (4 oz) ghee
2 large onions, peeled and thinly sliced
4 garlic cloves, peeled and thinly sliced
two 7.5 cm (3 inch) pieces fresh root ginger
15 cloves
15 cardamoms
two 5 cm (2 inch) cinnamon sticks
2 teaspoons turmeric
2 teaspoons black peppercorns
2 teaspoons garam masala
1 teaspoon salt
1.2 litres (2 pints) hot chicken stock from a cube
100 g (4 oz) sultanas
50 g (2 oz) slivered blanched almonds

Wash the rice well in at least 3 complete changes of cold water. Drain the rice, then pick it over to remove any stones or other 'undesirable' objects. Heat the ghee in a large, heavy-based saucepan, add the onions and garlic and fry gently for 4–5 minutes until soft. Peel the ginger and cut it into strips about 5 mm ($\frac{1}{4}$ inch) wide and 5 cm (2 inches) long. Add to the pan and fry for a further 2 minutes. Add the cloves, cardamoms and cinnamon, stir well to mix and fry for a further minute, then add the turmeric, peppercorns, garam masala and salt. Fry for a further 2 minutes, stirring constantly.

Add the rice and stir well to ensure it is coated with the spice mixture. Pour in the hot stock and bring to the boil. Boil gently, uncovered, until the rice is just hard in the centre, stirring from time to time to ensure that it does not stick to the bottom of the pan. If necessary, add a little more hot stock or water.

When the rice is ready, pour it into a large sieve and allow any liquid to drain away. Transfer the rice to a large oval platter and sprinkle over the sultanas and almonds. Serve immediately, or keep hot in a moderate oven (180°C/350°F, Gas Mark 4) until ready to serve.

Gobi Mussalum | Chapatti

Potato and Cauliflower Curry

Potatoes and cauliflower are both grown in India, but they tend to be found only in the more temperate, northern areas. This is a fairly dry curry, combining both vegetables in a hot spicy mixture.

SERVES 6–8 as an individual dish

450 g (1 lb) potatoes
450 g (1 lb) cauliflower
salt
75 g (3 oz) ghee
1 medium onion, peeled and finely chopped
2 garlic cloves, peeled and finely chopped
5 cm (2 inch) piece fresh root ginger, peeled and finely chopped
2 teaspoons coriander seeds
1 teaspoon kalonji (onion seeds)
1 teaspoon turmeric
1 teaspoon chilli powder
1 teaspoon freshly ground black pepper
50 g (2 oz) tomato purée
2 teaspoons garam masala

Peel the potatoes and cut into 2.5 cm (1 inch) pieces. Cut the cauliflower into small florets, discarding any thick stalks. Cook the potato and cauliflower in separate pans of boiling salted water until they just begin to soften.

Meanwhile, heat the ghee in a heavy-based saucepan, add the onion, garlic and ginger and fry gently for 4–5 minutes, or until soft. Add the coriander and kalonji and fry for a further 30 seconds. Add the turmeric, chilli powder, black pepper and 1 teaspoon salt, stir well and fry for a further 2 minutes. Stir the tomato purée into the mixture.

Drain the potato and cauliflower, reserving a little of the cauliflower water. Add the potato and cauliflower to the saucepan and toss gently in the spice mixture. If the curry is a little too dry, add some of the reserved cauliflower water. Cook for 5–6 minutes, then sprinkle in the garam masala and cook for a further minute. Serve hot.

Unleavened Bread

Chapattis are the easiest of the Indian breads to make, and they are probably the ones with which most people are familiar. They are in fact flat unleavened pancakes made with a wholemeal flour called *ata*. This flour is available at Indian food shops, and is also sometimes called *chapatti* flour, but if you are unable to get it, ordinary plain wholemeal flour is equally successful. If you follow the instructions in the recipe for wrapping the Chapattis in a teatowel after cooking, you can make them an hour or two in advance.

MAKES 8–10

350 g (12 oz) chapatti or wholemeal flour
¾ teaspoon salt

Sift the flour and salt into a bowl, then gradually add about 300 ml (½ pint) cold water and mix to a firm dough.

Turn the dough out on to a lightly floured surface and knead well until smooth and elastic. Break the dough into 8–10 pieces, then form each piece into a ball. Roll out each ball of dough to a thickness of 3 mm (⅛ inch).

Dust an ungreased heavy-based frying pan or griddle (preferably cast iron) with a little chapatti or wholemeal flour. Place the pan over the heat until very hot, then add a chapatti and cook for 3–4 minutes until blisters appear on the surface. Turn the chapatti over and cook for a further 3–4 minutes.

Remove the chapatti from the pan with tongs, then place under a preheated hot grill for a few seconds until black blisters appear and the chapatti swells up. Wrap immediately in a warm teatowel (to keep in the moisture) and place in a basket while making the remaining chapattis. Serve warm.

Shahi Korma

Royal Lamb Curry

This rich and exotic curry was created for the great Mogul Emperors.

SERVES 4 as an individual dish

1 kg (2–2¼ lb) lean boneless lamb (leg or shoulder)
juice of 1 lemon
225 g (8 oz) natural yogurt
75 g (3 oz) ghee
2 medium onions, peeled and thinly sliced
4 garlic cloves, peeled and thinly sliced
7.5 cm (3 inch) piece fresh root ginger, peeled and thinly sliced
7.5 cm (3 inch) cinnamon stick
10 cloves
10 cardamoms
2 teaspoons ground coriander
2 teaspoons ground cumin
2 teaspoons chilli powder
1 teaspoon turmeric
1 teaspoon freshly ground black pepper
1½ teaspoons salt
100 g (4 oz) whole blanched almonds
50 g (2 oz) shelled pistachios
150 ml (¼ pint) single cream
varak (silver leaf), to garnish (optional)

Cut the lamb into 4 cm (1½ inch) cubes, being careful to trim away excess fat and gristle. Put the cubes in a bowl, pour in the lemon juice and mix well. Mix in the yogurt, cover the bowl and leave the lamb to marinate in a cold place or the refrigerator for at least 2 hours.

Heat the ghee in a heavy-based saucepan, add the onions, garlic and ginger and fry gently for 4–5 minutes until soft. Add the cinnamon, cloves and cardamoms, stir well and fry for a further minute. Mix together the ground coriander, cumin, chilli powder, turmeric, black pepper and salt, add to the pan, stir well and cook for a further 2–3 minutes.

Add the lamb together with the marinade, stir well to ensure the cubes of meat are well coated in the spice mixture, then stir in 300 ml (½ pint) boiling water. Chop half of the almonds and stir into the lamb. Cover the pan and simmer gently for about 50 minutes, or until the meat is cooked.

Before serving, sprinkle in the remaining whole almonds and the pistachios, lower the heat and pour in the cream, stirring well to mix. Cook gently for a further 5–10 minutes, without allowing to boil. Transfer to a warmed serving dish, garnish with varak and serve hot.

BELOW: *From left to right; Royal Lamb Curry, Indian savoury snacks, Vermicelli Pudding (page 47), Fried Bread in Saffron and Pistachio Sauce (page 47).*

Shahi Tukra | Khir Sewian

Fried Bread in Saffron and Pistachio Sauce

This is very much a king of Mogul recipes. Although rich, it is refreshing to eat at the end of a large feast, when served chilled.

SERVES 6 as an individual dish

I small loaf white bread, crusts removed
vegetable oil, for deep-frying
I teaspoon saffron threads
600 ml (I pint) milk, warmed
225 g (8 oz) clear honey
50 g (2 oz) shelled pistachios, coarsely chopped
25 g (I oz) blanched almonds, chopped
300 ml (½ pint) single cream
5–6 drops rose water

Cut the bread into 2.5 cm (I inch) thick slices then cut each slice lengthways. Heat the oil in a deep-fat frier and deep-fry the bread until golden. Drain and keep hot.

Put the saffron in a cup and cover with some of the milk. Add the honey to the remaining milk and heat until melted, then add the nuts. Strain in the saffron-coloured milk, stir and remove from the heat. Cool slightly.

Stir in the cream and rose water. Put the bread in a serving bowl, pour over the sauce and chill in the refrigerator for at least I hour before serving.

Vermicelli Pudding

When Muslims visit each other, as is the tradition on Id-Ul-Fitr, they are always asked to partake of some food. Invariably, a large bowl of Khir Sewian is prepared, which is dipped into throughout the day as visitors come and go. It is not required to eat a great deal at one sitting; a small saucerful taken with a cup of tea is enough to show due respect for the hospitality.

SERVES 6 as an individual dish

100 g (4 oz) ghee
100 g (4 oz) vermicelli
750 ml (1¼ pints) milk
15 cardamoms
225 g (8 oz) clear honey
100 g (4 oz) sultanas

Heat the ghee in a heavy-based saucepan and add the vermicelli, breaking it into 10 cm (4 inch) pieces. Fry gently for 5–6 minutes, then pour on the milk and bring to the boil. Remove the seeds from the cardamoms, crush them in a mortar and pestle, then sprinkle into the pan and add the honey, spoon by spoon. Stir well until the honey has melted. Cook for a further 10–15 minutes, then stir in the sultanas. Serve hot or chilled.

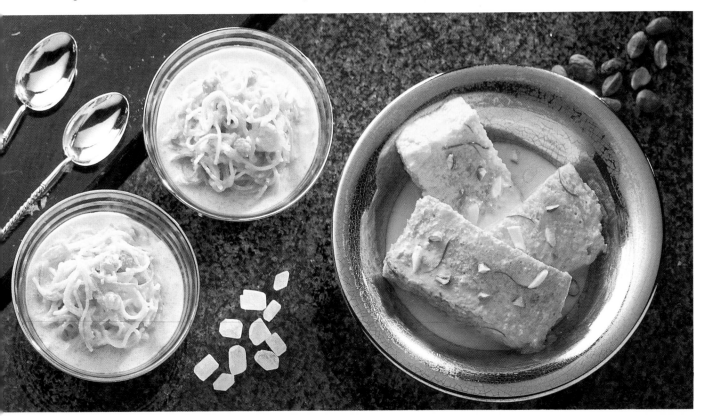

COCONUT FESTIVAL

Each year, around the coasts of India, a festival is held to give thanks for all the goodness supplied by the sea. The gods of the sea are responsible for the livelihood of millions, so it is perhaps not surprising that people go to great lengths, dressing up in their best clothes and, among other things, casting fresh coconuts into the waters.

By and large, the fish cooking of India has been overlooked by people in the West. The following menu includes mostly fish dishes, which makes it an interesting alternative to the more usual meat-based Indian meals.

FOR 10–12 PEOPLE

Steamed Mussels
Curried Crab
Rice Cooked with Chicken
Baked Fish
Prawn Curry with Coconut (page 20)
Egg and Coconut Curry
Mixed Vegetable Curry with Coconut (page 26)
Yogurt with Cucumber or Tomato (page 32)

Spiced Fruit Salad
Coconut Fudge
Indian Ice Cream with Pistachios (page 39)

Teesryo

Steamed Mussels
Traditionally, this dish is made with clams, but the recipe works equally well with mussels, which are far easier to buy in the West. Both are prepared in the same way.

SERVES 6 as an individual dish

1 kg (2–2¼ lb) mussels or clams
100 g (4 oz) ghee
1 large onion, peeled and finely chopped
2 garlic cloves, peeled and finely chopped
2 teaspoons desiccated coconut
2 teaspoons salt
1 teaspoon turmeric
1 teaspoon chilli powder
1 teaspoon freshly ground black pepper
150 ml (¼ pint) vinegar
450 g (1 lb) natural yogurt
2 teaspoons garam masala
juice of 2 lemons, to finish

Scrub the shellfish well under cold running water and remove the beards. Place in a large bowl, cover with fresh cold water and leave the mussels or clams to soak for 20–30 minutes.

Meanwhile, heat the ghee in a heavy-based saucepan, add the onion and garlic and fry gently for 4–5 minutes until soft. Add the desiccated coconut and salt and continue frying until the coconut begins to brown. Add the turmeric, chilli powder and pepper, stir well and fry for a further minute.

Drain the shellfish and discard any that are open, or that do not close when tapped sharply on the work surface. Add the vinegar to the pan with the shellfish, cover with a tight-fitting lid and increase the heat so that the mixture boils. Cook over high heat for about 5 minutes until the shells open, shaking the pan from time to time. Remove the saucepan from the heat.

Remove the empty half shells from the shellfish and discard. Arrange the shellfish on the half shells in a warmed serving bowl, one on top of the other. Pour the cooking liquid from the saucepan into a blender or food processor. Add the yogurt and garam masala, blend for 1 minute, then return to the saucepan and bring to just below boiling point. Pour the mixture over the shellfish, then sprinkle with the lemon juice and serve immediately.

Kaleacha Kari | Murgh Biryani

Curried Crab

The secret of this dish is to use coconut in two ways: firstly to add texture to the curry sauce by creating a thick milk from three-quarters of the coconut 'meat'; secondly to add texture towards the end of the cooking process by using the remaining coconut meat in slices.

SERVES 6 as an individual dish

1 fresh coconut
75 g (3 oz) ghee
1 large onion, peeled and thinly sliced
4 garlic cloves, peeled and thinly sliced
7.5 cm (3 inch) piece fresh root ginger, peeled and thinly sliced
2 teaspoons fenugreek seeds
2 teaspoons peppercorns
2 teaspoons chilli powder
2 teaspoons ground coriander
1 teaspoon turmeric
1 teaspoon salt
450 g (1 lb) natural yogurt
300 ml ($\frac{1}{2}$ pint) milk
450 g (1 lb) frozen crab meat, defrosted
2 tablespoons chopped coriander, to garnish

Make holes in the eyes of the coconut, then drain out the liquid and reserve. Crack open the coconut and separate the meat from the shell. Thinly slice one-quarter of the coconut meat and set aside. Put the remaining three-quarters of the coconut meat in a blender or food processor and chop very finely. (Alternatively, finely grate the meat.)

Transfer the chopped or grated coconut to a bowl, pour over 600 ml (1 pint) boiling water, stir for 5 minutes, then strain through a sieve lined with 2 thicknesses of cheesecloth held over a bowl. Gather up the cheesecloth and squeeze out as much of the coconut 'milk' as possible. Discard the coconut from inside the cloth. Stir the reserved liquid from the coconut into the coconut milk and set the bowl aside.

Heat the ghee in a heavy-based saucepan, add the onion, garlic and ginger and fry gently for 4–5 minutes until soft. Add the fenugreek seeds, peppercorns, chilli powder, coriander, turmeric and salt. Stir well and fry for 2–3 minutes, then add the coconut milk. Put the yogurt and fresh milk in a bowl and stir together until evenly mixed. Stir slowly into the pan, bring to just below boiling point and simmer for 5–6 minutes.

Add the crab meat and sliced coconut, folding the crab in gently so that the large pieces do not break up. Cook gently for a further 5 minutes, then turn into a warmed serving dish and sprinkle with the chopped coriander. Serve immediately.

Rice Cooked with Chicken

In recent years, biryani recipes have been adapted as a means of using up leftovers. This classic recipe goes back to first principles.

SERVES 6 as an individual dish

4 small onions, peeled and halved
2 bay leaves
1.5–1.75 kg (3–4 lb) boiling fowl
$\frac{1}{2}$ teaspoon saffron threads
750 g (1$\frac{1}{2}$ lb) Basmati rice
100 g (4 oz) ghee
5 garlic cloves, peeled and thinly sliced
10 cloves
10 cardamoms
two 7.5 cm (3 inch) cinnamon sticks
50 g (2 oz) blanched almonds
100 g (4 oz) sultanas
Garnish:
4 hard-boiled eggs, shelled and sliced
1 large onion, peeled, thinly sliced and fried until crisp

Put the onion halves and bay leaves into a large saucepan, pour in 1 litre (1$\frac{3}{4}$ pints) water and bring to the boil. Place the boiling fowl in the saucepan, cover and simmer gently for 1$\frac{1}{2}$–2 hours, until the bird is tender.

Remove the bird from the pan and reserve the cooking liquid and onions. Pull the flesh away from the carcass and discard the skin and bones. Place the flesh in a bowl, cover with foil and keep warm in the bottom of a preheated cool oven (150°C/300°F, Gas Mark 2). Bring 120 ml (4 fl oz) of the reserved cooking liquid to the boil in a saucepan. Put the saffron threads in a cup and pour over the boiling liquid. Leave to soak for 20 minutes.

Meanwhile, wash the rice well in at least 3 complete changes of water. Drain the rice, then pick it over to remove any stones or other 'undesirable' objects.

Heat the ghee in a clean, large saucepan. Remove the onions from the reserved cooking liquid with a perforated spoon and drain. Add to the ghee with the garlic, cloves, cardamoms and cinnamon. Fry for 5 minutes.

Add the rice and stir well so that each grain is coated in the ghee mixture. Strain in enough of the remaining cooking liquid to cover the rice, then strain in the saffron-coloured liquid and bring to the boil. Cook gently, uncovered, for 10–15 minutes until the rice has just softened, adding a little boiling cooking liquid or water if necessary.

When the rice is cooked, drain off any excess liquid, then tip the rice into a warmed large bowl. Mix in the almonds, sultanas and cooked chicken. Arrange the biryani on a warmed large platter and garnish with the sliced eggs and fried onion. Serve hot.

Tali Muchli | Narial Anday

Baked Fish

This dish is typical of southern India, where freshly caught fish are often coated with a fresh coconut masala. Traditionally, the cooking is done on an open beach fire, either directly on grey dying embers, or on a flat, heated stone, but a conventional oven gives equally good results. This recipe calls for plaice or sole, but any other flat fish could be used, or steaks cut from a larger fish such as cod.

SERVES 6 as an individual dish

1 kg (2–2¼ lb) plaice or sole, cleaned but left whole
juice of 2 lemons
1 fresh coconut
5 fresh green chillies, topped and tailed
2 garlic cloves, peeled
2 tablespoons vegetable oil
2 tablespoons chopped coriander
1 tablespoon clear honey
2 teaspoons ground cumin
2 teaspoons fenugreek powder
1 teaspoon salt
1 teaspoon freshly ground black pepper

Wash the fish well under cold running water, then pat dry with paper towels. Place the fish on a plate, sprinkle over half of the lemon juice and set aside while making the coconut masala.

Make holes in the eyes of the coconut and drain out the liquid. Crack open the coconut and separate the meat from the shell. Place the meat in a blender or food processor and work until smooth. Add the chillies, garlic and vegetable oil and work again until evenly mixed, then add the remaining lemon juice, the chopped coriander, honey, cumin, fenugreek powder, salt and black pepper.

Spread this masala over the fish, turning it so that all sides are coated. Place the fish on a baking tray, cover with foil and bake in a preheated moderately hot oven (190°C/375°F, Gas Mark 5) for 25 minutes or until cooked through. Remove the foil and transfer the fish to a warmed serving platter. Serve hot.

Egg and Coconut Curry

A very straightforward curry, calling for a tomato sauce enriched with coconut milk. Sliced coconut 'meat' adds texture. When boiling the eggs, take care not to overcook them or they will be hard and rubbery in the finished curry. Boil them for 8–9 minutes at the most.

SERVES 4–6 as an individual dish

1 fresh coconut
100 g (4 oz) ghee
1 large onion, peeled and thinly sliced
2 garlic cloves, peeled and thinly sliced
2 bay leaves
7.5 cm (3 inch) cinnamon stick
2 teaspoons ground ginger
2 teaspoons chilli powder
1 teaspoon fenugreek seeds
1 teaspoon ground coriander
1 teaspoon ground cumin
1 teaspoon salt
150 g (5 oz) tomato purée
8 hard-boiled eggs, shelled and halved

Make holes in the eyes of the coconut, then drain out the liquid and reserve. Crack open the coconut and separate the meat from the shell. Thinly slice one-third of the meat and set aside. Put the remaining two-thirds of the meat in a blender or food processor and chop very finely. (Alternatively, finely grate the meat.)

Transfer the chopped or grated coconut to a bowl, pour over 600 ml (1 pint) boiling water, stir for 5 minutes, then strain through a sieve lined with 2 thicknesses of cheesecloth held over a bowl. Gather up the cheesecloth and squeeze out as much of the coconut 'milk' as possible. Discard the coconut from inside the cloth. Stir the reserved liquid from the coconut into the coconut milk and set the bowl aside.

Heat the ghee in a heavy-based saucepan, add the onion and garlic and fry gently for 4–5 minutes until soft. Add the bay leaves, spices and salt, stir well and fry for a further 3–4 minutes. Stir in the coconut milk and bring to the boil, adding the tomato purée. Simmer for 5 minutes. Add the sliced coconut and the hard-boiled eggs and heat through gently for a further 2–3 minutes. Remove the eggs carefully from the sauce with a perforated spoon and arrange in a warmed serving dish. Pour over the sauce and serve hot.

LEFT: *Clockwise from top; Steamed Mussels (page 48), Curried Crab (page 49), Coconut Fudge (page 52), Rice Cooked with Chicken (page 49), Egg and Coconut Curry.*

Chaat | Narial ka Halwa

Spiced Fruit Salad

Chaat is often served as an appetizer in India, or even as a cooling accompaniment to a hot main course curry, but here it makes the most refreshing dessert, contrasting well with the rich Narial ka Halwa/Coconut Fudge (right). In central and northern India it is a common sight to see stalls by the roadside selling *chaat* and tea – a refreshing combination which quenches the thirst and refreshes the body. All kinds of different fruits are used; the following recipe includes those that are readily available in the West, but you can vary the combination according to individual taste and what is in season.

SERVES 4 as an individual dish

2 oranges
2 pears
1 eating apple
2 guavas
2 bananas
juice of 1 lemon
1 teaspoon ground ginger
1 teaspoon garam masala
$\frac{1}{2}$ teaspoon freshly ground black pepper
salt

Peel the oranges and divide into segments, removing all pith and pips. Peel, quarter and core the pears and apple, then cut into thick slices. Peel the guavas and cut into chunky slices, including the seeds. Peel the bananas and slice thinly.

Put the fruit in a serving bowl and sprinkle over the lemon juice. Mix together the spices and salt, then sprinkle over the fruit. Fold very gently until each piece of fruit is coated in the lemon and spice mixture, then cover the bowl tightly with cling film. Chill in the refrigerator for about 2 hours before serving.

Coconut Fudge

Most people in the West are familiar with coconut as the basis of a number of sweet confections, although many Indian recipes for halwa are based on semolina – and there is even a version which uses grated carrots. This particular recipe uses full-cream milk powder (baby milk formula), coconut and honey to produce a particularly rich sweetmeat; it will keep for several weeks in an airtight tin.

SERVES 6–8 as an individual dish

600 ml (1 pint) milk
100 g (4 oz) full-cream milk powder
75 g (3 oz) desiccated coconut
$\frac{1}{2}$ teaspoon ground mace
2 tablespoons clear honey
50 g (2 oz) shelled almonds

Heat the milk in a non-stick saucepan until slightly warmer than tepid. Put the milk powder in a bowl and stir in enough of the warmed milk to make a smooth, thick paste.

Add the desiccated coconut to the milk remaining in the saucepan and bring to the boil. Continue to boil until most of the liquid has evaporated and the mixture is virtually dry.

Sprinkle in the ground mace and stir in the honey, then add the milk powder paste and stir in well. Continue to evaporate the liquid until the mixture is very stiff.

Spread the mixture in a greased fudge tin, about 20 cm (8 inch) square and 2.5 cm (1 inch) deep. Leave to cool, then cut into the traditional diamond-shaped pattern with a sharp knife and decorate each piece with an almond. Remove from the tin before serving.

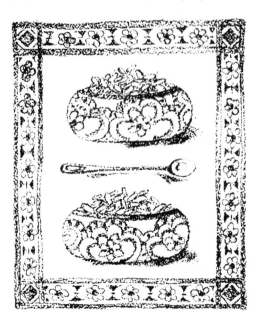

VEGETARIAN FEAST

Virtually all the great feast days of the Hindus are celebrated with a wide range of vegetarian dishes. Traditionally, Hindus eat off a special plate or *thali*, which in its most simple form might be a banana leaf or, on the richest of occasions, a solid silver platter. Samples of the various dishes will be arranged around the edge of the *thali* and drawn into the middle with the fingers, perhaps mixing one or two dishes before they are eaten, in a way reminiscent of an artist's palette.

As the feast cannot be enlivened by the addition of a meat dish, it is important to have a good blend of colours, consistencies and flavours. The following menu combines a pleasing variety of dishes, from crisp *pakoras* to aromatic *palao*.

FOR 8–10 PEOPLE

Chick Pea Flour Fritters (page 13)
Rice with Vegetables
Green Lentils
Banana Curry
Stuffed Aubergines
Aubergines with Tomato (page 25)
Courgette Curry
Dry-fried Spinach
Mint-flavoured Sauce (page 32)
Yogurt with Cucumber or Tomato (page 32)

Mango Ice Cream
Honey Squares

Kela Kari

Banana Curry

Bananas are plentiful in India, and often form a substantial part of a vegetarian diet. Be sure to use under-ripe bananas or they will disintegrate in the curry.

SERVES 4–6 as an individual dish

7.5 cm (3 inch) piece fresh root ginger
50 g (2 oz) ghee
1 tablespoon garam masala
2 teaspoons cumin seeds
1 teaspoon chilli powder
1 teaspoon turmeric
1 teaspoon salt
1 teaspoon freshly ground black pepper
750 g (1½ lb) under-ripe bananas
450 g (1 lb) natural yogurt
juice of 1 lemon
coriander or parsley, to garnish

Peel the fresh root ginger, then cut it into thin slices. Heat the ghee in a heavy-based saucepan, add the ginger and fry gently for 4–5 minutes until soft. Add the garam masala, cumin seeds, chilli powder, turmeric, salt and black pepper. Stir well to mix with the ginger and fry for a further 2 minutes.

Peel the bananas and cut them into 2.5 cm (1 inch) pieces. Add them to the pan and turn them gently so that they become coated with the spice mixture.

Mix the yogurt and lemon juice together in a bowl, pour slowly into the pan and mix with the pieces of banana. Bring to just below boiling point, stirring all the time. Reduce the heat and simmer gently for 10 minutes, until the bananas are softened but not broken up. Transfer carefully to a warmed serving dish and serve hot, garnished with coriander or parsley.

Goodhi Bjahhi

Courgette Curry

Marrow can be used instead of courgettes, but courgettes give a stronger flavour. If you have time, sprinkle the courgettes with salt after slicing, leave them to drain for 20 minutes, then rinse and pat dry with paper towels. This removes excess moisture and any bitterness. Extra piquancy is added by a masala of spices fried in sesame seed oil.

SERVES 4–6 as an individual dish

I kg (2–2¼ lb) courgettes
2 tablespoons sesame seed oil
I teaspoon mustard seeds
I teaspoon coriander seeds
I teaspoon aniseed
100 g (4 oz) ghee
I large onion, peeled and thinly sliced
2 garlic cloves, peeled and thinly sliced
7.5 cm (3 inch) piece fresh root ginger, peeled and thinly sliced
I tablespoon garam masala
I½ teaspoons turmeric
I teaspoon chilli powder
I teaspoon freshly ground black pepper
I teaspoon salt
2 tablespoons desiccated coconut, to finish

Top and tail the courgettes, then cut into I cm (½ inch) thick slices. Heat the sesame seed oil in a small frying pan until smoking, add the mustard seeds, coriander seeds and aniseed and fry for 30–40 seconds. Remove from the heat and set aside.

Heat the ghee in a heavy-based saucepan, add the onion, garlic and ginger and fry gently for 4–5 minutes until soft. Add the sesame seed oil together with the fried seeds, the garam masala, turmeric, chilli powder, black pepper and salt. Stir well and fry for a further 2–3 minutes, then add the courgette slices and toss them so that they become well coated in the spice mixture. Cook for 2–3 minutes, shaking the pan frequently to prevent the courgettes sticking.

Pour in enough boiling water to cover the courgette slices and cook gently for about 10 minutes, until the courgettes begin to soften but are not mushy. The dish should not be too moist, but a little extra water may be added if necessary. Sprinkle in the desiccated coconut and heat through, then transfer to a warmed serving dish and serve immediately.

Tali Saag

Dry-fried Spinach

Spinach is a popular vegetable in India. Fresh spinach is used in this recipe; if you are using frozen spinach you will need to halve the quantity.

SERVES 4–6 as an individual dish

50 g (2 oz) ghee
I small onion, peeled and thinly sliced
I teaspoon garam masala
I teaspoon salt
450 g (I lb) fresh spinach, washed

Melt the ghee in a heavy-based saucepan, add the onion and fry gently for 4–5 minutes until soft. Add the garam masala and salt and fry, stirring, for 2–3 minutes. Add the spinach and cook for about 5 minutes, stirring constantly. Transfer to a warmed serving dish and serve immediately.

Baigan

Stuffed Aubergines

For this recipe, use the long variety of aubergine rather than the shorter, rounded ones. As with all aubergine dishes, it is important to select firm, ripe aubergines, and not ones that are over-ripe.

SERVES 4–6 as an individual dish

4–6 medium aubergines, halved lengthways
1 bay leaf
100 g (4 oz) ghee
1 large onion, peeled and finely chopped
2 garlic cloves, peeled and finely chopped
2 teaspoons coriander seeds
1 teaspoon chilli powder
1 teaspoon lovage seeds
1 teaspoon salt
Garnish:
fresh coriander leaves
dried red chillies, chopped

ABOVE: *From left to right; Mango Ice Cream (page 57), Honey Squares (page 57), Green Lentils (page 56), Stuffed Aubergines, Banana Curry (page 53), Rice with Vegetables (page 56).*

Put the aubergines in a roasting tin with their cut sides upwards. Pour in 100 ml (3½ fl oz) water, add the bay leaf and cover the tin tightly with foil. Poach the aubergines in a preheated moderate oven (160°C/325°F, Gas Mark 3) for 25 minutes, or until soft.

Heat the ghee in a heavy-based saucepan. Add the onion and garlic and fry gently for 4–5 minutes until soft. Crush the coriander seeds slightly and add to the ghee with the chilli powder, lovage seeds and salt. Stir well and fry for a further 2–3 minutes.

Remove the poached aubergines from the water and pat them dry with paper towels. Using a sharp-edged teaspoon, scrape the flesh from inside the skins. Reserve the skins. Mash the aubergine flesh well and add to the spice mixture. Fry for a few minutes, stirring well.

Grill the aubergine skins for 5 minutes until dried out, then spoon in the fried aubergine mixture. Arrange the aubergines on a warmed serving dish, garnish with the chillies and coriander and serve.

Moongh Dal

Green Lentils

There are scores of different varieties of lentils to be found in India, but not so many are available in the West. Green lentils can be found at Indian stores and health food shops under the name of brown or continental lentils. They have an unusual 'earthy' flavour and hold their shape well, but if they are not available, ordinary red lentils can be used instead.

SERVES 4–6 as an individual dish

225 g (8 oz) green lentils
1 teaspoon salt
50 g (2 oz) ghee
1 medium onion, peeled and thinly sliced
2 garlic cloves, peeled and thinly sliced
2 teaspoons garam masala
1 teaspoon turmeric
1 teaspoon chilli powder
1 teaspoon cumin seeds
2 tablespoons chopped coriander

Wash the lentils well and soak them in cold water for about 1 hour. Drain, place in a saucepan with 900 ml (1½ pints) fresh cold water and the salt. Bring to the boil, then reduce the heat to a gentle simmer and cook for about 1 hour until the lentils have softened. Stir from time to time to prevent the lentils sticking to the bottom of the pan and add more water if necessary. When the lentils are cooked, keep them hot over the lowest possible heat while frying the spices.

Heat the ghee in a heavy-based frying pan, add the onion and garlic and fry gently for 4–5 minutes until soft. Sprinkle in the garam masala, turmeric, chilli powder and cumin seeds, stir well and fry for a further minute. Pour this mixture over the lentils and stir in with half of the chopped coriander. Transfer to a warmed serving dish, sprinkle over the remaining chopped coriander and serve immediately.

Subzi Palao

Rice with Vegetables

At any vegetarian feast, the rice dish usually forms the centrepiece. This recipe uses raw and pre-cooked vegetables, which are lightly sautéed before being added to the cooked rice.

SERVES 6–8 as an individual dish

225 g (8 oz) frozen diced mixed vegetables
100 g (4 oz) frozen diced red and green peppers
100 g (4 oz) courgettes, trimmed and sliced
2 tablespoons ground cumin
2 tablespoons ground coriander
1 tablespoon chilli powder
2 teaspoons turmeric
4 teaspoons black peppercorns, crushed
2 teaspoons salt
100 g (4 oz) ghee
4 large onions, peeled and thinly sliced
5 garlic cloves, peeled and thinly sliced
two 7.5 cm (3 inch) pieces fresh root ginger, peeled and thinly sliced
two 7.5 cm (3 inch) cinnamon sticks
20 cardamoms
20 cloves
1 tablespoon lovage seeds
750 g (½ lb) Basmati rice
75 g (3 oz) sultanas
50 g (2 oz) flaked almonds

Mix the frozen vegetables with the courgettes and allow to defrost. Mix together the spices and salt.

Heat half of the ghee in a heavy-based saucepan. Add half of the spice mixture and fry gently for 1–2 minutes, then add the vegetables and stir to coat in the ghee and spice mixture. Remove the vegetables from the pan with a perforated spoon and place in a bowl. Keep hot in a preheated cool oven (150°C/300°F, Gas Mark 2).

Heat the remaining ghee in the saucepan, add the onions, garlic and ginger and fry gently for 4–5 minutes until soft. Add the cinnamon, cardamoms, cloves and lovage seeds, stir well and fry for a further 3–4 minutes. Add the remaining spice mixture and fry for 2 minutes.

Wash the rice well in at least 3 complete changes of cold water. Drain the rice, then pick it over to remove any stones or other 'undesirable' objects. Add the rice to the saucepan and stir well to ensure it is coated with the spice mixture. Pour in 2 litres (3½ pints) boiling water and boil the rice gently, uncovered, until the rice is just hard in the centre, stirring from time to time so that it does not stick. If necessary, add a little boiling water.

When the rice is ready, pour it into a large sieve and allow any liquid to drain away. Mix with the vegetables and arrange on a warmed serving platter. Sprinkle over the sultanas and almonds and serve immediately.

Am ka Kulfi | Shehed Tukra

Mango Ice Cream

A very rich, but refreshing, dish which combines the aromatic flavour of mangoes with the richness of cream. In India, a rather poor-quality cream known as *malai* would be used, but fortunately in the West the cream is better quality and therefore makes kulfi even richer. This recipe can be made using fresh mangoes, but it is far easier to use canned mango pulp, and there is no noticeable difference in the flavour of the ice cream. If canned pulp is not available, used canned mango slices and liquidize them in a blender or food processor. Because of the richness of kulfi, rather smaller portions than normal are served.

SERVES 8 as an individual dish

400 g (14 oz) canned mango pulp
3 tablespoons clear honey
600 ml (1 pint) double cream
50 g (2 oz) ground almonds
4 egg whites

Warm the mango pulp in a saucepan and stir in the honey. Remove from the heat, stir in the cream and almonds until evenly mixed, then leave the mixture to become cool.

Pour the mixture into a freezer container and place in the freezer. Freeze for about 4 hours, or until the mixture is just beginning to freeze around the edges and become slushy. Remove the container from the freezer and turn the ice cream into a bowl. Break up with a fork.

Whisk the egg whites until stiff, then fold into the half-frozen mixture. Return to the freezer container, then freeze again for at least a further 4 hours, or until solid. Remove from the freezer at least 20 minutes before serving.

Honey Squares

These sweet honey squares are usually served as a snack in India, but they also make a good dessert for a special occasion. They are very simple to make, consisting of pastry squares coated in an aromatic spiced syrup. Like most pastries they are best eaten fresh, but will keep chilled in the refrigerator for up to 1 week.

SERVES 6–8 as an individual dish

225 g (8 oz) self-raising flour
50 g (2 oz) ghee or butter
½ teaspoon grated nutmeg
pinch of ground cinnamon
150 ml (¼ pint) milk
vegetable oil, for deep-frying
4 tablespoons clear honey
5 cm (2 inch) cinnamon stick
4 cloves
seeds of 4 cardamoms

Sift the flour into a bowl. Heat the ghee or butter gently in a saucepan and stir in the nutmeg and cinnamon. Add to the flour with the milk and mix to a firm dough with your fingers. Knead for at least 5 minutes.

Roll the dough to a thickness of 5 mm–1 cm (¼–½ inch). Cut into 2.5 cm (1 inch) squares. Heat enough oil in a deep, heavy-based frying pan to cover the squares of dough. Add the squares and deep-fry until they are golden brown.

Meanwhile, put the honey in a clean saucepan with the cinnamon stick, cloves and cardamom seeds. Heat gently until the honey has taken the flavour of the spices.

Remove the squares from the oil with a perforated spoon, drain quickly on paper towels, then arrange in a serving dish. Pour over the honey syrup, discarding the whole spices. Leave to cool before serving.

CHINA

The preparation and cooking of Chinese food has remained basically unchanged for thousands of years. Archaeological finds from the Bronze Age indicate that utensils like cleavers were used for cutting, and pots not unlike the modern wok were used for cooking. There is also textural data to prove that ingredients such as soy sauce, vinegar and rice wine were used at the time of the Zhou Dynasty (12th century BC) and by the time of Confucius in 551–479 BC it was recorded that harmony of flavours and the degree of heat applied were most important.

The harmonious blending of colour, aroma, flavour, shape and texture remains one of the main characteristics of modern Chinese cooking today. The choice of complementary or contrasting colours and flavours is a fundamental one – ingredients are never mixed indiscriminately. The cutting of ingredients is important to achieve the proper effect – slices are matched with slices and shreds with shreds, etc. The selection of different textures also contributes greatly to the character of Chinese cooking; for example, a dish may have just one or several contrasting textures such as tenderness, crispness and softness. These textures can only be achieved by the correct preparation techniques and cooking methods. Ingredients for stir-frying, for instance, are cut into small, thin shreds or slices, so that the maximum area is exposed and the food can cook quickly.

Chinese cooking methods can be divided into four main categories: water, oil, fire and steam cooking. The recipes in this chapter are grouped according to these methods, which also determine their serving order.

CHINA
STARTERS & SOUPS

Chinese starters traditionally consist of a small portion of several different dishes. (If you prefer you can serve just one dish.) They are served either hot or cold, just like hors d'oeuvre. Most of them can be prepared and cooked well in advance.

Chinese soups are mostly clear broths in which thinly sliced or shredded vegetables or meat, or a mixture of both, are rapidly boiled for a very short time, then seasonings are added just before serving.

Baiqie Ji

White-cut Cantonese Chicken
There are a number of variations of this famous Cantonese dish; this is one of the simplest. Always use a fresh, not frozen, chicken.

SERVES 4–6

1.5 kg (3½ lb) fresh young chicken
2–3 slices fresh root ginger
2–3 spring onions, trimmed
3 tablespoons Chinese rice wine, or dry sherry
1 tablespoon salt
Sauce:
2–3 tablespoons light soy sauce
1 teaspoon sugar
1 tablespoon sesame seed oil
2 spring onions, finely chopped

Wash the chicken well, inside and out, in cold running water, then place in a large saucepan and cover with cold water. Add the ginger, spring onions and rice wine or sherry, cover the pan with a tight-fitting lid and bring to the boil. Skim off the scum, reduce the heat and simmer for 10 minutes. Add the salt, cover the pan tightly again and place heavy weights on top to prevent the heat from escaping. Turn off the heat and let the chicken cook gently in the hot water for 4–6 hours, or until the liquid is cool. Do *not* lift the lid off the pan during this time.

To serve, remove the chicken and chop it into 20–24 pieces, then re-assemble the chicken on a serving dish.

Mix the sauce ingredients with a few tablespoons of the chicken stock, then pour it all over the chicken, or pour it into a bowl and serve as a dip.

Bon Bon Ji

Chicken Salad with Spicy Dressing
This very popular dish from Sichuan is also known as Bang-Bang Chicken in some Peking restaurants, because the chicken meat is tenderized by being banged with a rolling pin (*bon* in Chinese).

SERVES 4

275 g (10 oz) boneless chicken breast, skinned
1 lettuce heart
Sauce:
1 tablespoon sesame paste (tahini), or peanut butter creamed with 1 teaspoon sesame seed oil
1 tablespoon light soy sauce
1 tablespoon vinegar
2 teaspoons chilli sauce
1 teaspoon sugar

Put the chicken in a saucepan and cover with cold water. Bring to the boil, then reduce the heat and simmer gently for 10 minutes. Remove the chicken from the pan, reserving the liquid. Beat the chicken with a rolling pin until soft, then pull the meat into shreds with your hands. Leave to cool.

Cut the lettuce leaves into shreds and place on a serving dish. Arrange the chicken shreds on top.

Mix the sauce ingredients with a few tablespoons of the reserved cooking liquid. Pour evenly over the chicken. Toss the ingredients just before serving or at the table.

Cha Wahn Tan | Baiqie Rou

Deep-fried Wontons

In China, Wontons are always served as a snack, either in a clear stock (page 64) or soup. The deep-fried crispy version served as an appetizer in some Cantonese restaurants is, like Chop Suey, purely a Western invention. Wonton skins are readily available, fresh or frozen, from most oriental stores.

SERVES 4

24 wonton skins
vegetable oil, for deep-frying
Filling:
100 g (4 oz) minced pork
50 g (2 oz) peeled prawns, finely chopped
2 teaspoons finely chopped spring onions
1 tablespoon Chinese rice wine, or dry sherry
1 teaspoon sugar
½ teaspoon salt
Sauce:
1 tablespoon cornflour
1 tablespoon tomato purée
1 tablespoon sugar
2 tablespoons vinegar
1 tablespoon soy sauce
1 tablespoon vegetable oil

Put the ingredients for the filling in a bowl and blend thoroughly together to form a smooth mixture. Place about 1 teaspoon of the filling in the centre of a wonton skin, fold over from corner to corner, wetting a small part of the skin on the sides immediately around the filling, then press them together. Repeat with the remaining filling and skins.

Heat the oil in a deep-fat frier or hot wok until very hot, then turn down the heat to allow the oil to cool a little. Deep-fry the wontons in batches for 2–3 minutes or until crispy. Remove the wontons and drain on paper towels. Keep hot in a preheated oven (150°C/300°F, Gas Mark 2).

Make the sauce: put the cornflour in a bowl and mix to a paste with 4–5 tablespoons cold water. Stir in the remaining sauce ingredients, except the oil. Heat the oil in a wok or heavy-based saucepan, pour in the sauce mixture and stir over moderate heat for 3–4 minutes until smooth. Serve immediately, with the wontons.

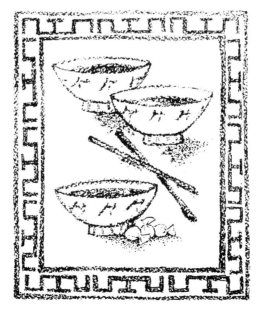

White-cut Pork with Garlic Dressing

'White-cut' is a traditional Chinese cooking method used for white meats such as pork or chicken that are very fresh and tender. They are cooked in large pieces in a relatively short time, then the heat is turned off and the remainder of cooking is done by the residual heat. Modern cookers and Western cooking pots do not retain heat to the same extent as traditional Chinese ones, but a similar effect can be obtained by lowering the heat after the initial period of rapid boiling, then simmering very gently until the required tenderness is achieved. If you are using frozen meat, make sure it is thoroughly defrosted before cooking.

SERVES 6–8

1 kg (2–2¼ lb) leg of pork, boned but not skinned
Sauce:
3 tablespoons light soy sauce
1 tablespoon dark soy sauce
1 tablespoon sesame seed oil
1–2 garlic cloves, peeled and finely chopped
2 spring onions, finely chopped
1 teaspoon finely chopped fresh root ginger
1 teaspoon sugar
1 teaspoon chilli sauce (optional)

Tie the piece of pork together with string if necessary. Bring 2 litres (3½ pints) water to a rapid boil in a large saucepan. Add the pork, skim off the scum, then cover the saucepan and simmer gently for about 1 hour.

Remove the meat from the liquid and leave to cool for 4–6 hours if it is not to be served at once, otherwise soak the pork in cold water for 20–30 minutes.

To serve, cut the skin off the pork, leaving a thin layer of fat on top. Cut the meat into small, thin slices across the grain and arrange them neatly in rows on a plate. Mix together all the ingredients for the sauce and drizzle over the pork.

Ban Zajin | Xun Yu

Mixed Vegetable Salad with Chinese Dressing

Most so-called 'salads' are in fact lightly cooked vegetables, which are served cold. This recipe, using raw vegetables, is an exception to the rule.

Shanghai Smoked Fish

In this recipe the term 'smoked' does not mean that the fish is actually smoked, but that it acquires a smoky flavour from being marinated twice in soy sauce, wine and spices.

SERVES 4–6

½ head Chinese leaves, or 1 celery heart
1 green pepper, cored and seeded
1 red pepper, cored and seeded
Salad dressing:
1 teaspoon salt
1 teaspoon sugar
4 tablespoons light soy sauce
2 tablespoons sesame seed oil

SERVES 4

450 g (1 lb) white fish fillets (plaice, cod, haddock or sole)
3 tablespoons Chinese rice wine, or dry sherry
2 tablespoons light soy sauce
1 tablespoon dark soy sauce
2 tablespoons sugar
3–4 spring onions, finely chopped
3 slices fresh root ginger, peeled and finely chopped
1 tablespoon five-spice powder
1 teaspoon salt
600 ml (1 pint) vegetable oil, for deep-frying
1 spring onion, shredded, to garnish

Remove and discard any tough outer parts of the Chinese leaves then cut into thick slices. (If using celery, separate the sticks, then cut each one into thick slices.) Cut the green and red pepper diagonally into thin slices.

Place the Chinese leaves or celery in a bowl and arrange the red and green pepper on top. Sprinkle the salt and sugar evenly over the salad; leave to stand for a few minutes. Just before serving, sprinkle over the soy sauce and sesame seed oil and toss well.

Put the fish in a shallow dish. Mix together the rice wine or sherry, soy sauces, sugar, spring onions, ginger, spice and salt. Pour over the fish, cover and leave to marinate for at least 2 hours.

Remove the fish from the marinade. Pour the marinade into a saucepan, add 85 ml (3 fl oz) water and bring to the boil. Simmer gently for 10–15 minutes, then strain through a sieve into a shallow dish; cool.

Heat the oil in a hot wok until very hot, then turn down the heat to allow the oil to cool a little. Deep-fry the fish for 4–5 minutes or until crisp and golden, stirring gently with chopsticks to keep the pieces separate. Remove gently with a perforated spoon and immerse in the cold marinade for 10–15 minutes.

Remove the fish from the marinade with a perforated spoon and chill in the refrigerator for at least 2–3 hours. Serve garnished with the shredded spring onion.

Fengwei Xia

Poached Prawns with Piquant Dip Sauce
If you cannot buy uncooked prawns, use cooked prawns, but omit the poaching part and simply serve them with the dip sauce.

SERVES 4

450 g (1 lb) headless uncooked prawns, defrosted if frozen
1 teaspoon salt
4–5 slices unpeeled fresh root ginger
Dip sauce:
2 tablespoons vegetable oil
2–3 slices fresh root ginger, peeled and thinly shredded
2–3 spring onions, thinly shredded
2–3 fresh green and red chillies, seeded and thinly shredded
3 tablespoons light soy sauce
1 tablespoon vinegar
1 tablespoon Chinese rice wine, or dry sherry
pinch of sugar
1 teaspoon sesame seed oil

Wash the prawns and trim off the whiskers and legs, but leave the tail pieces firmly attached.

Bring 2 litres (3½ pints) water to the boil in a large saucepan with the salt and sliced ginger. Add the prawns and poach for 1–2 minutes only; drain well.

Make the dip sauce: heat the vegetable oil in a small saucepan until very hot. Put the shredded ginger, spring onions and fresh chillies in a bowl. Pour the hot oil slowly into the bowl, then mix in the remaining ingredients. Serve with the prawns.

ABOVE: *Poached Prawns with Piquant Dip Sauce.*
OPPOSITE: *Left, Shanghai Smoked Fish. Right, Mixed Vegetable Salad with Chinese Dressing.*

Lu Niurou

Soy-braised Beef
In this dish, the meat is cooked slowly in soy sauce and spices over low heat, a method also known as '*red-cooking*'.

SERVES 6–8

750 g (1½–1¾ lb) braising steak, trimmed
25 g (1 oz) fresh root ginger, unpeeled
3–4 spring onions
50 ml (2 fl oz) Chinese rice wine, or dry sherry
25 ml (1 fl oz) brandy
2 teaspoons five-spice powder
3 tablespoons light soy sauce
2 tablespoons dark soy sauce
1 tablespoon brown sugar

Cut the beef into 2–3 large pieces. Cut the ginger into thick slices, the spring onions into short lengths.

Put the beef, ginger and spring onions in a large saucepan. Add the rice wine or sherry, the brandy, five-spice powder and light soy sauce and stir well to mix. Marinate for 1 hour, turning the meat occasionally.

Pour enough water into the pan to cover the beef. Bring to the boil, skim off the scum, then cover the pan with a lid and simmer gently for 45 minutes. Add the dark soy sauce and the sugar, cover the pan again and simmer for a further 30–45 minutes.

Remove the beef from the liquid and leave to cool. When cold, slice thinly and arrange on a plate.

Qing Tang

Clear Stock

Although described as a soup in Chinese, this is really a basic stock, the very first item a Chinese cook prepares when commencing duty in the kitchen every morning. It is used for cooking throughout the day, and is the basis for most soups.

Qing Tang can also be served as a clear soup on its own like a consommé, with the addition of seasonings: for every 600 ml (1 pint), add 2 teaspoons finely chopped spring onions, 1 tablespoon light soy sauce and 1 teaspoon salt.

MAKES 2 LITRES (3½ PINTS)

1 kg (2–2¼ lb) chicken pieces
750 g (1½–1¾ lb) pork spareribs
50 g (2 oz) fresh root ginger, unpeeled and cut into large chunks
4–5 spring onions
50 ml (2 fl oz) Chinese rice wine or dry sherry (optional)

Trim off the excess fat from the chicken and pork, then place the meat in a large saucepan with the ginger and spring onions. Pour in 2.75 litres (5 pints) water, bring to the boil, then skim off the scum. Reduce the heat to a rolling boil and cook, uncovered, for at least 1½–2 hours.

Strain the stock and return to the rinsed-out pan. Add the rice wine or sherry (if using) and bring the soup back to the boil. Simmer for 5 minutes or so before using. Any leftover soup should be stored in a covered container in the refrigerator, where it will keep for up to 4–5 days.

Xihongshi Dan Tang

Tomato and Egg Soup

If homemade stock is not available, a chicken stock cube dissolved in water may be substituted, but remember to reduce the amount of soy sauce by half because of the saltiness of most brands of stock cubes.

SERVES 4

250 g (9 oz) tomatoes
1–2 eggs
pinch of salt
2 spring onions, finely chopped
600 ml (1 pint) Clear Stock (above)
2 tablespoons light soy sauce
1 teaspoon cornflour

Skin the tomatoes: dip them in boiling water for a minute or so, then peel off the skins with your fingers. Cut the flesh into large chunks. Put the eggs in a bowl with the salt and about half of the finely chopped spring onions. Beat well to mix.

Pour the stock into a saucepan and bring to a rolling boil. Add the tomatoes and the soy sauce, then very slowly stir in the beaten egg mixture. Mix the cornflour to a smooth paste with 1 tablespoon cold water, then add to the boiling soup, stirring constantly until smooth.

Serve the soup in individual soup bowls. Sprinkle each dish with the remaining finely chopped spring onions as a garnish.

Jishi Fuotui Tang

Chicken and Ham Soup

This is a delicious and nourishing soup, yet very simple to make. The type of ham you use is of vital importance: the better the quality of the ham, the better the flavour of the soup. The sesame seed oil, although optional, does add a delicate 'nutty' flavour to the soup.

SERVES 4

100 g (4 oz) boneless cooked chicken meat, skinned
100 g (4 oz) cooked ham
100 g (4 oz) can bamboo shoots, or fresh bean-sprouts
600 ml (1 pint) Clear Stock (left)
1 teaspoon finely chopped spring onion
1 teaspoon sesame seed oil (optional)
salt
freshly ground pepper

Thinly shred the chicken, ham and bamboo shoots. (If using bean-sprouts, wash them in cold water, discarding the husks and any little bits that float to the surface; it is not necessary to top and tail each sprout.)

Pour the stock into a saucepan and bring to a rolling boil. Add the chicken, ham and bamboo shoots or bean-sprouts. Cook for 1 minute.

Divide the chopped spring onion between 4 individual soup bowls or place in a warmed serving bowl and pour in the hot soup. Sprinkle in the sesame seed oil (if using) and salt and pepper to taste. Serve hot.

Donggu Tang | Huntun Tang

Mushroom and Cucumber Soup

Since this is a pure vegetarian soup, water is used as the basic liquid rather than stock, but you may use Clear Stock (page 64) if you prefer. If using water, the addition of monosodium glutamate in the seasoning accentuates the flavour of the soup, but it is optional. Dark field mushrooms have plenty of flavour. If this type of mushroom is used, then the monosodium glutamate is not necessary. Vegetable stock cubes are available from some supermarkets and health food stores and, if preferred, vegetable stock may be used in place of the water and monosodium glutamate.

SERVES 4

100 g (4 oz) flat or open mushrooms
½ cucumber
2 spring onions
2 tablespoons vegetable oil
1 teaspoon salt
1 tablespoon soy sauce
¼ teaspoon monosodium glutamate (optional)
¼ cucumber, finely shredded, to garnish

Wash the mushrooms, but do not peel them. Pat the mushrooms dry with paper towels, then slice them. Cut the cucumber in half lengthways, then slice thinly. Finely chop the spring onions.

Heat the oil in a wok or large, heavy-based saucepan, add the spring onions to flavour the oil, then add the mushrooms. Stir for a few minutes, then add a pinch of the salt, with 600 ml (1 pint) water. Drop in the cucumber and bring to the boil. Add the remaining salt and the soy sauce and cook for about 1 minute. If using monosodium glutamate, stir it into the soup just before serving. Serve hot, garnished with the shredded cucumber.

Wonton Soup

In China, Wontons are traditionally served in a clear broth as a snack rather than as a soup. The skin of Wontons should be wafer thin, and the filling should consist of a teaspoonful of coarsely chopped (not finely minced) meat.

SERVES 4

24 wonton skins
600 ml (1 pint) Clear Stock (page 64)
1 tablespoon light soy sauce
Filling:
100 g (4 oz) leafy green vegetable (spinach or cabbage)
175 g (6 oz) boneless pork sparerib, coarsely chopped
1–2 spring onions, finely chopped
1 tablespoon light soy sauce
1 tablespoon Chinese rice wine, or dry sherry
1 teaspoon sesame seed oil
1 teaspoon salt
1 teaspoon sugar
Garnish:
2 teaspoons finely chopped spring onion
1 teaspoon sesame seed oil

First make the filling: plunge the green leaves into boiling water and blanch until soft. (Blanching times will vary according to the type of vegetable used – spinach will take only a few seconds, whereas cabbage may take up to 2 minutes.) Drain thoroughly and chop coarsely. Place in a bowl with the pork, spring onions, soy sauce, rice wine or sherry, sesame seed oil, salt and sugar. Blend all the ingredients thoroughly together to form a smooth mixture.

Place about 1 teaspoon of the filling in the centre of a wonton skin, then bring the opposite corners together. Seal by pinching the top edges together firmly, then fold the other 2 corners towards each other and pinch to seal. Repeat with the remaining filling and skins to make 24 wontons altogether.

Pour the stock into a saucepan and bring to a rolling boil. Drop in the wontons and boil rapidly for 2–3 minutes, then add the soy sauce. Pour the soup into 4 individual soup bowls and garnish with the chopped spring onion and sesame seed oil. Serve hot.

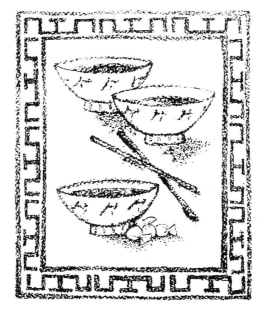

Doufu Roupian Tang

Pork and Bean Curd Soup

Since both the pork and bean curd are pale in colour, a touch of brightness is introduced by adding watercress or spinach leaves. Prawn crackers can be served at the same time as the soup. To cook prawn crackers: heat approximately 150 ml ($\frac{1}{4}$ pint) vegetable oil in a preheated wok until it is moderately hot. Reduce the heat and allow the oil to cool slightly before deep-frying 5–6 prawn crackers at a time. The crackers will expand to 4–5 times their original size. Allow them to turn from translucent to opaque white, then remove them with a perforated spoon and drain on paper towels. The crackers can be kept warm in a low oven and will stay crisp for several hours.

SERVES 4

100 g (4 oz) pork fillet (tenderloin)
1 tablespoon Chinese rice wine, or dry sherry
1 tablespoon light soy sauce
225 g (8 oz) firm or silken bean curd (tofu)
$\frac{1}{2}$ bunch watercress, or 50–75 g (2–3 oz) fresh spinach leaves
600 ml (1 pint) Clear Stock (page 64)
1 teaspoon salt
1 teaspoon sesame seed oil

Thinly slice the pork. Place in a bowl with the rice wine or sherry and the soy sauce and leave to marinate for at least 10 minutes. Cut each cake of bean curd into 16 small pieces. Wash the watercress or spinach leaves. Trim the stalk ends and discard any coarse stalks or ribs. If using watercress, reserve a few leaves to garnish the finished soup.

Pour the stock into a saucepan and bring to a rolling boil. Add the pork, stirring to keep the slices separate. Boil rapidly for 30 seconds, then add the bean curd pieces and salt and boil for another minute. Finally, add the watercress or spinach and the sesame seed oil. Stir well, then pour the soup either into a warmed serving bowl or 4 individual soup bowls. Serve hot, garnished with the reserved watercress leaves.

Yupian Yungcai Tang

Fish and Watercress Soup

It is unnecessary to skin the fish fillets; the skin helps to keep the fish together during cooking.

SERVES 4

225 g (8 oz) white fish fillets (plaice, sole or cod)
1 tablespoon cornflour
1 egg white, lightly beaten
600 ml (1 pint) Clear Stock (page 64)
1 teaspoon finely chopped fresh root ginger
1 bunch watercress, washed and trimmed
salt
freshly ground pepper
1 teaspoon finely shredded spring onion
1 teaspoon sesame seed oil

Cut the fish into large slices. Dust with the cornflour, then coat with the egg white.

Pour the stock into a saucepan, add the ginger and bring to a rolling boil. Add the fish a slice at a time. As soon as the slices float to the surface, add the watercress and seasoning. Reduce the heat and simmer for 1 minute.

Pour the soup into warmed serving bowls and sprinkle the tops with the shredded spring onion and sesame seed oil. Serve hot.

Suan La Tang

Hot and Sour Soup

This very popular soup, served frequently in Peking and Sichuan restaurants, is one of the few thick Chinese soups. It is made hot and sour by the addition of plenty of freshly ground pepper and vinegar.

Chinese, or Donggu mushrooms are the most widely used mushrooms in the Orient. They are grown on the wood of dead deciduous trees, then dried in the sun. They provide texture and flavour and are extremely nutritious.

SERVES 4

3–4 Chinese dried mushrooms
100 g (4 oz) boneless cooked chicken meat, skinned
100 g (4 oz) firm bean curd (tofu)
75 g (3 oz) bamboo shoots
1 egg
salt
600 ml (1 pint) Clear Stock (page 64)
50 g (2 oz) fresh or frozen garden peas
2 tablespoons vinegar
1 tablespoon dark soy sauce
2 teaspoons freshly ground pepper
3 tablespoons cornflour

Soak the mushrooms in warm water to cover for 20–25 minutes, then drain and reserve the soaking liquid. Squeeze the mushrooms dry, discard the hard stalks, then cut the mushrooms into thin shreds.

Thinly shred the chicken, bean curd and bamboo shoots. Put the egg in a bowl with a pinch of salt and beat lightly together.

Pour the stock into a saucepan. Add the reserved soaking liquid from the mushrooms and bring to a rolling boil. Add the shredded mushrooms, chicken, bean curd, bamboo shoots, peas and 1 teaspoon salt. Cook for 2–3 minutes, then add the vinegar, soy sauce and freshly ground pepper.

Mix the cornflour to a smooth paste with 6 tablespoons cold water. Add to the soup and stir for 1 minute, or until the soup has thickened. Add the beaten egg very slowly in a thin, steady stream, pouring it evenly all over the surface of the soup.

Transfer the soup to a warmed serving bowl or individual serving dishes and serve hot.

BELOW: *Left, Fish and Watercress Soup. Centre, Pork and Bean Curd Soup. Right, Hot and Sour Soup.*

CHINA
QUICK COOKING DISHES

The Chinese cooking method known as quick stir-frying has become very popular in Western kitchens in recent years; doubtlessly, this is because most stir-fried dishes are comparatively simple and easy to cook.

There are a number of variations in stir-frying, generally they can be classified as follows:

Pure stir-frying Ingredients are not pre-cooked or marinated during preparation; they are just stir-fried in hot oil and seasoned towards the end of cooking. Most vegetables are cooked in this way.

Rapid stir-frying This method is known in Chinese as *bao*, which literally means 'to explode'. The ingredient or ingredients are first deep-fried or rapid-boiled, then they are quickly stir-fried over intense heat for a very short time. The vital point is to have all the ingredients and seasonings such as soy sauce, rice wine, sugar, etc, ready in advance, so that each step can be performed in quick succession.

Braising stir-frying The main and supplementary ingredients are cooked separately first, then brought together with the addition of seasonings and stock or a thickening agent (usually cornflour mixed with water), and braised very quickly before serving.

Tangcu Daxia

Rapid-fried Prawns in Sweet and Sour Sauce
Traditionally these prawns are cooked in their shells then braised in a sweet and sour sauce. It is easier if you use chopsticks or your fingers to pick up the prawns rather than a knife and fork.

SERVES 4

450 g (1 lb) headless uncooked prawns, defrosted if frozen
600 ml (1 pint) vegetable oil, for deep-frying
2 teaspoons cornflour
fresh coriander leaves, or parsley, to garnish
Sauce:
2 tablespoons Chinese rice wine, or dry sherry
2 tablespoons soy sauce
2 tablespoons vinegar
1 tablespoon sugar
1 teaspoon finely chopped spring onion
1 teaspoon finely chopped fresh root ginger

Make sure the prawns are thoroughly defrosted. Wash and trim off the whiskers and legs, but leave the tail pieces firmly attached. Pat dry with paper towels.

Heat the oil in a hot wok until smoking, then turn down the heat to allow the oil to cool a little. Deep-fry the prawns until they become bright pink, stirring all the time with chopsticks to keep them separated. Scoop the prawns out with a perforated spoon and drain on paper towels.

Pour off all but 1 tablespoon oil from the wok. Increase the heat to high. Mix together the ingredients for the sauce, then add to the wok with the prawns and cook for about 1 minute. Mix the cornflour to a smooth paste with 1 tablespoon cold water, add to the wok and stir a few times until each prawn is coated with the sauce.

To serve, arrange the prawns neatly on a warmed serving dish and garnish with coriander or parsley. Serve hot or cold as part of a main meal. This dish could also be served as a starter.

Zhuachao Haixian

Scallops and Prawns with Mixed Vegetables

This is a very colourful Cantonese dish. You can use both scallops and prawns as suggested here, or use one or the other.

SERVES 3–4

4–6 fresh scallops
100–175 g (4–6 oz) headless uncooked prawns, defrosted if frozen
1 egg white
1 tablespoon cornflour
3 celery sticks, trimmed
1 red pepper, cored and seeded
1–2 carrots, peeled
2 slices fresh root ginger, peeled
2–3 spring onions
600 ml (1 pint) vegetable oil, for deep-frying
2 tablespoons Chinese rice wine, or dry sherry
1 tablespoon light soy sauce
2 teaspoons chilli bean paste (optional)
1 teaspoon salt
1 teaspoon sesame seed oil, to finish

Cut each scallop into 3–4 pieces. Shell the prawns, leave them whole if small, otherwise cut each one into 2 or 3 pieces. Put the fish in a bowl with the egg white and about half of the cornflour and mix together.

Cut the celery, red pepper and carrots into small pieces; finely shred the ginger and spring onions.

Heat the oil in a hot wok, then deep-fry the scallops and prawns for 1 minute, stirring them all the time with chopsticks to keep the pieces separate. Scoop them out with a perforated spoon and drain on paper towels.

Pour off all but 2 tablespoons oil from the wok. Increase the heat to high and add the ginger and spring onions. Add the vegetables and stir-fry for about 1 minute, then return the scallops and prawns to the wok and stir in the rice wine or sherry, soy sauce, chilli bean paste (if using) and season with the salt.

Mix the remaining cornflour to a smooth paste with a little stock or water, then add to the wok and blend all the ingredients until thickened. Sprinkle over the sesame seed oil and serve immediately.

Zaolui Yupian

Peking-style Fish in Wine Sauce

In this very popular Peking dish, filleted fish slices are coated with a light batter, then deep-fried and braised briefly in a delicious wine sauce flavoured with garlic, ginger and spring onions. To add a dash of bright colour to contrast with the whiteness of the fish, serve on a bed of lettuce.

SERVES 2–3

450 g (1 lb) white fish fillets (sole, plaice or haddock)
1 egg white
2 tablespoons cornflour
600 ml (1 pint) vegetable oil, for deep-frying
1–2 garlic cloves, peeled and chopped
2 spring onions, white parts only, finely chopped
2 slices fresh root ginger, peeled and chopped
2 teaspoons salt
1 teaspoon sugar
4–5 tablespoons Chinese rice wine, or dry sherry
50 ml (2 fl oz) Clear Stock (page 64)
1 teaspoon sesame seed oil, to finish

Cut the fish into fairly large pieces, leaving the skin on in order to keep the slices intact during cooking. Put the fish in a bowl and mix in the egg white. Mix the cornflour to a smooth paste with 5 tablespoons cold water, add to the fish and mix together.

Heat the oil in a hot wok until fairly hot then turn down the heat to allow the oil to cool a little. Add the fish slices one by one, reserving the leftover cornflour mixture in the bowl. Deep-fry the fish slices for about 1 minute, stirring them with chopsticks. Remove the slices and drain on paper towels.

Pour off the oil from the wok. Increase the heat to high and add the garlic, spring onions, ginger, salt, sugar, rice wine or sherry, and the stock. Bring the sauce to the boil, return the fish to the wok and simmer for 1 minute.

Pour the reserved cornflour mixture evenly all over the fish slices. As soon as the sauce starts to thicken, add the sesame seed oil. Lift the fish slices on to a warmed serving dish and serve immediately.

69

Chinchao Yutiao

Fillets of Sole with Mushrooms

This dish is not unlike the French *filets de sole bonne femme*. The fish can be skinned if preferred, but leaving the skin on helps to keep the fillets together. Use 3–4 Chinese dried mushrooms can be used instead of button mushrooms. Soak them for 20–25 minutes in warm water then squeeze dry, remove the stalks and slice the mushrooms.

SERVES 3–4

450 g (1 lb) sole fillets
1 egg white
1 tablespoon cornflour
225 g (8 oz) button mushrooms
2–3 spring onions
1 slice fresh root ginger, peeled
600 ml (1 pint) vegetable oil,
for deep-frying
1 teaspoon salt
1 teaspoon sugar
1 tablespoon soy sauce
1 tablespoon Chinese rice wine, or dry sherry
120 ml (4 fl oz) Clear Stock (page 64)
1 teaspoon sesame seed oil, to finish (optional)

Leave the fish fillets whole if they are small and simply trim off the soft bones along the edges; if the fillets are very large, cut in half. Put the fillets in a bowl with the egg white and cornflour. Mix together. Thinly slice the mushrooms. Cut the spring onions into 5 cm (2 inch) sections and finely shred. Cut the ginger into fine shreds.

Heat the oil in a hot wok until fairly hot, then turn down the heat to allow the oil to cool a little. Deep-fry the fish until golden and crisp, stirring all the time with chopsticks. Remove them and drain on paper towels.

Pour off all but 2 tablespoons oil from the wok. Increase the heat to high and add the mushrooms, spring onions and ginger. Stir a few times and then add the salt, sugar, soy sauce, rice wine or sherry and the stock. Bring to the boil, return the fish to the wok and simmer for 2 minutes. Sprinkle over the sesame seed oil and serve.

Haoyou Niurou

Cantonese Beef Steak

Oyster sauce is a speciality of Canton, and the special feature of this dish is its extreme savouriness and tenderness.

SERVES 2–3

275–350 g (10–12 oz) beef steak
1 teaspoon salt
1 teaspoon sugar
1 tablespoon soy sauce
1 tablespoon Chinese rice wine, or dry sherry
1 tablespoon cornflour
1 spring onion
1 slice fresh root ginger, peeled
1 head Chinese leaves, or Cos lettuce
4 tablespoons vegetable oil
1 tablespoon oyster sauce

Cut the beef into thin slices about the size of a large postage stamp. Place in a bowl with a pinch of the salt, the sugar, soy sauce, rice wine or sherry and cornflour. Mix well, then leave to marinate for at least 30 minutes.

Chop the spring onion and ginger. Wash the Chinese leaves or lettuce and cut each leaf into 2 or 3 pieces.

Heat 2 tablespoons of the oil in a hot wok until smoking, add the Chinese leaves or lettuce and the remaining salt and stir-fry until the leaves are limp. Remove with a perforated spoon and arrange on a warmed serving dish.

Heat the remaining oil in the wok until hot, toss in the spring onion and ginger to flavour the oil, then add the beef and marinade and stir vigorously. When the colour of the meat changes, blend in the oyster sauce and cook for 1 minute. Transfer to the serving dish.

Kung Bao Jiding

Diced Chicken with Walnuts in Hot Sauce

A highly popular dish from Sichuan, which is made hot by the addition of whole dried red chillies. The amount of chillies added to this dish can be adjusted according to personal taste. If the chillies remain whole the dish will be less hot, as the seeds are the 'hottest' part of the chilli. The walnuts can be substituted with almonds, cashew nuts or peanuts.

SERVES 2–3

275–350 g (10–12 oz) boneless chicken breast, skinned
½ teaspoon salt
1 egg white
1 tablespoon cornflour
1 green pepper, cored and seeded
50 g (2 oz) shelled walnuts
4 tablespoons vegetable oil
2 spring onions, cut into short sections
2 slices fresh root ginger, peeled
3–4 dried red chillies, sliced into rings
1 tablespoon yellow or black bean sauce
1 teaspoon sugar
2 tablespoons Chinese rice wine, or dry sherry
1 teaspoon cornflour

ABOVE: *Left, Diced Chicken with Walnuts in Hot Sauce. Right, Stir-fried Mixed Vegetables (page 73).*
OPPOSITE: *Fillets of Sole with Mushrooms.*

Remove the white tendons and membranes from the chicken breasts, then cut the chicken into small cubes about the size of sugar lumps. Place in a bowl and first mix with the salt, then the egg white and finally the cornflour. Cut the green pepper and walnuts to roughly the same size as the chicken cubes.

Heat the oil in a hot wok, add the chicken cubes and stir-fry for a few seconds until the colour changes from pink to white. Remove from the oil with a perforated spoon and set aside.

Add the spring onions, ginger, chillies and walnuts to the hot oil in the wok, then add the bean sauce. Stir a few times, then add the green pepper. Return the chicken cubes to the wok, stir a few times more, then add the sugar and rice wine or sherry. Cook for about 1 minute.

Mix the cornflour to a smooth paste with 1 tablespoon cold water, add to the wok and blend well until thickened. Transfer to a warmed dish and serve hot.

Chao Yaohua

Stir-fried Kidneys Sichuan Style

Time and again people who normally do not like the taste of kidneys cannot help falling for this particular dish. It is typically Sichuan in that it has a complexity of different flavours: savoury, sweet, sour and hot. Pig's kidneys are traditionally used in China, but there is no reason why lamb's or calf's kidneys cannot be used if preferred. The traditional Chinese technique of scoring the kidneys before cooking gives them an attractive appearance.

SERVES 2–3

225–275 g (8–10 oz) kidneys
½ teaspoon salt
½ teaspoon freshly ground pepper
1 tablespoon Chinese rice wine, or dry sherry
2 teaspoons cornflour
3–4 dried red chillies
1 slice fresh root ginger, peeled
2 spring onions
1 garlic clove, peeled
600 ml (1 pint) vegetable oil,
for deep-frying
1 teaspoon sesame seed oil, to finish (optional)
Sauce:
1 tablespoon sugar
1 tablespoon soy sauce
1½ tablespoons vinegar
2 teaspoons cornflour
1½ tablespoons stock or water

Split each kidney in half; discard the fat and the white parts in the centre. Score the surface of each piece of kidney diagonally in a criss-cross pattern, cutting about two-thirds of the way down. Cut each half into several small pieces, then place in a bowl with the salt, pepper, rice wine or sherry and the cornflour. Mix well together.

Cut the chillies into small pieces, discarding the seeds. Finely chop the ginger, spring onions and garlic. Mix the ingredients for the sauce in a jug or bowl.

Heat the oil in a hot wok until hot. Deep-fry the kidney pieces for about 1 minute, then scoop them out with a perforated spoon and drain on paper towels.

Pour off all but about 1 tablespoon oil from the wok, add the chillies, ginger, spring onions and garlic to flavour the oil, then add the kidney pieces. Stir for a few times, add the sauce mixture and blend well. As soon as the sauce starts to bubble, sprinkle in the sesame seed oil. Transfer to a warmed serving dish and serve hot.

Congbao Yangrou

Rapid-fried Lamb and Leeks

There are well over 4 million Chinese Muslims; although Chinese speaking, they are distinguished from ethnic Chinese by their affiliation with the Sunni branch of Islam. Together with about 6 million other national minorities (the Uygur and the Mongols, all non-pork eaters), they form the Muslim school of cooking in China. This simple Peking-style recipe is a fine example of that school.

SERVES 2

225–275 g (8–10 oz) leg of lamb fillet
1–2 spring onions
1 tablespoon soy sauce
1 tablespoon Chinese rice wine, or dry sherry
2 teaspoons vinegar
½ teaspoon freshly ground pepper
1 tablespoon cornflour
600 ml (1 pint) vegetable oil,
for deep-frying
225 g (8 oz) leeks
1 garlic clove, peeled and crushed
1 teaspoon salt
1 teaspoon sesame seed oil, to finish

Trim off all the fat from the lamb and cut the meat as thinly as possible into small strips. Cut the spring onions in half lengthways, then slice them diagonally. Put the lamb and spring onions in a bowl with the soy sauce, rice wine or sherry, vinegar, pepper, cornflour and about 1 tablespoon of the oil. Stir well to mix, then cover and leave to marinate for at least 30 minutes, longer if possible (several hours would be ideal).

When ready to cook, wash the leeks well and cut them into 2.5 cm (1 inch) lengths. Heat the oil in a hot wok until moderately hot, add the lamb, together with the marinade and spring onions, and deep-fry for 1–1½ minutes at the very most, stirring all the time with chopsticks to keep the strips separate. Do not overcook. Scoop out the strips of lamb with a perforated spoon and drain on paper towels.

Pour off all but about 2 tablespoons oil from the wok. Add the crushed garlic to flavour the oil, then add the leeks and stir-fry for about 1 minute. Add the salt, return the lamb to the wok and continue stirring for another minute or so. Add the sesame seed oil and blend well. Serve hot.

Zahui Liji | Zhi Wu Si Bao

Stir-fried Pork and Vegetables
This is a basic recipe for cooking any meat (pork, beef or chicken) with vegetables – usually several different kinds, according to seasonal availability.

SERVES 3–4

225 g (8 oz) pork fillet
1 tablespoon soy sauce
1 tablespoon Chinese rice wine, or dry sherry
1 teaspoon sugar
2 teaspoons cornflour
225 g (8 oz) Chinese leaves, spring greens, spinach, or Cos lettuce
100 g (4 oz) French beans, or mangetout
100 g (4 oz) cauliflower, or broccoli florets
1–2 carrots
1–2 spring onions
4 tablespoons vegetable oil
2 teaspoons salt

Cut the pork into thin slices about the size of an oblong postage stamp. Place in a bowl with the soy sauce, rice wine or sherry and sugar. Mix the cornflour to a smooth paste with 1 tablespoon cold water, add to the bowl and mix well.

Wash the green vegetables and cut them into pieces about the same size as the pork. Peel the carrots and cut them into thin slices of the same size. Cut the spring onions into short lengths.

Heat about half of the oil in a hot wok, add the pork mixture and stir-fry for about 1 minute or until the colour changes. Scoop out the pork with a perforated spoon and set aside.

Heat the remaining oil in the wok. Toss in the spring onions to flavour the oil, then add the vegetables. Stir-fry for about 1 minute, add the salt and stir a few more times. Return the partly-cooked pork to the wok and continue stirring for another minute or so, adding a little stock or water to moisten if necessary. Serve when the sauce starts to bubble.

Stir-fried Mixed Vegetables
The Chinese never mix ingredients indiscriminately: different ingredients are carefully selected with the aim of achieving a harmonious balance of colour, aroma, flavour and texture.

SERVES 4

5–6 Chinese dried mushrooms, or
50 g (2 oz) button mushrooms
225 g (8 oz) Chinese leaves, or Cos lettuce
175 g (6 oz) carrots, peeled
100 g (4 oz) mangetout, or French beans
4 tablespoons vegetable oil
1 teaspoon salt
1 teaspoon sugar
1 tablespoon light soy sauce

Soak the dried mushrooms in warm water to cover for 25–30 minutes, then drain and squeeze dry. Discard the hard stalks and cut the mushrooms into thin slices. If using fresh mushrooms, do not peel them, just wash and slice them.

Cut the Chinese leaves or lettuce and the carrots diagonally into thin slices. Top and tail the mangetout or French beans, leave them whole if small, otherwise cut them in half.

Heat the oil in a hot wok until smoking, add the Chinese leaves, lettuce or cabbage and the carrots, stir-fry for 30 seconds, then add the mangetout or beans and the mushrooms. Continue stirring for 30 seconds or so, then add the salt and sugar. Toss and turn all the ingredients until well blended, then add the soy sauce.

There should be enough natural juice from the vegetables to form a small amount of sauce, therefore no extra liquid should be needed. Cook for another minute at the very most. Transfer to a warmed serving dish and serve hot.

CHINA
LONG COOKING DISHES

After the cold starters, soups and quick stir-fried dishes, the main courses in the serving sequence of a grand Chinese meal are usually long-cooked, therefore most of them can be prepared and cooked well in advance, avoiding a last-minute rush.

Some of these dishes can even be served cold, so they are ideal buffet party food. Practically all of them blend well with Western food and can therefore also be served as part of a menu in conjunction with non-Chinese food.

Hui Gou Rou

Twice-cooked Pork with Chilli Bean Sauce
To be authentic, the cut of meat usually used is the belly of pork, known as 'five-flower' pork in China because the alternate layers of fat and meat form a pretty pink and white pattern when viewed in cross-section. Serve with deep-fried rice noodles and stir-fried baby sweetcorn and green beans.

SERVES 3–4

350 g (12 oz) belly pork in one piece, not too lean
100 g (4 oz) bamboo shoots
100 g (4 oz) celery sticks
3 tablespoons vegetable oil
2 spring onions, cut into short lengths
1 garlic clove, peeled and finely chopped
2 tablespoons Chinese rice wine, or dry sherry
1 tablespoon soy sauce
1 tablespoon chilli bean sauce

Place the whole piece of pork in a saucepan of boiling water and cook for 25–30 minutes. Remove the meat, leave to cool. Cut across the grain of the meat, into thin slices about 5 x 2.5 cm (2 x 1 inch) in size. Cut the bamboo shoots and celery into chunks of roughly the same size.

Heat the oil in a hot wok until smoking, add the spring onions and garlic to flavour the oil, then add the vegetables and stir a few times. Add the pork, followed by the rice wine or sherry, soy and chilli bean sauces. Stir-fry for about 1–2 minutes. Serve hot.

Ching Zheng Yu

Cantonese Steamed Fish
Most fish can be steamed successfully. Use whole sea bass, trout, grey mullet, whiting, plaice or sole. Do not fillet or skin the fish.

SERVES 4

750–800 g (1½–1¾ lb) fish, either whole or in one piece, cleaned and scaled
1 teaspoon salt
½ teaspoon freshly ground pepper
5 spring onions
4 slices fresh root ginger, peeled and thinly shredded
2 tablespoons Chinese rice wine, or dry sherry
1 tablespoon crushed salted black beans, or 2 tablespoons soy sauce
1 tablespoon vegetable oil

Rub the salt and pepper all over the fish. Place 3 whole spring onions on a heatproof dish, then place the fish on top. Mix together about half of the ginger with the rice wine or sherry and the crushed black beans or soy sauce. Cover the fish with this mixture and leave to marinate for about 30 minutes.

Place the dish on a rack in a wok, or in the top half of a steamer. Cover and steam vigorously above fast-boiling water for 15–20 minutes only.

Meanwhile, thinly shred the remaining spring onions. Heat the oil in a small saucepan and add the shredded spring onions and the remaining ginger to flavour it. Remove the dish from the wok or steamer, pour the flavoured oil all over the length of the fish and serve.

Su Shijin

Chinese Vegetarian Casserole

The various ingredients for this casserole are carefully selected to provide a contrast and balance of colour, aroma, flavour and texture.

SERVES 4

2–3 tablespoons dried wood ears (black fungus),
or 5–6 Chinese dried mushrooms
225 g (8 oz) firm bean curd (tofu)
salt
4 tablespoons vegetable oil
100 g (4 oz) carrots, peeled and sliced
100 g (4 oz) mangetout, trimmed
100 g (4 oz) Chinese leaves, sliced
100 g (4 oz) canned, sliced bamboo shoots or
whole baby sweetcorn
1 teaspoon sugar
1 tablespoon light soy sauce
1 teaspoon cornflour
1 teaspoon sesame seed oil, to finish (optional)

Soak the wood ears or Chinese dried mushrooms in water to cover for 20–25 minutes; discard the hard roots, then rinse. Cut the mushrooms into small slices.

Cut each cake of bean curd into about 12 small pieces, then put them in a saucepan of lightly salted boiling water for 2–3 minutes, so that they become firm. Remove with a perforated spoon and drain.

Heat about half of the oil in a flameproof casserole or heavy-based saucepan until hot. Add the pieces of bean curd and fry until lightly browned on both sides. Remove the bean curd then heat the remaining oil in the pan. Add the vegetables and stir-fry for about 1–2 minutes. Return the bean curd to the pan, add 1 teaspoon salt, the sugar and soy sauce and stir well. Cover, reduce the heat and braise for 2–3 minutes.

Meanwhile, mix the cornflour to a smooth paste with 1 tablespoon cold water. Pour the paste over the vegetables and stir. Increase the heat to high to thicken the sauce, then sprinkle in the sesame seed oil (if using).

BELOW: *Twice-cooked Pork with Chilli Bean Sauce (page 74).*

Tangcu Yukuai

Braised Fish in Sweet and Sour Sauce

The best fish for this recipe are monkfish tails; otherwise use the small cutlets from the tail ends of cod or haddock. Halibut is also suitable, but it is very expensive.

SERVES 4

1 kg (2–2¼ lb) fish steaks
1 egg
2 tablespoons cornflour
about 1 litre (1¾ pints) vegetable oil, for deep-frying
1 teaspoon sesame seed oil, to finish
fresh coriander or parsley leaves, to garnish
Sauce:
2 slices fresh root ginger, peeled and finely chopped
2 spring onions, finely chopped
2 tablespoons Chinese rice wine, or dry sherry
2 tablespoons sugar
3 tablespoons vinegar
2 tablespoons soy sauce
250 ml (8 fl oz) Clear Stock (page 64), or water
1 tablespoon cornflour

Pat the fish steaks dry with paper towels, leaving the skin on. If they are large, cut them into pieces, no smaller than half the size of a postcard. In a bowl, beat the egg with the cornflour, whisking in just enough water to make a thin batter.

Heat the vegetable oil in a hot wok. Meanwhile, mix the ingredients for the sauce in a jug or bowl.

When the oil is hot, turn down the heat to allow the oil to cool a little. Dip the fish steaks in the batter and turn to coat well, then slide gently into the oil one by one. Increase the heat to high and deep-fry for about 2 minutes until crisp and golden. Remove the fish with a perforated spoon and drain.

Pour off all but about 1 tablespoon oil from the wok. Add the sweet and sour sauce mixture, stir over moderate heat until smooth, then return the fish to the wok and braise for about 2 minutes. Sprinkle in the sesame seed oil and serve immediately, garnished with coriander or parsley.

Shaguo Doufu Yu

Fish and Bean Curd Casserole

This dish is light in texture, low in calories and extremely high in protein. It is also very delicious, really simple to prepare and cook – and economical into the bargain! Serve it as part of a Chinese meal, as a complete meal with rice or pasta, or you may find it substantial enough to be served on its own. There is a fair amount of liquid, which can be served with the casserole, or separately as a soup if thinned down with hot stock or water.

SERVES 4

450 g (1 lb) firm white fish fillets (cod, lemon sole, or haddock)
1 tablespoon cornflour
1 egg white
450 g (1 lb) firm bean curd (tofu)
a few Chinese, or Cos lettuce leaves
3 tablespoons Chinese rice wine, or dry sherry
2 tablespoons light soy sauce
1 teaspoon sugar
2 slices fresh root ginger, peeled
3 spring onions, cut into 5 cm (2 inch) lengths
1 teaspoon salt
freshly ground pepper
300 ml (½ pint) Clear Stock (page 64), or water
50 g (2 oz) cooked ham, finely chopped
1 teaspoon sesame seed oil, to finish

Cut the fish into small pieces, leaving the skin on if wished. In a bowl, mix the cornflour to a paste with 2 tablespoons cold water, then mix with the egg white and use to coat the pieces of fish. Cut the bean curd into small cubes.

Line a flameproof casserole with the Chinese leaves or lettuce. Add the bean curd and fish pieces together with the rice wine or sherry, the soy sauce, sugar, ginger, spring onions, salt and pepper to taste. Pour over the stock or water, then sprinkle on the finely chopped ham as a garnish. Bring the casserole to the boil over high heat, then reduce the heat to low and cover with a tight-fitting lid. Simmer gently for 15–20 minutes; do not overcook.

Sprinkle in the sesame seed oil and serve straight from the casserole, or transfer to a warmed deep serving dish. Serve hot.

Yuxiang Qiezi

Braised Aubergine with Garlic and Chilli

This highly popular Sichuan dish is also known as 'fish-fragrant' or 'sea-spice aubergine'. The interesting point is that neither fish nor shellfish is used in the dish; the seasonings, however, are normally used for cooking fish dishes, hence the term *yuxiang*, which means 'fish flavour'.

SERVES 3–4

750 g (1½–1¾ lb) aubergines
100 g (4 oz) pork fillet
1 litre (1¾ pints) vegetable oil, for deep-frying
3–4 spring onions, finely chopped, with white and green parts separated
1 slice fresh root ginger, peeled and finely chopped
1 garlic clove, peeled and finely chopped
1 teaspoon salt
1 teaspoon sugar
1 tablespoon soy sauce
1 tablespoon Chinese rice wine, or dry sherry
1 tablespoon vinegar
1 tablespoon chilli bean paste
2 teaspoons cornflour
1 teaspoon sesame seed oil, to finish

Cut the aubergines into strips about the size of potato chips. Cut the pork into matchstick shreds.

Heat the oil in a hot wok until hot, add the aubergine strips and deep-fry for about 3–4 minutes or until soft, stirring all the time with chopsticks to keep the strips separate. Remove with a perforated spoon and drain on paper towels. Pour off all but about 1 tablespoon oil from the wok. Add the finely chopped white parts of the spring onions, the ginger and garlic, then the shredded pork. Stir-fry for a few seconds, then add the aubergines together with the salt, sugar, soy sauce, rice wine or sherry, vinegar and chilli bean paste. Blend well, then braise for 2–3 minutes. Mix the cornflour to a smooth paste with 1 tablespoon cold water, then stir into the wok to thicken the gravy. Finally, sprinkle in the green parts of the spring onions and the sesame seed oil. Serve hot.

Hong Shao Ji

Soy Braised Chicken (Red-cooked Chicken)

This is one of the most popular ways of preparing poultry in China. If preferred, use an assortment of different chicken pieces instead of the whole chicken suggested here.

SERVES 4

1.5 kg (3–3½ lb) fresh young chicken
1 teaspoon salt
1 tablespoon sugar
3 tablespoons light soy sauce
2 tablespoons dark soy sauce
3 tablespoons Chinese rice wine, or dry sherry
1 tablespoon cornflour
3 tablespoons vegetable oil
2 slices fresh root ginger, peeled
2–3 spring onions, cut into short lengths
1 garlic clove, peeled and crushed
300 ml (½ pint) Clear Stock (page 64), well-flavoured stock, or water
450 g (1 lb) carrots, peeled
225 g (8 oz) mushrooms, wiped
fresh coriander, to garnish

Joint the chicken, then cut it into about 20–24 pieces, leaving the skin on. Place them in a bowl with the salt, sugar, soy sauces, rice wine or sherry and cornflour. Mix well, then cover and leave to marinate for 10–15 minutes, turning the pieces once or twice.

Heat the oil in a hot wok or large, heavy-based saucepan. Add the ginger, spring onions and garlic to flavour the oil, then remove the chicken pieces from the marinade with a perforated spoon and add to the wok. Stir-fry for about 5 minutes until the chicken pieces are lightly browned on all sides.

Add the marinade to the wok with the stock or water, bring to the boil, then reduce the heat and cover with a lid. Simmer gently for about 25–30 minutes, stirring now and again to make sure that the chicken pieces do not stick to the bottom of the pan.

Slice the carrots and mushrooms and add to the chicken. Increase the heat to high and cook for a further 10–15 minutes, or until the liquid has almost all evaporated. Serve hot, garnished with coriander.

Wuxiang Paigu

Five-spice Pork Spareribs
This is a very versatile dish; it can be cooked in the oven, under a grill, or outside on a barbecue.

SERVES 4

1 kg (2–2¼ lb) pork spareribs
1 teaspoon salt
2 tablespoons sugar
2 tablespoons brandy, whisky, rum or vodka
2 tablespoons light soy sauce
2 tablespoons hoisin sauce
1 tablespoon dark soy sauce
1 teaspoon five-spice powder
1 teaspoon curry powder (optional)

Cut the pork into individual ribs if this has not already been done by the butcher. Place in a bowl, add the remaining ingredients and blend together. Leave to marinate for 1 hour, turning them over once or twice.

Cook the ribs in the marinade in a preheated moderately hot oven (200°C/400°F, Gas Mark 6) for 40–45 minutes, turning them once, halfway during cooking. Alternatively, remove the ribs from the marinade and grill for 15–20 minutes, turning them every 5 minutes or so, until browned all over. If cooking on a barbecue, slightly less time is required, but the ribs will need to be turned over more frequently.

Chop each rib into 2 or 3 bite-sized pieces if you have a meat cleaver, otherwise serve them whole, with the sauce poured over them. If you have grilled or barbecued the ribs, make the sauce by bringing the marinade to the boil in a saucepan with a little stock or water.

Baipa Erbai

Braised Chinese Leaves and Mushrooms
Chinese straw mushrooms are available both canned and fresh in this country. Should you have difficulty obtaining them use small button mushrooms instead.

SERVES 4

450 g (1 lb) Chinese leaves
350 g (12 oz) canned straw mushrooms, or 225 g (8 oz) fresh straw or button mushrooms
4 tablespoons vegetable oil
2 teaspoons salt
1 teaspoon sugar
1 tablespoon cornflour
50 ml (2 fl oz) milk

ABOVE: *Left, Soy-braised Chicken (Red-cooked Chicken) (page 77). Centre, Braised Chinese Leaves and Mushrooms. Right, Fish and Bean Curd Casserole (page 76).*

Separate and wash the Chinese leaves, then cut each leaf in half lengthways. Drain the canned straw mushrooms. If using fresh straw or button mushrooms, do not peel them, simply wash or wipe them clean and then trim off the stalk ends.

Heat about half of the oil in a hot wok, add the Chinese leaves and stir-fry for about 1 minute. Add 1½ teaspoons of the salt and the sugar and continue stirring for another minute or so. Remove the Chinese leaves and arrange them neatly on a warmed serving dish. Keep hot while making the sauce.

Mix the cornflour to a smooth paste with 3 tablespoons cold water. Heat the remaining oil in the wok until hot, add the mushrooms with the remaining salt and stir-fry for about 1 minute.

Add the cornflour paste and the milk to the mushrooms and stir constantly until the sauce is smooth, white and thickened. Pour the sauce evenly over the Chinese leaves and serve immediately.

Guangdong Shao Ya

Cantonese Roast Duck

When the Cantonese roast duck or chicken, they fill it with a liquid stuffing and rub the skin with soy sauce, honey and red colouring. These are the shining red ducks you see hanging in the windows of Chinese restaurants.

SERVES 4

2–2.5 kg (4½–5¾ lb) duckling
1 teaspoon salt
1 tablespoon vegetable oil
2 slices fresh root ginger, peeled and finely chopped
2 spring onions, finely chopped
1 tablespoon sugar
2 tablespoons Chinese rice wine, or dry sherry
1 tablespoon crushed yellow bean sauce
1 tablespoon hoisin sauce
1 teaspoon five-spice powder
3 tablespoons clear honey
2 tablespoons dark soy sauce
1 teaspoon red powder, or cochineal food colouring

Clean the duck well inside and out, then pat thoroughly dry with a clean cloth or paper towels. Rub both inside and out with the salt, then tie the neck tightly with string so that no liquid will drip out of the duck when it is hanging head downwards.

Make the stuffing: heat the oil in a pan over moderate heat, add the ginger and spring onions, then the rest of the ingredients except the honey, soy sauce and colouring. Bring to the boil, stirring all the time.

Pour the liquid stuffing into the cavity of the duck and truss it securely with string or thread. Plunge the whole duck into a large saucepan of boiling water for a few seconds only, then take it out. Mix the remaining ingredients with 150 ml (¼ pint) cold water and brush thoroughly all over the duck. Hang the duck up on a meat hook to dry, head downwards, in a well-ventilated spot. Leave for at least 4–5 hours, ideally overnight.

When ready to cook, hang the duck on the meat hook (still with its head down) in a preheated moderately hot oven (200°C/400°F, Gas Mark 6). Place a tray of cold water in the bottom of the oven to catch the drips. Roast for 25 minutes, then roast at 180°C/350°F, Gas Mark 4 for a further 30 minutes, basting once or twice with any remaining coating mixture.

Remove the string or thread and pour the liquid stuffing into a jug or bowl. Chop the duck into bite-sized pieces, arrange on a serving plate and pour over the liquid stuffing. Serve hot or cold.

CHINA

RICE, NOODLES & SWEET DISHES

Plain boiled rice forms the bulk food in a Chinese meal, while fried rice and noodles (fried or in soup) are often served on their own as a light meal or snack. The Chinese do not eat bread as such, but steamed buns and pancakes, both sweet and savoury, are very popular.

In China, everyday meals do not normally finish with a dessert; most sweet dishes are served either as a snack or, on more formal occasions, between courses to cleanse the palate, rather like the role of a sorbet in the West.

Bai Fan

Boiled Rice

Fan, the Chinese term for cooked rice or other cereals, has a wide range of meanings in everyday usage, since it is synonymous with the word 'meal', just as in the West the word 'bread' is used in 'give us our daily bread' or 'bread-winner'. Should you prefer your rice to be softer and less fluffy, use short grain or round pudding rice and reduce the amount of water by a quarter.

SERVES 4

350 g (12 oz) long grain rice
½ teaspoon salt

Wash and rinse the rice in cold water just once, then drain and place in a saucepan. Add about 450 ml (15 fl oz) fresh cold water, to cover the rice by 2.5 cm (1 inch). Bring to the boil, then add the salt and use a spoon to give the rice a stir in order to prevent it sticking to the bottom of the pan.

Reduce the heat to very low, cover the saucepan with a tight-fitting lid and cook for 15–20 minutes. Turn off the heat and let the rice stand for 10 minutes or so. Just before serving, fluff up the rice with a fork or spoon.

Chao Fan

Special-fried Rice

This is a meal or a snack in its own right. To make a less substantial dish, simply stir-fry cold cooked rice in a little oil, adding beaten eggs, a few finely chopped spring onions and a pinch of salt.

SERVES 4

2–3 eggs
2 spring onions, finely chopped
2 teaspoons salt
3 tablespoons vegetable oil
100 g (4 oz) peeled prawns
100 g (4 oz) cooked meat (chicken, pork or ham), cut into small cubes
4 tablespoons fresh or frozen peas, cooked
1 tablespoon light soy sauce
350–450 g (12 oz–1 lb) cold cooked rice

Lightly beat the eggs with about 1 teaspoonful of the finely chopped spring onions and a pinch of the salt. Heat about 1 tablespoon of the oil in a hot wok, add the eggs and scramble until set, then remove and set aside in a bowl.

Heat the remaining oil in the wok, add the prawns, meat and peas, stir a few times, then add the soy sauce. Stir-fry for a few minutes, then add the rice and scrambled eggs with the remaining spring onions and salt. Stir to separate each grain of rice. Serve hot.

Mayi Shangsu

Ants Climbing Trees

This strangely named dish is quite simply transparent noodles with minced pork – the noodles are the 'trees' and the pieces of minced pork are the 'ants'.
Small red chillies, including the seeds, are used for their hot 'bite', but if you prefer a milder flavour to the dish, choose the larger green chillies, or simply omit the seeds.

SERVES 4

225 g (8 oz) minced pork
2 tablespoons soy sauce
1 tablespoon sugar
1 teaspoon cornflour
½ teaspoon chilli sauce
3 tablespoons vegetable oil
1 small fresh red chilli, chopped
2 spring onions, chopped
75 g (3 oz) transparent noodles, soaked in warm water for 30 minutes
120 ml (4 fl oz) chicken stock
shredded spring onions, to garnish

Put the minced pork in a bowl with the soy sauce, sugar, cornflour and chilli sauce. Stir well to mix, then cover and leave to marinate in a cold place for about 20 minutes.

Heat the oil in a hot wok or deep, heavy-based frying pan. Add the chopped fresh chilli (including the seeds) and the spring onions and stir-fry for a few seconds to flavour the oil. Add the pork mixture and stir-fry for a further few minutes, until the meat changes colour from pink to white.

Drain the transparent noodles thoroughly, then add to the pan and blend well with the pork. Pour in the chicken stock and stir gently with chopsticks to combine with the other ingredients in the pan. Stir-fry until the pork is cooked and all of the liquid has been absorbed by the pork and noodles.

Transfer to a warmed serving dish and garnish with the shredded spring onions. Serve hot.

Tang Mian

Noodles in Soup

In China, noodles are more commonly served in soup than fried as Chao Mian/Chow Mein (page 82) – a popular dish in the West. It is hard to explain why, as there is so little difference in the basic ingredients used in both dishes. Peeled prawns have been used in this recipe, but if you prefer you can use strips of pork, lamb, ham or chicken instead.

SERVES 4

225 g (8 oz) peeled prawns
salt
1 teaspoon cornflour
100 g (4 oz) bamboo shoots, or button mushrooms
100 g (4 oz) spinach leaves, Chinese leaves, or Cos lettuce
350 g (12 oz) egg noodles or spaghettini
600 ml (1 pint) well-flavoured chicken stock
2 tablespoons light soy sauce
3 tablespoons vegetable oil
2 spring onions, thinly shredded
2 tablespoons Chinese rice wine, or dry sherry
1–2 teaspoons sesame seed oil, to finish (optional)

Place the prawns in a bowl with a pinch of salt. Mix the cornflour to smooth paste with 1 tablespoon cold water, then stir into the prawns. Thinly shred the bamboo shoots or mushrooms and the green leaves.

Cook the noodles or spaghettini in a large saucepan of boiling salted water according to packet instructions, then drain and place in a warmed large serving bowl or 4 individual bowls. Bring the stock to the boil and pour over the cooked noodles, with about half of the soy sauce. Keep hot.

Heat the oil in a hot wok, add the shredded spring onions to flavour the oil, then add the prawn mixture and the shredded vegetables. Stir a few times, add 1½ teaspoons salt, the remaining soy sauce and the rice wine or sherry. Cook for about 1–2 minutes, stirring constantly. Pour the mixture over the noodles and sprinkle with the sesame seed oil if using. Serve hot.

Chao Mian

Chow Mein (Fried Noodles)

Noodles have been eaten in China for more than 2000 years, and it is believed that Marco Polo learnt the art of making spaghetti and ravioli in China in the 14th century.

SERVES 4

450 g (1 lb) egg noodles or spaghettini
salt
4 tablespoons vegetable oil
1 medium onion, peeled and thinly sliced
100 g (4 oz) cooked meat (pork, chicken or ham), cut into thin shreds
100 g (4 oz) mangetout, or French beans
100 g (4 oz) fresh bean-sprouts
2–3 spring onions, thinly shredded
2 tablespoons light soy sauce
1 tablespoon sesame seed oil or chilli sauce, to finish

Cook the noodles or spaghettini in a large saucepan of boiling salted water according to packet instructions, then drain and rinse under cold running water until cool; set aside.

Heat about 3 tablespoons of the oil in a hot wok, add the onion, meat, mangetout or beans and the bean-sprouts and stir-fry for about 1 minute. Add 1 teaspoon salt and stir a few times more, then remove from the wok with a perforated spoon and keep hot.

Heat the remaining oil in the wok and add the spring onions and the noodles, with about half of the meat and vegetable mixture. Mix with the soy sauce, then stir-fry for 1–2 minutes, or until heated through.

Transfer the mixture from the wok to a warmed large serving dish, then pour the remaining meat and vegetable mixture on top as a dressing. Sprinkle with the sesame seed oil or chilli sauce (or both if preferred). Serve immediately.

BELOW: *Left, Chow Mein (Fried Noodles). Top, Special-fried Rice (page 80). Right, Noodles in Soup (page 81).* OPPOSITE: *Top, Chinese Fruit Salad. Bottom, Almond Junket.*

Xingren Doufu

Almond Junket

Also known as Almond Float, the *doufu* is in fact
made from agar-agar, isinglass or gelatine.

SERVES 4

*15 g (½ oz) agar-agar or isinglass, or 25 g (1 oz)
powdered gelatine
4 tablespoons sugar
300 ml (½ pint) milk
1 teaspoon almond flavouring
400 g (14 oz) can apricots, or mixed fruit salad
50 g (2 oz) white grapes, peeled and seeded*

Dissolve the agar-agar or isinglass in 300 ml (½ pint) water
over gentle heat. (If using gelatine, dissolve in the water
according to packet instructions.) Dissolve the sugar in
300 ml (½ pint) water in a separate saucepan, then
combine with the dissolved setting agent and add the
milk and almond flavouring. Pour this mixture into a
large serving bowl. Leave until cold, then chill in the
refrigerator for at least 2–3 hours, until set.

To serve, cut the junket into small cubes and place in a
serving bowl. Pour the canned fruit and syrup over the
junket, add the grapes and mix well. Serve chilled.

Shuiguo Shala

Chinese Fruit Salad

Choose from kiwi fruit, lychees, strawberries,
pineapple, pears, apples, peaches, grapes,
cherries and tangerines. For the best effect, you
should have at least 4 different types of fruit.

SERVES 4

*1 large honeydew melon
4–5 types of fresh and canned fruit, with the
syrup from the can*

Cut the honeydew melon in half and scoop out the inside
of the fruit, discarding the seeds. Cut the flesh of the
melon into small chunks. Reserve the shell.

Prepare the other fruit, leaving it whole if small,
otherwise separating it into segments or cutting it into
small chunks as with the melon.

Mix the pieces of melon with the fruit and canned
syrup. Pack the melon shell with this mixture, then
cover tightly with cling film. Chill in the refrigerator for
at least 2 hours before serving.

Hong Dousha Bing

Red Bean Paste Pancakes

Sweetened chestnut purée can be used as a
substitute for red bean paste.

MAKES 8

*225 g (8 oz) plain flour
3 tablespoons vegetable oil
1 egg, beaten
100 g (4 oz) sweetened red bean paste*

Sift the flour into a bowl, then very gently pour in 125 ml
(4 fl oz) boiling water. Add about 1 teaspoon of the oil and
the beaten egg. Knead the mixture into a firm dough,
then divide it into 2 equal portions. Roll out each portion
into a long 'sausage' on a lightly floured surface and cut
each sausage into 4 pieces. Press each piece into a flat
pancake with the palm of your hand, then roll gently to a
15 cm (6 inch) circle with a rolling pin.

Place an ungreased frying pan over high heat. When
hot, reduce the heat to low and place 1 pancake in the
pan. Cook until brown spots appear on the underside,
then turn and cook the other side. Transfer to a plate and
cover with a damp cloth. Continue cooking the remaining pancakes, stacking them under the cloth.

Spread about 1 tablespoon red bean paste over about
three-quarters of 1 pancake, then roll the pancake over 3
or 4 times to form a flattened roll. Repeat with the
remaining bean paste and pancakes, until all are used up.
Heat the remaining oil in the frying pan and shallow-fry
the rolls until golden brown, turning once.

CHINA
MENUS & CUSTOMS

The main distinctive feature in Chinese cuisine is the harmonious balance of colours, aromas, flavours and textures as well as shapes and forms, not only in a single dish, but also in a course of different dishes. This aspect of serving Chinese food often puzzles people in the West, partly because the order of different courses served at a Chinese meal bears no resemblance to the Western custom of not mixing meat and fish in the same course.

On closer examination, one soon realizes that a Chinese meal is served according to a carefully worked out programme based on the *yin-yang* principle in Chinese culture. This ancient Chinese philosophy believes that harmony arises from the blending of opposites; not of irreconcilable opposites, but of complementary pairs. Therefore, the order in which different courses or dishes are served depends more on the method of cooking, and the way the ingredients are prepared before cooking, rather than on the food itself.

Due to the multi-course nature of a Chinese meal, eating and dining have always been very much a family or communal event. Chinese food is best eaten in this way, for only then can a variety of dishes be enjoyed. Separate tables were unheard of in China until very recent times, since a Chinese meal is essentially a buffet-style affair, with more hot dishes than cold served on the table at the same time, to be shared by everyone. Dishes are served singly, or in groups, only at banquets and formal dinner parties. For example a typical menu of 10–12 dishes for 8–10 people would be served as follows:

First course: 3–4 cold starters or an assorted hors d'oeuvre dish.

Second course: 2–3 quick stir-fried dishes, deep-fried or braised dishes; the exact number and variety of dishes depends on the occasion and what is to follow.

Main course: 1, 2 or 3 long-cooked dishes, which can be steamed, braised (red-cooked) or roasted, usually consisting of a whole duck, chicken, fish and a joint of meat. Again, the number and variety of dishes served will depend on the scale of the occasion.

Rice course: is served towards the end of the main course, so too are noodles and dumplings.

Dessert: only served at formal banquets in China; soup is often served at the end of less grand banquets, instead of a dessert course.

Fresh fruit and China tea: traditionally served right at the end. In fact, fruit and nuts as well as tea are also served at the beginning of a dinner, rather like crudités with aperitifs in the West. Tea is seldom served during a Chinese meal; tea with *dim sum* is a different matter, since they are snacks served between meals.

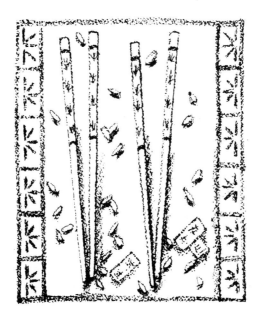

84

Planning A Chinese Menu

When it comes to planning a Chinese menu, allow two dishes for 2–4 people, three dishes for 4–6, and four dishes for 6–8 and so on. The Chinese never serve an individual dish to each person; all the dishes on the table are shared. The only exception to this is when a light snack such as a dish of *chow mein* or a bowl of noodles in soup is served, in which case each person is given his or her own portion.

When eating out in a Chinese restaurant, order one more dish than there are people, since the portions are usually much smaller than you would cook at home. Therefore, order 3 dishes for two people, 5 dishes for four people and so on; and do not duplicate the order for one or two particular personal favourites, since that will only overcrowd the table unnecessarily. Be sure to have a variety of dishes by selecting from the wide range of foods available, always bearing in mind the underlying principle of harmonious balance and contrast in colour, aroma, flavour, shape and texture.

The recipes in the Chinese chapter are grouped under the general heading of cooking methods, which more or less determine the serving order, so as to simplify the process of menu planning.

The sample menus on this page should help you select dishes that combine to produce well-balanced meals.

What To Drink With A Chinese Meal

In China, people drink tea almost all day long, but they very rarely drink it during their meals. Soups are usually served throughout an everyday meal in order to help wash down savoury foods, but when it comes to formal dinners or when entertaining, wine and spirits are an essential part of the fare. The Chinese, in contrast to their sophisticated approach to food, are remarkably unparticular about alcoholic drinks – with the exception of the true connoisseurs. On the whole, Chinese people do not distinguish between fermented wine, in which the alcoholic content is low, and distilled spirit, in which it is high. In everyday usage, the word *jiu* or *chiew* means any alcoholic beverage, including beer. Many Chinese people drink whisky and brandy with their meals as if they are table wines.

Many people in the West seem to think that table wine and Chinese food do not go together, but there is no reason why not. Do not feel confined to drinking only white wines, as most people seem to prefer. By all means start the meal with a white wine, but then go on to red if there are enough guests to warrant opening more than one bottle of wine.

If you are eating alone, or there are only a small number of people at the table, good red wines to serve throughout a Chinese meal are: a light and fruity Beaujolais or Mâcon, or a red from the Loire (Chinon, Bourgueil), California (Cabernet Sauvignon, Pinot Noir), Italy (Valpolicella, Bardolino) and Spain (Rioja).

For those people who prefer not to drink wine with Chinese food, chilled lager or a light beer can be served. At the end of the meal, lend an authentic touch by serving China or jasmine tea without sugar or milk; it is most refreshing.

— Sample Menus —

SIMPLE SUPPER
Fish and Watercress Soup
Twice-cooked Pork with
Chilli Bean Sauce
Boiled Rice

STIR-FRY DINNER
Chicken and Ham Soup
Stir-fried Pork and Vegetables
Cantonese Steamed Fish
Boiled Rice

LIGHT LUNCH
Chicken Salad with Spicy Dressing
Scallops and Prawns with
Mixed Vegetables
Boiled Rice

DINNER PARTY
White-cut Pork with Garlic Dressing
Fillets of Sole with Mushrooms
Cantonese Roast Duck
Boiled Rice
Fruit Fritters

CANTONESE DINNER
White-cut Cantonese Chicken
Rapid-fried Prawns in Sweet and
Sour Sauce
Rapid-fried Lamb and Leeks
Fish and Bean Curd Casserole
Boiled Rice

SUMMER BUFFET
Deep-fried Wontons
Mixed Vegetable Salad with
Chinese Dressing
Poached Prawns with Piquant Dip Sauce
Special Fried Rice
Five-spice Pork Spareribs
Cantonese Steamed Fish
Chicken Salad with Spicy Dressing
Lychee Sorbet
Chinese Fruit Salad

NOTE: Adjust quantities of individual dishes according to the number of people being served.

BIRTHDAY DINNER PARTY

This simple menu is perfect for an informal dinner with friends. The
starter and dessert can be prepared in advance, so too can the ingredients
for the main course. All you have to do when guests arrive is light
the charcoal – then let your guests do their own cooking!

FOR 4–6 PEOPLE

*Mixed Vegetable Salad with Chinese
Dressing (page 62)
Mongolian Hot Pot
Chinese Fruit Salad (page 83)*

Shijin Huoguo

Mongolian Hot Pot
Inexpensive hot pots or 'fire kettles' for
cooking this dish at the table can be bought at
Chinese supermarkets. Alternatively, use an
electric wok or rice cooker. Fondue sets are not
suitable because their burners are not
hot enough.

SERVES 4–6 as an individual dish

*225 g (8 oz) lamb, pork or beef fillet, or a
mixture of all 3 meats
225 g (8 oz) boneless chicken breast, skinned
225 g (8 oz) prawns or scallops, or a mixture
of both
225 g (8 oz) fish fillets (sole, cod or haddock)
225 g (8 oz) button mushrooms
450 g (1 lb) Chinese leaves or Cos lettuce
350 g (12 oz) firm bean curd (tofu)
225 g (8 oz) cellophane noodles, or 450 g (1 lb)
egg noodles
1.75 litres (3 pints) Clear Stock (page 64)
1 teaspoon salt
2–3 tablespoons Chinese rice wine or dry sherry
Dip sauce:
4 tablespoons light soy sauce
4 tablespoons dark soy sauce
1 tablespoon sugar
2 teaspoons sesame seed oil
3–4 spring onions, finely shredded
3–4 slices fresh root ginger, peeled and
finely shredded
1–2 garlic cloves, peeled and crushed
1 tablespoon chilli sauce (optional)*

Thinly slice the meat and chicken. Leave the prawns
whole; cut the scallops (if using) and the fish into thin
slices. Wash the vegetables and cut into small pieces with
the bean curd.

Soak the noodles in boiling hot water until soft, rinse
under cold running water, then drain. Arrange all these
ingredients on separate plates or in bowls, then place
them on the table.

Mix all the ingredients for the dip sauce together, then
divide equally between 4–6 saucers. Place them on the
table at individual place settings.

Place the hot pot in the centre of the table. Light the
charcoal in the funnel and fill the moat with the stock.
Add the salt and rice wine or sherry, a little of the
Chinese leaves or lettuce, mushrooms, noodles and bean
curd. Bring to the boil. Each person picks up a few pieces
of meat or fish and swirls them in the stock for a few
seconds. When the slices begin to curl and change
colour, they should be removed from the liquid and
dipped into the sauce before eating.

More vegetables and noodles can be added to the pot
from time to time, and eaten with the meat, fish and bean
curd. When the meat and fish have been eaten, top up the
pot with more stock, add the remaining vegetables and
noodles, and recharge with more charcoal if necessary.
Bring to the boil and cook for about 1–2 minutes, then
ladle out the contents into individual bowls. Serve as a
soup with the remaining dip sauce, to finish off the meal.

RIGHT: *Mongolian Hot Pot and Mixed Vegetable Salad
with Chinese Dressing (page 62).*

NEW YEAR'S EVE BANQUET

All Chinese festivals are based on the lunar calendar, which is why the
Chinese New Year falls on a different day each year: it can be as early
as mid January or as late as mid February. Whatever the date, the
New Year also signals the coming of spring, which is why it is
also called the Spring Festival. Traditionally it is a big event
and, for the well-off, celebrations can start weeks beforehand.
The official celebration begins about a week before, with the ritual
of sending the kitchen god to heaven for the annual report on the
family's good behaviour. The celebrations reach their climax on
New Year's Eve, when the return of the kitchen god to his rightful
place above the stove is enthusiastically celebrated, in the
form of a truly grand banquet such as this one.

FOR 10–15 PEOPLE

Shanghai Smoked Fish (page 62)
Deep-fried Prawn Balls
Sichuan Chicken
Whole Fish in Garlic and Chilli Sauce
Cantonese Beef Steak (page 70)
Eight-treasure Soup
Soy-braised Duck
Crispy Seaweed
Chicken Slices in Egg White
Braised Meatballs
Stir-fried Mixed Vegetables (page 73)
Stewed Beef with Carrots
Five-spice Pork Spareribs (page 78)
Plum Blossom and Snow

Zha Xia Wan

Deep-fried Prawn Balls
Cook these balls up to 3 hours in advance, then
deep-fry or crisp in the oven before serving.

SERVES 4 as an individual dish

450 g (1 lb) peeled cooked prawns
50 g (2 oz) pork fat
1 egg white
2 tablespoons cornflour
1 tablespoon brandy or rum
1 teaspoon finely chopped fresh root ginger
salt
freshly ground pepper
600 ml (1 pint) vegetable oil, for deep-frying
coriander leaves or parsley, to garnish

Finely chop the prawns with the pork fat. Place in a bowl
with the remaining ingredients except the oil and the
garnish, adding pepper to taste. Mix together, then stir
in one direction until stiff and smooth. Leave to stand for
about 30 minutes.

Form the mixture into about 24 small balls. Heat the
oil in a hot wok, then turn down the heat slightly or take
the wok off the heat for a while to cool the oil down a
little. Deep-fry the prawn balls in batches over moderate
heat until they turn golden, then scoop out with a
perforated spoon and drain on paper towels.

Just before serving, reheat the oil to hot and fry the
prawn balls for a few seconds or place in a hot oven, until
crisp. Arrange in a warmed serving dish. Sprinkle with
salt and pepper to taste, garnish with coriander leaves or
parsley and serve hot.

Guaiwei Ji | Furong Ji

Sichuan Chicken

Also known as 'Strange-flavoured Chicken', this dish is simplicity itself to cook. The sesame paste for the sauce is available at oriental stores, and also at health food shops and Greek, Cypriot and Middle Eastern stores under the name of tahini. If you cannot find it, use peanut butter mixed with a little sesame seed oil instead.

SERVES 2–3 as an individual dish

450 g (1 lb) chicken portions, with the skin on
Sauce:
1 tablespoon sesame seeds
1 tablespoon sesame paste (tahini)
1 tablespoon light soy sauce
2 teaspoons chilli sauce
1 tablespoon sugar
1 tablespoon sesame seed oil
2–3 spring onions,
finely chopped
2 slices fresh root ginger, peeled and
finely chopped
1 teaspoon freshly ground pepper
1 garlic clove, peeled and crushed or finely
chopped (optional)

Put the chicken in a saucepan and cover with cold water. Bring to the boil, then reduce the heat, cover and simmer gently for 10 minutes. Turn off the heat and leave the chicken in the water until cool.

Meanwhile, make the sauce: toast the sesame seeds under the grill or dry-roast them in a frying pan until they turn golden, then crush them coarsely with a pestle and mortar or rolling pin. Mix them with the remaining sauce ingredients in a bowl.

Take the chicken out of the saucepan and pat dry with paper towels. Remove the bones from the chicken and cut the flesh into small pieces, keeping the skin on. Arrange the chicken pieces on a serving plate, pour over the sauce and mix thoroughly. Serve cold.

Chicken Slices in Egg White

The original recipe for this Shanghai dish contains a few items which are not so readily available in the West; these have been substituted without altering the main feature of the dish — it remains very colourful and delicious.

SERVES 2 as an individual dish

2 chicken breasts, boned and skinned
1 teaspoon salt
1 egg white, lightly beaten
2 teaspoons cornflour
225 g (8 oz) mangetout or courgettes
100 g (4 oz) button mushrooms
4 tablespoons vegetable oil
2 spring onions, cut into short lengths
1 slice fresh root ginger, peeled and
finely chopped
1 teaspoon sugar
1 tablespoon Chinese rice wine or dry sherry
1 tablespoon light soy sauce
1 teaspoon sesame seed oil, to finish

Remove the white tendons and membranes from the chicken breasts, then cut the meat into thin slices about the size of a large postage stamp. Place them in a bowl and mix first with a pinch of the salt, then the egg white. Mix the cornflour to a smooth paste with 1 tablespoon cold water, then stir into the chicken.

Top and tail the mangetout. If using courgettes, trim off the ends, cut each one in half lengthways, then cut diagonally into diamond-shaped chunks. Wipe the mushrooms, leave them whole if small, otherwise cut them in half or into neat slices.

Heat the oil in a hot wok, add the chicken slices and stir-fry over moderate heat until the colour turns white. Remove them with a perforated spoon and drain.

Increase the heat to high, add the spring onions and ginger to flavour the oil, then add the vegetables and stir a few times. Return the chicken slices to the wok, add the remaining salt, the sugar, rice wine or sherry and the soy sauce. Stir and blend well, then sprinkle in the sesame seed oil. Serve while hot.

Babao Tang

Eight-treasure Soup

Everyday soups are usually clear, this one is thick and therefore a festival dish. The ingredients can be varied according to seasonal availability.

SERVES 10–15

175 g (6 oz) boneless chicken breast, skinned
175 g (6 oz) pork fillet
175 g (6 oz) cooked ham
175 g (6 oz) peeled cooked prawns, or 3 tablespoons dried shrimps
350 g (12 oz) firm bean curd (tofu)
175 g (6 oz) button mushrooms, wiped
3.6 litres (6 pints) Clear Stock (page 64) or water
175 g (6 oz) fresh or frozen garden peas
175 g (6 oz) sweetcorn
3 eggs, beaten
3 tablespoons light soy sauce
3 tablespoons cornflour
salt
freshly ground pepper

Thinly shred the chicken, pork and ham. If using dried shrimps, soak them in warm water to cover for 20 minutes, then drain. Slice the tofu and mushrooms.

Bring the stock or water to the boil in a large saucepan. Add the meats, fish, bean curd and vegetables. When they start to float to the surface, gently pour in the beaten eggs, then add the soy sauce and cook for 1 minute stirring constantly.

Mix the cornflour to a smooth paste with 1 tablespoon cold water. Add to the soup and stir until thickened, then season with salt and pepper to taste. Pour into warmed individual bowls and serve hot.

Jiang Ya

Soy-braised Duck

The whole duck can be served hot in its own juice, or it can be served cold, in which case it should be taken out of the cooking liquid, cut into small pieces and arranged neatly on a plate.

SERVES 4 as an individual dish

1 duckling, weighing about 2.25 kg (5–5¼ lb)
3–4 spring onions
3–4 slices fresh root ginger
5 tablespoons dark soy sauce
3 tablespoons brandy
2 tablespoons brown sugar

ABOVE: *Clockwise from top; Whole Fish in Garlic and Chilli Sauce (page 93), Crispy Seaweed (page 91), Deep-fried Prawn Balls (page 88), Eight-treasure Soup (page 90), Stewed Beef with Carrots (page 92), Plum Blossom and Snow (page 93).*

Bring 2.5 litres (4½ pints) water to the boil in a large saucepan. Place the duckling in the pan and par-boil for 4–5 minutes, turning it over once. Discard about two-thirds of the water, then add the spring onions, ginger, soy sauce and brandy.

Bring the liquid back to the boil, then reduce the heat, cover and simmer gently for 30 minutes, turning the duck over once or twice.

Add the brown sugar and continue simmering for a further hour or until the flesh feels tender when pierced with a skewer. Turn the duck over in the cooking liquid several times during this final simmering. Serve hot, or leave in the cooking liquid until cold.

Cai Soong

Crispy Seaweed

The very popular 'seaweed' often served as a starter in Chinese restaurants is, in fact, green cabbage! Choose fresh, young spring greens which have pointed heads, so that even the deep-green, outer leaves are quite tender. If liked, sprinkle the 'seaweed' with a few deep-fried split almonds before serving.

SERVES 10–12 as an individual dish

750 g (1½ lb) spring greens
600 ml (1 pint) vegetable oil, for deep-frying
1½ teaspoons caster sugar
1 teaspoon salt

Separate the spring green leaves, then wash and pat dry with paper towels or a clean teatowel. Using a very sharp knife, shred into the thinnest possible shavings. Spread the shavings out on paper towels for about 30 minutes, until thoroughly dry.

Heat the oil in a hot wok or deep-fat frier. Turn off the heat for 30 seconds, then add a batch of spring green shavings. Turn the heat on to moderate and deep-fry the greens until they begin to float to the surface of the oil, stirring them with chopsticks all the time. Scoop them out with a perforated spoon. Drain on paper towels while deep-frying the remaining batches of spring green shavings in the same way.

When all the seaweed is cooked and well drained, place in a large bowl and sprinkle over the sugar and salt. Toss gently to mix. Serve cold.

Hongshao Rouwan

Braised Meatballs

This dish is sometimes known as 'Lion's Head' because the meatballs are supposed to resemble the shape of a lion's head and the cabbage to look like its mane.

SERVES 4 as an individual dish

3 Chinese dried mushrooms
350 g (12 oz) boneless pork, finely minced
1 egg white
2 tablespoons soy sauce
1 tablespoon Chinese rice wine or dry sherry
1 tablespoon cornflour
1 teaspoon sugar
3 tablespoons vegetable oil
2.5 cm (1 inch) piece fresh root ginger, peeled and finely chopped
2 spring onions (white part only), finely chopped
350 g (12 oz) Chinese leaves, shredded
1 teaspoon salt
about 450 ml (¾ pint) chicken stock
100 g (4 oz) transparent noodles

Soak the mushrooms in warm water to cover for 20–25 minutes. Meanwhile, put the minced pork in a bowl with the egg white, soy sauce, rice wine or sherry, cornflour and sugar. Mix well, then form into 10–12 balls.

Drain the mushrooms, squeeze dry and discard the hard stalks. Heat the oil in a heavy-based saucepan or flameproof casserole, add the meatballs and fry until golden on all sides. Remove with a perforated spoon and set aside to drain on paper towels.

Add the ginger and spring onions to the pan and fry for a few minutes to flavour the oil, then add the shredded Chinese leaves, the mushrooms and salt.

Return the meatballs to the pan and pour in just enough stock to cover. Bring to the boil, then lower the heat and cover the pan. Simmer for 25 minutes.

Meanwhile, put the noodles in a bowl and pour in enough boiling water to cover. Leave to soak for 10 minutes, then drain. Stir into the pan of meatballs and simmer for a further 3 minutes. Serve hot.

Luopu Men Niunan

Stewed Beef with Carrots

This recipe has a familiar English name, yet is very typically Chinese in taste, texture and appearance. Shin or brisket of beef can be used instead of stewing steak for a more economical dish, but the cooking time should be increased in order to tenderize the meat.

This dish tastes even better when reheated; this will also give you the chance to remove any excess fat once the sauce has cooled.

SERVES 4 as an individual dish

2 tablespoons vegetable oil
2.5 cm (1 inch) piece fresh root ginger, peeled and finely chopped
1 spring onion, chopped
1 garlic clove, peeled and crushed
750 g (1½ lb) stewing steak, trimmed of fat and cut into 1 cm (½ inch) squares
4 tablespoons soy sauce
1 tablespoon medium or dry sherry
1 tablespoon sugar
½ teaspoon five-spice powder
450 g (1 lb) carrots

Heat the oil in a heavy-based saucepan or flameproof casserole. Add the chopped root ginger and spring onion, together with the crushed garlic, stirring well to mix. Fry gently for a few minutes to flavour the oil, stirring constantly.

Add the beef and the remaining ingredients, except the carrots. Toss gently to mix, then pour in just enough cold water to cover. Bring to the boil, then lower the heat, cover the pan and simmer for 1½ hours. Lift the lid occasionally during this time and stir the ingredients to ensure that the beef cooks evenly.

Meanwhile, scrape or peel the carrots and cut diagonally into diamond shapes. Add to the beef and simmer for a further 30 minutes, or until both beef and carrots are tender. Turn into a warmed serving dish or on to a platter and serve while hot.

Ganshao Yu | Meixue Zhengchun

Whole Fish in Garlic and Chilli Sauce

In China, fish weighing less than 1 kg (2 lb) are often cooked whole, head and tail intact, and served right at the end of a banquet. The reason for this is partly because the word for fish is *yu*, pronounced the same as the Chinese character for 'to spare'; the Chinese like to think that there is always something on the table to spare.

SERVES 4 as an individual dish

1 large, or 2 small grey mullet, carp or sea bass
3 tablespoons vegetable oil
1 garlic clove, peeled and crushed or
finely chopped
2 slices fresh root ginger, peeled and
finely chopped
2 tablespoons chilli bean paste
2 tablespoons Chinese rice wine or dry sherry
1 tablespoon soy sauce
1 teaspoon sugar
1 tablespoon vinegar
a little stock or water, if necessary
2 teaspoons cornflour
2 spring onions, finely shredded, to finish

Scale and clean the fish. Using a sharp knife, slash both sides of the fish diagonally as deep as the bone, at about 2 cm (¾ inch) intervals.

Heat the oil in a hot wok until smoking. Add the fish and fry for about 3–4 minutes, turning it over once. Push the fish to one side, add the garlic, ginger, chilli bean paste, rice wine or sherry and soy sauce and stir until these ingredients are mixed to a smooth sauce.

Push the fish back to the centre of the wok, add the sugar and vinegar and a little stock or water to moisten, if necessary. Cook for 2–3 minutes, turning the fish over once more. Mix the cornflour to a smooth paste with 1 tablespoon cold water, stir into the sauce and cook until thickened. Transfer the fish to a warmed serving dish and spoon over the sauce. Sprinkle the shredded spring onions over the fish before serving.

Plum Blossom and Snow

This dessert is correctly called 'Plum Blossom and Snow Competing for Spring'. The fruit symbolizes the first blossom of spring, and the egg white topping the layer of snow leftover from winter. It is the perfect dessert for a banquet serving a large number of people.

SERVES 12

6 eating apples
6 bananas
2 lemons
6 eggs, separated
350 g (12 oz) sugar
9 tablespoons milk
9 tablespoons cornflour
thinly pared rind of 1 lime, to decorate

Peel and core the apples and slice thinly. Peel the bananas and slice thinly. With a potato peeler, thinly pare the rind of 1 lemon and set aside for the decoration. Squeeze the juice of both lemons. Arrange the apple and banana in alternate layers in 12 individual ovenproof dishes, sprinkling each layer with a little of the lemon juice.

Put the egg yolks in a heavy-based saucepan with the sugar, milk, cornflour and 135 ml (4½ fl oz) cold water. Stir well to mix, then heat very gently, stirring all the time, until smooth.

Pour the custard mixture over the fruit. Beat the egg whites until stiff, then spread over the top. Bake in a preheated hot oven (220°C/425°F, Gas Mark 7) for 5 minutes, or until the top is crisp and golden. Remove the dishes from the oven and leave until completely cold.

Meanwhile, prepare the decoration. Plunge the pared lemon rind and the lime rind into a saucepan of boiling water and blanch for 2 minutes. Drain; refresh under cold running water, then pat dry with paper towels and cut into thin strips. Sprinkle evenly over the top of the cold desserts just before serving.

NEW YEAR'S DAY LUNCH

On New Year's Day, people call on each other in the morning to
exchange the season's greetings. Hot tea is offered to visitors, usually
accompanied by a box of 'treasures' – dried dates and other
fruits and nuts.
For those well-to-do Chinese families who have feasted themselves
the night before, the palate and stomach really need a rest on New Year's
Day; this simple vegetarian lunch fits the bill perfectly.

FOR 6–8 PEOPLE

Stir-fried Bean-sprouts and Green Beans
Tomato and Egg Soup (page 64)*
Sweet and Sour Cucumber
Braised Bean Curd
Braised Chinese Leaves and Mushrooms (page 78)
Chinese Vegetarian Casserole (page 75)
Boiled Rice (page 80)*
Almond Junket (page 83)*

*Make double quantity

Douya Chao Caidou

Stir-fried Bean-sprouts and Green Beans
Only fresh bean-sprouts should be used. Canned
bean-sprouts do not have a crunchy texture,
which is the main characteristic of this very
popular vegetable.

SERVES 4 as an individual dish

450 g (1 lb) fresh bean-sprouts
225 g (8 oz) dwarf French beans
3–4 tablespoons vegetable oil
1 spring onion, finely chopped
1 teaspoon salt
1 teaspoon sugar
sesame seed oil, to finish

Wash and rinse the bean-sprouts in cold water. It is not
necessary to top and tail each sprout; just discard the
husks and other bits and pieces that float to the surface.
Drain well. Top, tail and halve the French beans.

Heat the oil in a hot wok until smoking, add the spring
onion to flavour the oil, then add the beans and stir a few
times. Add the bean-sprouts, stir-fry for 30 seconds,
then add the salt and sugar and stir-fry for another
minute. Sprinkle with sesame seed oil before serving.

Tangcu Huanggua

Sweet and Sour Cucumber
Select a dark green and slender cucumber; the
overgrown, pale-coloured fat ones contain too
much water and have far less flavour.

SERVES 4 as an individual dish

1 cucumber
1 teaspoon salt
2 tablespoons caster sugar
2 tablespoons vinegar
1 tablespoon sesame seed oil
strips of red and yellow pepper, to garnish
(optional)

Cut the cucumber in half lengthways, but do not peel.
Cut each half lengthways into 3 long strips, then cut
these into 2.5 cm (1 inch) lengths. Place the slices in a
bowl, add the salt, sugar and vinegar and leave to
marinate for 10–15 minutes.

To serve, place the cucumber strips in a serving bowl,
add the sesame seed oil and mix well. Garnish with the
red and yellow pepper strips, if liked. Serve at room
temperature, or chilled.

Doufu

Braised Bean Curd

When this bean curd is sliced after cooking and cooling, the texture resembles honeycomb. To provide a crunchy contrast to the tofu, garnish with shredded spring onions and carrot flowers, which will also make the dish look more attractive. To make carrot flowers, peel a medium carrot and cut into 7.5 cm (3 inch) chunks. Make a V-shaped cut down the length of each chunk and remove the strip of carrot from the centre of the cut. Repeat at regular intervals around the carrot, then cut crossways into thin slices, which will resemble flowers. If not using immediately, keep in a bowl of iced water.

SERVES 4 as an individual dish

450 g (1 lb) firm bean curd (tofu)
300 ml (½ pint) vegetable stock
2 spring onions, trimmed
5 cm (2 inch) piece fresh root ginger, peeled
3 tablespoons soy sauce
2 tablespoons Chinese rice wine or dry sherry
1 tablespoon sugar

Put the bean curd in a saucepan, cover with cold water and bring to the boil. Cover the pan with a lid and cook over high heat for 10 minutes.

Meanwhile, put the stock in a separate saucepan with the spring onions and ginger. Bring to the boil and simmer gently for 5 minutes, so that the stock becomes flavoured with the onions and ginger.

Drain the bean curd and add to the pan of stock with the remaining ingredients. Bring to the boil again, then cover and simmer gently for 30 minutes. Turn off the heat and leave the bean curd to cool in the cooking liquid until it is completely cold.

To serve, remove the bean curd from the liquid with a perforated spoon, cut into slices and arrange on a serving plate. Serve cold.

BELOW: Left, Braised Bean Curd. Centre, Stir-fried Bean-sprouts and Green Beans (page 94). Right, Sweet and Sour Cucumber (page 94).

—— SUMMER BARBECUE ——

Chinese food lends itself beautifully to informal
outdoor eating as most dishes can be prepared in advance and served
at room temperature or even cold. Barbecue parties, as such, do not exist
in China but for very special occasions like large wedding parties, food
such as sucking pig is often roasted on a spit in the open air – very
few Chinese kitchens have ovens. Do not worry if the weather
looks uncertain, as all of the barbecued food in this menu
can be cooked in the oven or under the grill, then
finished off for the last few minutes on the barbecue if wished.

FOR 10–15 PEOPLE

Marinated Beef Steaks
Cantonese Barbecued Pork
Crispy Meatballs
Soy Chicken Drumsticks
Five-spice Pork Spareribs (page 78)
Duck on Skewers
Cantonese Steamed Fish (page 74)
Braised Eggs
Celery and Chicken Liver Salad
Bean-sprout Salad
Ten-variety Rice Salad
Fruit Fritters
Lychee Sorbet

Shao Nipai

Marinated Beef Steaks

T-bone or sirloin steaks can be used instead of
fillet, if preferred. Lamb and pork chops and
chicken portions can also be cooked this way,
but they will need a longer cooking time. Pork
chops and chicken portions, should be well-
cooked and not at all rare

SERVES 4–6 as an individual dish

1 kg (2–2¼ lb) fillet steak, in one piece
four 2.5 cm (1 inch) pieces fresh root ginger,
peeled and finely shredded
4 spring onions, finely chopped
4 tablespoons Chinese rice wine or dry sherry
4 tablespoons soy sauce
2 tablespoons vegetable oil
2 tablespoons brandy
2 tablespoons sugar

Cut the fillet steak into 10–15 slices, each one about 1 cm
(½ inch) thick. Place in a shallow dish. Put the remaining
ingredients in a jug, mix well together, then pour over
the slices of steak. Cover and leave to marinate in a cool
place for at least 2–3 hours, or overnight in the
refrigerator. Spoon the marinade over the slices of steak
several times during marinating so that they become
evenly coated.

When ready to cook, drain the steak and reserve the
marinade. Place the steak on the grid of a moderately hot
barbecue and cook for 2–3 minutes on each side, or until
cooked to your liking. Baste frequently with the reserved marinade so that the steak does not dry out.
When cooked, transfer the steak slices to a serving dish.
Serve hot or cold.

Cha Rouyuan

Crispy Meatballs

These meatballs can be served cold; spear each one on to a cocktail stick and arrange on a serving platter with a bowl of chilli sauce dip in the centre.

SERVES 6 as an individual dish

750 g (1½ lb) boneless pork, not too lean
2 tablespoons light soy sauce
1 tablespoon Chinese rice wine or dry sherry
2 teaspoons freshly ground Sichuan or black pepper
1 teaspoon finely chopped fresh root ginger
1 teaspoon finely chopped spring onion
1 teaspoon sugar
1 teaspoon salt
1 egg
about 3 tablespoons cornflour
12–18 bamboo skewers, soaked in water for 30 minutes

Finely chop the pork in a food processor, then place in a bowl with the remaining ingredients, except the cornflour. Mix well together, then add 2 tablespoons of the cornflour and mix again until slightly thickened.

Form the mixture into 24–36 small balls and coat each one with a little more cornflour. Drain the skewers, then thread 2 meatballs on each one. Place on the grid of a moderately hot barbecue and cook for 6–8 minutes, turning the skewers halfway through cooking. Transfer to a serving plate and serve hot.

Zha Jitui

Soy Chicken Drumsticks

If there is any marinade left after cooking the chicken, dilute it with a few spoonfuls of stock or water and pour it over the drumsticks before serving.
These drumsticks are also ideal for packed lunches or picnics, as it is not essential for them to be finished on the barbecue.

SERVES 6 as an individual dish

12–18 chicken drumsticks
4 tablespoons soy sauce
2 spring onions, finely chopped
2 tablespoons Chinese rice wine or dry sherry
2 tablespoons sesame seed oil
½ teaspoon freshly ground black pepper

Slash each drumstick in several places with a sharp knife, cutting through the skin into the flesh. Place in a shallow dish. Put the remaining ingredients in a jug, mix well together, then pour over the chicken. Cover and leave to marinate in a cool place for at least 20 minutes, or in the refrigerator overnight if more convenient. Turn the drumsticks in the marinade several times.

Drain the drumsticks well, reserving the marinade. Arrange the drumsticks side by side in a single layer on a baking tray. Roast in a preheated moderate oven (180°C/350°F, Gas Mark 4) for 15–20 minutes, then remove and cool.

To finish cooking the drumsticks, brush with the reserved marinade and place on the grid of a moderately hot barbecue. Cook for 5–10 minutes, turning the drumsticks halfway through cooking. Serve hot or cold.

Cha Shao

Cantonese Barbecued Pork

Cha Shao is traditionally served cold; if you think it will be easier not to have to cook lots of different things on the barbecue at the same time, barbecue this pork dish before guests arrive and serve it cold. Sliced thinly and arranged on a serving platter, it looks most attractive.

SERVES 4–6 as an individual dish

1 kg (2–2¼ lb) pork fillet, in one piece
2 tablespoons Chinese rice wine or dry sherry
2 tablespoons hoisin (barbecue) sauce
2 tablespoons light soy sauce
1 tablespoon dark soy sauce
1 tablespoon brandy
3 tablespoons clear honey

Put the pork fillet in a shallow dish. Put the Chinese rice wine or sherry in a jug with the hoisin sauce, light and dark soy sauces and the brandy. Mix well together, then pour over the pork. Cover and leave to marinate in a cool place for at least 45 minutes, or in the refrigerator overnight. Turn the meat in the marinade several times to ensure that it is evenly coated.

When ready to cook, lift the pork out of the dish and place on the grid of a moderately hot barbecue. Cook for 30–45 minutes, turning frequently. Remove from the barbecue, leave to stand for 3 minutes, then brush with the honey. Return to the barbecue and cook for a further 2 minutes. Transfer to a board and cut diagonally into thin slices before serving.

Jigan Ban Qincai | Kao Chuan Ya

Celery and Chicken Liver Salad

In China, the gizzards of duck and chicken are almost regarded as the best part of the bird. This recipe uses chicken livers, but the gizzards can be used instead. If gizzards or chicken livers are not available, lamb's or pig's kidneys may be substituted.

SERVES 4 as an individual dish

225 g (8 oz) chicken livers, trimmed and cleaned
2 teaspoons Chinese rice wine or dry sherry
1 teaspoon cornflour
½ teaspoon salt
50 g (2 oz) dried wood ears (black fungus)
1 head celery, sliced diagonally
1 cm (½ inch) piece fresh root ginger, peeled and finely shredded, to garnish
Dressing:
4 tablespoons soy sauce
4 tablespoons vinegar
2 tablespoons sesame seed oil
1 cm (½ inch) piece fresh root ginger, peeled and finely shredded
freshly ground pepper

Put the chicken livers in a bowl and sprinkle with the rice wine or sherry, the cornflour and salt. Mix well, then cover and leave to marinate in a cool place for at least 30 minutes, turning them occasionally.

Meanwhile, cover the wood ears with warm water and soak for 20–25 minutes. Rinse; discard the hard stalks, if any, then plunge into a saucepan of boiling water and blanch for 1 minute. Drain, rinse under cold running water, then drain again.

Plunge the chicken livers into a pan of fresh boiling water, blanch for 2 minutes and drain. Arrange on a serving platter with the wood ears and celery. Mix together the ingredients for the dressing, with pepper to taste. Pour over the salad and garnish with the shredded ginger. Serve cold.

Duck on Skewers

Filleted duck breasts, which are available at large supermarkets, are meaty and tender, and convenient to use for kebabs and barbecues. This recipe makes either 8 small or 4 large skewers. If cooking on the larger, metal skewers, remove the pieces of duck after cooking and skewer one or two pieces on to wooden cocktail sticks to serve.

SERVES 8 as an individual dish

4 duck breasts, boned and skinned
Marinade:
2 tablespoons brown sugar
1 teaspoon salt
4 tablespoons soy sauce
1 tablespoon sesame seed oil
1 cm (½ inch) piece fresh root ginger, peeled and finely chopped
1 teaspoon sesame seeds

Cut the duck breasts into 32 small pieces. In a large bowl mix together the ingredients for the marinade, then stir in the duck. Cover and leave to marinate for 3–4 hours in a cool place, or overnight in the refrigerator. Spoon the marinade over the duck several times so that the pieces become evenly coated. Remove the duck with a perforated spoon and thread on to 8 bamboo skewers or 4 large metal skewers.

Place on the grid of a moderately hot barbecue and cook the small skewers for 8–10 minutes, the larger ones for 10–12 minutes. Turn the skewers several times during cooking and baste with the remaining marinade. Serve the barbecued duck hot or cold, either on or off the skewers.

LEFT: *Clockwise from top: Duck on Skewers, Lychee Sorbet (page 101), Fruit Fritters (page 101), Bean-sprout Salad (page 100), Five-spice Pork Spareribs (page 78), Braised Eggs (page 100).*

Lu Dan

Braised Eggs

'Marbled' braised eggs make an attractive addition to any menu. The effect is simple to achieve by gently cracking the shells all over before braising in the soy-based sauce. The sauce remaining after cooking may be stored in the refrigerator for several weeks and used again.

SERVES 6 as an individual dish

300 ml (½ pint) Clear Stock (page 64)
3 tablespoons soy sauce
1 tablespoon Chinese rice wine or dry sherry
5 cm (2 inch) piece fresh root ginger, peeled
½ teaspoon five-spice powder
6 eggs

Bring the stock to a gentle boil in a medium-sized saucepan. Add the soy sauce, rice wine or sherry, the ginger and five-spice powder. Stir well to mix.

Cook the eggs in a separate saucepan of boiling water for 5 minutes, then drain. Remove the shells from 3 of the eggs and lightly crack the shells of the remaining eggs to give a 'marbled' effect. Add both the shelled and unshelled eggs to the stock and simmer over gentle heat for 20 minutes, turning the eggs over now and then to ensure even cooking. Leave the eggs to cool in the stock.

To serve, lift the eggs out of the stock with a perforated spoon, remove the remaining shells, then cut into halves or quarters. Serve cold.

Laingban Douyar

Bean-sprout Salad

Use fresh not canned bean-sprouts in this salad as the sprouts should still retain their crispness. Try to buy good-quality bean-sprouts that do not require trimming, as this would be very time-consuming.

SERVES 8–10 as an individual dish

450 g (1 lb) fresh bean-sprouts
salt
2 eggs
1 tablespoon vegetable oil
100 g (4 oz) boiled ham, cut into thin strips
Dressing:
2 tablespoons soy sauce
2 tablespoons vinegar
1 tablespoon sesame seed oil
freshly ground black pepper

Wash the bean-sprouts under cold running water. Plunge into a large saucepan of boiling salted water and blanch for 1 minute. Drain, rinse under cold running water, then drain again and set aside.

Put the eggs in a bowl with a pinch of salt and beat lightly. Heat the oil in an omelette pan or heavy-based frying pan, add the eggs and cook to make a thin omelette. Remove from the pan, leave to cool, then cut into thin strips.

To serve, put all the ingredients for the dressing in a jug, with pepper to taste, and mix well together. Put the bean-sprouts in a bowl, pour over the dressing and toss gently to mix. Transfer the salad to a serving platter and arrange the ham and omelette strips on top. Serve cold.

Shijin Fan

Ten-variety Rice Salad

This salad is really a superior version of the Chinese-American dish *chop suey*, which means 'bits and pieces'. The ingredients can be varied according to taste and availability.

SERVES 8–10 as an individual dish

3 Chinese dried mushrooms
450 g (1 lb) long grain rice
salt
2 tablespoons vegetable oil
4 spring onions, finely chopped
100 g (4 oz) peeled cooked prawns
100 g (4 oz) boneless cooked chicken, skinned and diced
100 g (4 oz) boiled ham, diced
100 g (4 oz) canned bamboo shoot, drained and diced
100 g (4 oz) frozen peas, defrosted
2 tablespoons light soy sauce

Soak the mushrooms in warm water to cover for 20–25 minutes. Meanwhile, wash and rinse the rice in cold water, then drain and place in a large saucepan. Add enough fresh cold water to cover the rice by about 2.5 cm (1 inch). Bring to the boil, then add ¼ teaspoon salt and stir. Reduce the heat to very low, cover the saucepan with a tight-fitting lid and cook for 15–20 minutes.

Meanwhile, drain the mushrooms and squeeze them dry. Discard the hard stalks and dice the caps. Set aside.

Heat the oil in a hot wok or heavy-based frying pan, add the spring onions and fry gently for a few minutes to flavour the oil, then add the mushrooms, prawns, chicken, ham, bamboo shoot and peas. Stir-fry until the peas are cooked but still crisp, then add the cooked rice and soy sauce and mix well. Turn into a bowl and leave until cold.

Basi Shuiguo

Fruit Fritters

Undoubtedly, fruit fritters are one of the most famous Chinese dessert dishes served in Peking-style restaurants. Apple and banana seem to be the most popular fruits, but any other firm-fleshed fresh or canned fruit may be used, such as pineapple. The pieces of fruit are coated with batter and deep-fried, then coated with caramel and dipped in cold water, which results in a wickedly delicious confection – crispy on the outside, yet soft on the inside.

SERVES 8 as an individual dish

2 large, firm eating apples
2 medium bananas
1 egg
4 tablespoons cornflour
600 ml (1 pint) vegetable oil, for deep-frying
100 g (4 oz) sugar
3 tablespoons sesame seed oil
1 tablespoon sesame seeds
To serve:
lime slices
banana slices

Peel and core the apples, then cut each one into 8 pieces. Peel the bananas, cut in half lengthways, then cut each half into 3–4 sections. Beat the egg in a bowl, then blend in the cornflour and enough cold water to make a smooth batter.

Heat the oil in a hot wok, dip each piece of fruit in the batter and deep-fry in the hot oil for 2–3 minutes. Remove with a perforated spoon and drain. Heat the sugar and sesame seed oil in a heavy-based saucepan over low heat for 5 minutes, add 3 tablespoons water and stir for a further 2 minutes. Add the fruit fritters and the sesame seeds and stir slowly, until each fritter is covered with syrup. As soon as the syrup has caramelized, remove the fritters and plunge them into a large bowl of cold water to harden the 'toffee'.

To serve, arrange the fritters on a plate and decorate with lime and banana slices. Serve hot or cold, according to taste.

Lichi Bian Choz Ling

Lychee Sorbet

This is an unusual way of serving lychees and the delicate flavour of this exotic fruit makes a most refreshing sorbet. Serve on its own or as the perfect accompaniment to the crunchy-sweet Fruit Fritters (left).

SERVES 6 as an individual dish

450 g (1 lb) can lychees
100 g (4 oz) granulated sugar
2 tablespoons lemon or lime juice
2 egg whites
thinly pared rind of 1 lime, to decorate

Drain the juice from the lychees into a measuring jug and make up to 300 ml (½ pint) with cold water. Pour into a saucepan and stir in the sugar. Heat gently until the sugar has dissolved, then bring to the boil. Simmer gently, without stirring, for 10 minutes, then remove from the heat. Set aside and allow to cool slightly.

Purée the lychees in a blender or food processor or press through a sieve, then mix with the sugar syrup and lemon or lime juice. Pour the mixture into a shallow freezer container and place in the freezer for 1–2 hours, or until nearly frozen.

Whisk the egg whites in a clean, dry bowl until fairly stiff. Cut the frozen mixture into small pieces and either work in a blender or food processor, or place in a mixing bowl and mash with a fork, to break down the crystals. Without allowing the mixture to melt, quickly fold in the whisked egg white until evenly incorporated, then pour into a slightly deeper freezer container. Return to the freezer for 2–3 hours or until firm.

Meanwhile, prepare the decoration. Plunge the lime rind into a saucepan of boiling water and blanch for 2 minutes. Drain, refresh under cold running water, then pat dry with paper towels and cut into thin strips.

To serve the sorbet: remove from the freezer 10 minutes before serving. Scoop the sorbet into individual glass dishes and sprinkle with the lime rind. Serve immediately.

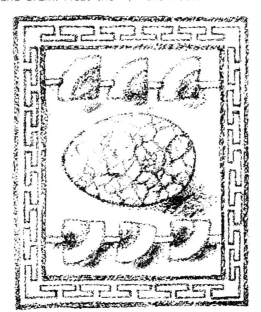

JAPAN & KOREA

Japanese food is renowned for the care and effort taken over its presentation. But it offers far more than mere appearances. A major characteristic of the cuisine of Japan is its reliance on natural flavours: only the best and freshest of ingredients are used, and cooking and seasoning are kept to a minimum.

Formal cooking is very distinct from home cooking. Formal dishes, called *kaiseki ryori*, are mainly served at special restaurants and tea ceremony parties, whereas home cooking is less formal. However, there are still similarities with kaiseki; for example, in the freshness of ingredients, meticulous preparation, the minimal use of seasoning during cooking and in careful presentation. The Japanese are close to nature, and the four seasons are always present in the imagination of the cook. There is also a strong vegetarian tradition in modern-day Japan, despite a decline in Buddhism, and in most Japanese meals you will find three times as many vegetable dishes as meat, which is a relatively recent innovation. Fish from the seas surrounding Japan are plentiful and fresh fish plays a major part in the diet and cuisine. Rice however, is the most important food of all, and is the staple diet of all Japanese people, who refer to rice and meal with one and the same word – *gohan*

Korean food and cooking methods are similar to that of Japan, since both countries have such strong historical and cultural links. Korea is the older of the two civilizations, however, and many people believe that Japanese food developed from Korean. The main difference between the two lies in the greater use of spices and sugar by the Koreans.

JAPAN & KOREA
SOUPS & STOCKS

Almost every Japanese meal includes a soup, indeed most Japanese start the day with a hot and nourishing bowl of Miso-Shiru/Bean Soup (below). There are two main types of soup: clear soups, which are light and delicate and demonstrate uncluttered Japanese artistry, and thick soups, which are almost a meal in themselves and are based on the ingredient miso, a fermented soy bean paste.

Dashi/Soup Stock (page 105) is probably the most essential ingredient in any Japanese kitchen, as it is responsible for adding the subtle but distinctive flavour familiar to Japanese food. It is based on two ingredients, dried fish and dried kelp. Dashi is easy to make, but for added convenience, sachets of instant dashi are available.

Sumashi-Jiru

Clear Soup with Prawns/Japan
Uncooked prawns are available (usually frozen) from oriental stores and high-class fishmongers. They are full of flavour, and they look very pretty if the tail shells are left on.

SERVES 4

4 headless uncooked prawns, defrosted if frozen
1 teaspoon salt
a little cornflour, for coating
40 g (1½ oz) somen (fine noodles)
600 ml (1 pint) Dashi/Soup Stock (page 105)
½ teaspoon soy sauce
4 sprigs watercress, trimmed, to garnish

Wash and shell the prawns, retaining the shell on the end of the tail. Take the black vein out of the back of the prawns. Pat dry with paper towels. Season the prawns with a little of the salt, then dust with cornflour. Plunge them into a saucepan of boiling water for 30 seconds, then drain and set aside. Cook the noodles in a saucepan of boiling water for 3 minutes, drain and rinse in cold water, then drain again.

Bring the dashi to the boil in a medium-sized saucepan. Season with the soy sauce and remaining salt. Divide the prawns and noodles equally between 4 warmed soup bowls and pour over the dashi. Garnish with sprigs of watercress and serve.

Miso-Shiru

Bean Soup/Japan
Miso (soy bean paste) soups are traditional for family meals in Japan, mainly because they are so nutritious and filling.

SERVES 4

25 g (1 oz) niboshi (dried small whole sardines)
1–2 packets wakame (dried young seaweed)
4 tablespoons miso (soy bean paste)
50 g (2 oz) firm tofu (bean curd)
2 spring onions, finely chopped

Make the stock. Put the niboshi in a saucepan, add 600 ml (1 pint) water and place over high heat. Bring quickly to the boil and simmer for 5–10 minutes, depending on the strength of flavour required. Remove from the heat, strain through a clean teatowel, then return to the rinsed-out pan. Discard the niboshi.

Put the wakame in a bowl and cover with cold water. Leave to soak for 5–10 minutes, or until fully expanded; drain and set aside. Put the miso in a small bowl and dilute with a few spoonfuls of the stock. Return the pan of stock to the heat. Just before boiling point is reached, add the diluted miso and turn down the heat to low so that the stock does not boil. Cut the tofu into small cubes and add to the pan with the wakame. Bring to the boil, then remove the soup from the heat and add the finely chopped spring onions. Serve hot, in warmed individual soup bowls.

Dashi

Soup Stock / Japan

Dashi is an essential flavouring used extensively in Japanese cooking. It is easy to make, requiring only two basic ingredients to give it its characteristic flavour. Instant dashi, or *dashi-no-moto*, is available from oriental stores.

MAKES 800 ml (1⅓ pints)

25 g (1 oz) konbu (dried kelp)
25 g (1 oz) katsuo-bushi (dried bonito flakes)

Put the konbu in a medium saucepan, add 800 ml (1¾ pints) cold water and leave to soak for about 10 minutes. Place the pan over gentle heat and bring slowly to boiling point. Take out the konbu just before the water boils.

Immediately add the katsuo-bushi and bring to a rapid boil. Boil for a few seconds only, then remove the pan from the heat. Leave to stand for about 1 minute, or until the katsuo-bushi settle down to the bottom. Strain the dashi through a clean teatowel into a bowl.

Safuran Sumashi

Saffron Soup with Chicken / Japan
The addition of saffron gives this soup a delicate yellow colour which contrasts well with the white of the chicken.

SERVES 4

100 g (4 oz) boneless chicken breast, skinned
a little cornflour, for coating
600 ml (1 pint) chicken stock
1 whole bone from a flat white fish
pinch of saffron threads
salt
freshly ground black pepper
4 sprigs watercress, trimmed, to garnish

Cut the chicken breast into 2.5 cm (1 inch) squares, then coat lightly with cornflour. Plunge the chicken into a saucepan of boiling water for 5 minutes, or until cooked.

Meanwhile, bring the chicken stock to the boil in a separate saucepan, add the fish bone and boil gently for 5 minutes. Remove the bone and discard. Add the saffron to the stock, with salt and pepper to taste.

Drain the chicken pieces, divide equally between 4 warmed individual soup bowls and pour over the saffron-coloured soup. Garnish with watercress and serve.

Chawan Mushi

Thick Egg Soup / Japan
Traditional *chawan mushi* cups are available at Japanese and other oriental stores. They vary in price according to the quality and design of the china, but there are many inexpensive sets to choose from, which lend this soup an authentic touch and look very pretty on the table if you are serving guests. If you do not want to go to the expense of buying them, you can use coffee mugs instead, as long as the circumference of the rim is the same as that of the base, so the soup sets evenly.

SERVES 4

100 g (4 oz) boneless chicken breast, skinned
4 teaspoons sake (rice wine)
1½ teaspoons soy sauce
8 unpeeled prawns
salt
4 mangetout
500 ml (18 fl oz) Dashi / Soup Stock (left)
1 teaspoon mirin (sweet rice wine)
3 eggs, beaten
8 small button mushrooms, wiped

Thinly slice the chicken, then sprinkle with 1 teaspoon of the sake and ½ teaspoon of the soy sauce. Wash and shell the prawns, taking the black vein out if necessary. Sprinkle the prawns with the remaining sake and a pinch of salt. Plunge the mangetout into a saucepan of lightly salted water for 1 minute, then drain.

Bring the dashi to the boil in a medium-sized saucepan. Add ½ teaspoon salt, the mirin and the remaining soy sauce. Remove from the heat and leave to cool for 5 minutes, then add the beaten eggs. Divide the chicken equally between 4 chawan mushi cups or coffee mugs and pour in the egg soup. Add 2 mushrooms, 2 prawns and 1 mangetout to each cup.

Put the cups in a steamer and steam vigorously for 2 minutes. Lower the heat and steam for a further 12–15 minutes, or until the juice runs clear when the thickened soup is pierced with a skewer or fork. Alternatively, if you do not have a steamer, put the cups or mugs in a shallow baking dish, half-filled with hot water. Cover with foil and cook in the oven at 220°C/425°F, Gas Mark 7 for 5 minutes, then at 180°C/350°F, Gas Mark 4 for 20–25 minutes, or until set. Serve the soup immediately.

JAPAN & KOREA
MEAT DISHES

For centuries Japan was predominantly a Buddhist country, and the eating of meat was strictly forbidden. Prior to 1868 and the end of the 300-year-long Tonkugawa era, Japan was closed to foreign visitors. The exception was the trading port of Nagasaki, where foreigners were allowed to mix with the Japanese. These *nanban*, or barbarians as they were known, introduced the habit of eating meat. Today, meat is still a luxury, as the mountainous landscape does not lend itself to rearing large herds of cattle. This is also true of Korea, although beef is immensely popular with the Koreans, and Bulgogi/Marinated Beef with Sweet Sauce (page 112) is one of Korea's most famous dishes.

Yakitori

Grilled Skewered Chicken/Japan

Japanese bamboo skewers, unlike their Chinese equivalents, do not need soaking in water before use as they are very strong.

SERVES 4

2 chicken legs
2 thin leeks, white part only, or 2 large spring onions
Tare sauce:
65 ml (2½ fl oz) soy sauce
65 ml (2½ fl oz) mirin (sweet rice wine)
2 tablespoons sugar
2 teaspoons plain flour

Bone the chicken legs, then cut the meat into 24 bite-sized pieces. Cut the leeks or spring onions into 16 pieces. Put all the ingredients for the tare sauce in a small saucepan. Bring to the boil, stirring, then simmer for 10 minutes, or until the sauce reduces to about two-thirds of its original volume. Remove from the heat.

Thread 3 pieces of chicken and 2 pieces of leek or spring onion alternately on to 8 Japanese bamboo skewers. Grill over a charcoal barbecue or under a conventional grill until browned, then remove from the heat and spoon on the tare sauce. Return to the heat for a few more minutes, then remove and coat with more sauce. Repeat this process a few times until all of the tare sauce is used and the chicken is cooked.

Shoga-Yaki

Grilled Ginger Pork/Japan

An easy, economical dish, which nonetheless is delicious enough to be served at dinner parties. Serve with French beans and plain boiled rice if wished. Garnish with grated daikon.

SERVES 4

2 pork fillets, each weighing 175–225 g (6–8 oz)
5 cm (2 inch) piece fresh root ginger, peeled and grated
4 tablespoons soy sauce

Put the pork fillets in a shallow dish, add the grated ginger and soy sauce. Leave to marinate in a cold place for at least 30 minutes.

Wrap each fillet in foil, seal the edges and reserve any marinade in the dish. Place under a preheated hot grill for 5 minutes, then turn the grill down to low and continue cooking for a further 20–25 minutes, or until the pork is thoroughly cooked.

Unwrap the pork and cut each fillet into 1 cm (½ inch) slices. Place on warmed individual plates. Pour the meat juices from the foil into a small saucepan and add any reserved marinade. If there is not enough sauce add a few spoonfuls of water and soy sauce to taste. Bring to the boil and simmer for about 5 minutes, then pour over the meat. Serve hot.

Torino Teriyaki

Chicken Teriyaki/Japan

In Japan, hashi (chopsticks) are used both as cooking utensils and for eating. For this recipe they are used to test if the chicken meat is tender. Ginger juice is obtained by grating fresh root ginger, then squeezing out the juice.

SERVES 4

4 chicken legs
3 tablespoons vegetable oil
I tablespoon mirin (sweet rice wine)
I tablespoon sugar
watercress sprigs, to garnish
sansho powder, to serve
Marinade:
3 tablespoons soy sauce
I tablespoon sake (rice wine)
I tablespoon mirin (sweet rice wine)
I teaspoon ginger juice

Bone the chicken legs, then spike the skin with a fork to prevent the skin shrinking during cooking. Put the chicken in a shallow dish. Mix together the ingredients for the marinade, pour over the chicken and leave to marinate for 20–30 minutes.

Heat the oil in a heavy-based frying pan. Remove the chicken from the marinade, place skin side down in the pan and fry until the skin is lightly browned. Turn the chicken over and continue frying for about 10 minutes, until the chicken is tender when pierced with hashi (chopsticks).

Remove the chicken from the pan and pour off any excess oil. Add the marinade to the pan, then the mirin and sugar. Simmer for 2–3 minutes, then return the chicken legs to the pan and turn them over so that they are completely soaked in the pan juices.

Transfer the chicken to a board and slice thinly. Arrange the slices on a warmed serving platter and garnish with watercress. Serve hot, with sansho powder.

BELOW: *Left, Grilled Ginger Pork (page 106). Centre, Vinegared Cucumber (page 129). Right, Grilled Skewered Chicken (page 106).*

Iridori | Sukiyaki

Chicken cooked with Vegetables/Japan

Iridori looks most attractive in its serving bowl, when garnished with boiled carrot 'flowers' and cooked fresh garden peas. Ginnan or ginkgo nuts could also be used as a garnish.

SERVES 4

2 dried shiitake mushrooms
100 g (4 oz) canned gobo (burdock root), drained, or fresh parsnip
100 g (4 oz) canned bamboo shoots, drained
75 g (3 oz) canned renkon (lotus root) or water chestnuts, drained
1 medium carrot, peeled
½ cake kon-nyaku (arum root)
5 tablespoons vegetable oil
6½ tablespoons soy sauce
1 chicken leg, boned
1 teaspoon finely chopped fresh root ginger
a little sake (rice wine)
4 tablespoons sugar
Dashi/Soup Stock (page 105) or water
2 tablespoons mirin (sweet rice wine)

Soak the mushrooms in warm water for 20–25 minutes, then drain and cut into bite-sized pieces. Cut the vegetables into bite-sized pieces. The carrot can be cut decoratively into small flower shapes, if liked. Break the kon-nyaku into bite-sized pieces. Heat 1 tablespoon of the oil in a heavy-based frying pan, add the kon-nyaku pieces and fry for 1–2 minutes, sprinkling on ½ tablespoon of the soy sauce. Remove from the pan and set aside.

Chop the chicken meat into slightly larger pieces than the vegetables. Heat another tablespoon of the oil in the frying pan. Add the chicken pieces and chopped ginger. Sprinkle with a little sake, half of the sugar and 3 tablespoons of the remaining soy sauce. Stir-fry for about 2 minutes, or until lightly browned. Remove the chicken from the pan with a perforated spoon and set aside. Reserve the pan juices.

Heat the remaining oil in a shallow saucepan. Add the mushrooms, vegetables and the kon-nyaku and fry for 1 minute. Add the reserved pan juices from the chicken and enough dashi or water to just cover the vegetables. Put an otoshi-buta (small wooden lid) or small upturned plate inside the pan so that the vegetables are held down tightly. Cover the pan with a lid and simmer for 5–8 minutes, until the vegetables are lightly cooked.

Add the remaining sugar, replace the otoshi-buta or plate and the pan lid and cook for a further 10 minutes. Add the mirin and the remaining soy sauce, cover and continue cooking until the juice has been absorbed. Add the chicken pieces, cook over high heat for 30 seconds, then leave until cold before serving.

Pan-cooked Beef with Vegetables/Japan

Most Japanese families have special sukiyaki pans to cook this popular dish at the table, but a heavy-based frying pan and a portable cooking stove will do the job just as well. Sukiyaki is very informal – the host or hostess cooks the first amount of meat and vegetables at the table, adding flavouring ingredients to his or her taste. After the first 'cooking' it is every man for himself, and ingredients are selected, cooked and flavoured according to individual tastes. Bowls of plain boiled rice are served to each guest to be eaten alongside the Sukiyaki.

SERVES 4

450 g (1 lb) sirloin or topside of beef
4 heads of Chinese leaves
1 bunch watercress
2 thin leeks, white part only
8 button mushrooms
100 g (4 oz) firm tofu (bean curd)
200 g (7 oz) shirataki (yam-flour noodles), or fine vermicelli
1 small piece of beef fat (suet)
To serve:
Dashi/Soup Stock (page 105)
soy sauce
mirin (sweet rice wine)
sake (rice wine)
sugar
4 eggs

Freeze the meat for 45 minutes, leave for 10 minutes on a board, then cut into wafer-thin slices with a very sharp knife. Arrange the meat on a platter. Cover and chill in the refrigerator.

Wash the Chinese leaves, cut in half lengthways, then cut into 5 cm (2 inch) lengths. Wash and trim the watercress. Slice the leeks diagonally. Wipe and trim the mushrooms. Cut the tofu into 4 cm (1½ inch) cubes. Cook the shirataki (if using) in boiling water for 3 minutes, then drain. If using vermicelli, soak it in boiling water for 10 minutes, then drain. Arrange the vegetables, tofu and noodles on a platter.

Place a cast-iron frying pan on a portable cooking stove in the centre of the dining table. Surround with the platters of raw ingredients and with jugs of dashi, soy sauce, mirin and sake, and a pot of sugar.

Melt a little beef fat in the pan, then add a few slices of meat and cook until lightly browned. Add a selection of the other raw ingredients, then pour in dashi, soy sauce, mirin, sake and sugar to taste. Each diner beats an egg lightly in his or her bowl, takes a selection of the cooked ingredients and mixes them with the egg.

Wafu Roast Beef

Japanese 'Roast' Beef/Japan

Wafu Roast Beef is traditionally served with finely chopped spring onions and grated fresh root ginger. Each person mixes a little spring onion and ginger with some of the sauce, then dips a slice of meat into it before eating. If you prefer, mustard can be substituted for the ginger and spring onion. Japanese mustard, which is very hot, is available from Japanese supermarkets and other oriental stores.

SERVES 4

750 g (1½ lb) sirloin of beef
1 garlic clove, peeled and sliced
100 ml (3½ fl oz) soy sauce
100 ml (3½ fl oz) sake (rice wine)
1½ teaspoons sugar
To serve:
2 spring onions, trimmed and finely chopped
2.5 cm (1 inch) fresh root ginger, peeled and grated
parsley sprigs, to garnish

Put the beef in a deep saucepan with the garlic, soy sauce, sake and sugar. Put an otoshi-buta (small wooden lid) or small upturned plate on top of the joint, cover the pan with a lid, place over high heat and bring to the boil. Lower the heat and simmer for 10 minutes, shaking the saucepan occasionally so that the meat does not stick.

Transfer the meat to a board, cut in half and check the extent of the cooking. If the meat is too rare for your liking, return it to the saucepan and cook for a further few minutes. When the meat is cooked, remove the saucepan from the heat. Leave the meat to cool in the liquid, covered with the lid.

Slice the meat thinly, then arrange on individual plates and garnish with parsley sprigs. Serve cold, with the cooking liquid from the meat served in individual bowls, and the prepared spring onions and ginger.

Kakuni

Simmered Pork with Soy Sauce/Japan

This dish originated in the port of Nagasaki. Unlike the rest of Japan this port has been open to foreign visitors for many centuries, and it was due to the influence of Chinese and Western traders that the first meat dishes – contravening the Japanese Buddhist law that forbids the eating of meat – came from this area. In Japan, belly pork is normally used for Kakuni, but this may be too fatty for most Western tastes. Leg or loin of pork is leaner, and it will be beautifully soft and tender at the end of the long cooking time.

SERVES 4

450 g (1 lb) boneless leg or loin of pork
200 ml (7 fl oz) sake (rice wine)
about 400 ml (14 fl oz) Dashi/Soup Stock (page 105) or water
2 tablespoons mirin (sweet rice wine)
2 tablespoons sugar
7 tablespoons soy sauce
100 ml (3½ fl oz) katsuo-bushi (dried bonito flakes)

Put the pork in a saucepan and pour over the sake. Leave to marinate for 30 minutes, turning the pork over from time to time so that it absorbs the sake evenly.

Pour enough dashi or water into the pan to cover the pork. Place over high heat and bring to the boil, then skim with a perforated spoon. Lower the heat, cover the pan and simmer for about 1 hour.

Lift out the pork, reserving 450–600 ml (¾–1 pint) cooking liquid. Cut the pork into 4 equal pieces, then place in a clean saucepan with the reserved cooking liquid. Add the mirin and sugar and bring to the boil, then lower the heat, cover and simmer for 30 minutes. Add 4 tablespoons of the soy sauce and the katsuo-bushi, cover again and simmer for a further 2 hours, adding the remaining soy sauce after 1 hour. Transfer the meat to a warmed serving dish and serve hot.

Shabu Shabu

Beef and Vegetables Cooked in Broth/Japan

The ingredients for Shabu Shabu are basically the same as for Sukiyaki/Pan-cooked Beef with Vegetables (page 108), but they are cooked in a broth. The name Shabu Shabu is an onomatopoeia describing the sound of washing. Wafer-thin slices of beef are picked up with hashi (chopsticks), dipped into broth and swished from side to side as if washing clothes in water. The skill of eating Shabu Shabu lies in not losing the meat in the broth, which requires dexterity with chopsticks, giving the Japanese an unfair advantage over any foreigners eating at the same table!

SERVES 4

750 g (1½ lb) sirloin or topside of beef
4 heads of Chinese leaves
2 thin leeks, white part only
1 bunch watercress
8 medium button mushrooms
100 g (4 oz) firm tofu (bean curd)
150 g (5 oz) canned bamboo shoots, drained
10 cm (4 inch) square konbu (dried kelp)
2 spring onions, finely chopped
1 small daikon (Japanese radish), peeled and grated, or momiji-oroshi (page 114)
4 lemon wedges
150 ml (¼ pint) soy sauce
Sesame sauce:
3 tablespoons sesame paste (tahini)
100 ml (3½ fl oz) Dashi/Soup Stock (page 105)
2 tablespoons soy sauce
1 tablespoon mirin (sweet rice wine)
1½ teaspoons sugar
1 tablespoon sake (rice wine)
1 teaspoon chilli sauce (optional)

Prepare the meat, Chinese leaves, leeks, watercress, mushrooms and tofu as for Sukiyaki (page 108). Cook the bamboo shoots in boiling water for 3 minutes, drain, then cut into half-moon shapes about 5 mm (¼ inch) thick, if not already sliced. Arrange the meat, tofu and vegetables on a large serving platter.

Make the sesame sauce: put the sesame paste in a serving bowl and add the dashi, soy sauce, mirin, sugar and sake. Mix well and add the chilli sauce, if liked, for a slightly more pungent flavour.

Put the konbu in a donabe (earthenware pot) or flameproof casserole and fill two-thirds full with cold water. Bring to the boil and immediately remove the konbu. Transfer the pot or casserole to a portable cooking stove in the centre of the dining table and bring the water to the boil again.

Put the platter of meat, tofu and vegetables on the table, with the bowl of sesame sauce and separate bowls of chopped spring onions, grated daikon or momiji-oroshi and lemon wedges. Pour the soy sauce into a small jug. Set the table so that each guest has 2 sauce bowls, one for the sesame sauce and the other for a sauce which guests make themselves by mixing together spring onions, daikon or momiji-oroshi, a squeeze of lemon juice and soy sauce to taste. Guests then help themselves to ingredients, cook them in the broth and dip them in the sauce of their choice before eating.

BELOW: *Left, 'Roast Beef' (page 109). Right, ingredients for Pan-cooked Beef with Vegetables (page 108).*

Yukhwe

Raw Beef/Japan

Yukhwe is served as a starter. The yolk of a raw egg is mixed with the meat before eating.

SERVES 4

225 g (8 oz) sirloin steak
1 garlic clove, peeled and crushed
2 teaspoons sesame seed oil
½ teaspoon sesame seeds
1½ teaspoons sugar
½ teaspoon salt
¼ teaspoon freshly ground white pepper
1 firm pear
½ cucumber
4 quail's or hen's egg yolks

Freeze the meat for 45 minutes, leave for 10 minutes on a board, then shred with a very sharp knife. Leave the shredded meat in the refrigerator until thoroughly defrosted.

Mix the meat with the crushed garlic, sesame seed oil, sesame seeds, sugar, salt and pepper.

Peel and core the pear, then shred finely. Peel the cucumber, then cut in half lengthways and scoop out the seeds with a sharp-edged teaspoon. Finely shred the flesh. Divide the pear and cucumber shreds equally between 4 individual plates.

Spoon one-quarter of the meat mixture on each bed of pear and cucumber. Top each serving with an egg yolk and serve immediately.

Bulgogi

Marinated Beef with Sweet Sauce/Korea

In Korean restaurants, this famous dish is cooked at the table in a special bulgogi pan over a charcoal burner. The resulting smoky atmosphere is considered part of the enjoyment of eating! In the absence of a special pan and burner, a heavy-based frying pan can be used, in which case the Bulgogi can be cooked in the kitchen and brought to the table on a serving platter or individual plates.

SERVES 4

450–750 g (1–1½ lb) sirloin steak
1½ tablespoons sugar
3 tablespoons soy sauce
3 tablespoons sesame seed oil
1 tablespoon finely chopped garlic
1 teaspoon freshly ground black pepper
1 teaspoon sesame seeds
To garnish:
parsley sprigs
grated daikon

Freeze the meat for 45 minutes, leave for 10 minutes on a board, then with a very sharp knife, slice the meat as thinly as possible into 5 cm (2 inch) squares. Place in a shallow dish and sprinkle with the sugar. Cover the dish and leave the meat to stand in a cold place for about 30 minutes.

Add the soy sauce to the meat with 1 tablespoon of the sesame seed oil, the garlic, black pepper and sesame seeds. Mix well, cover and leave to marinate in the refrigerator for at least 24 hours.

Heat the remaining sesame seed oil in a heavy-based frying pan. Fry the meat with the marinade, until cooked to your liking.

Serve either on a warmed large serving platter or individual plates, garnished with parsley sprigs and grated daikon.

Tonkatsu

Pork with Shredded White Cabbage/Japan

This deep-fried, breaded pork is a popular family supper or lunch dish in Japan. It is simple, economical and filling, yet also extremely delicious.

SERVES 4

750 g (1½ lb) pork fillet
salt
freshly ground black pepper
plain flour, for coating
2 eggs, lightly beaten
about 100 g (4 oz) dried breadcrumbs
10 cm (4 inch) wedge hard white cabbage
vegetable oil, for deep-frying
Tonkatsu sauce:
soy sauce
sake (rice wine)
Worcestershire sauce
Japanese mustard

Cut the pork fillet crossways into 1 cm (½ inch) slices. Sprinkle lightly with salt and pepper, then dust with flour, shaking off any excess. Dip each piece of pork into the beaten eggs, then coat in the breadcrumbs. Press lightly so that the breadcrumbs adhere to the meat.

Separate the cabbage leaves, then cut each one in half, discarding the thick and tough central stalks. Pile the leaves on top of each other, then cut into fine shreds. Arrange one-quarter of the shredded cabbage on each of 4 individual plates so that half of the plate is covered.

Make the tonkatsu sauce: in a bowl or jug, combine all the ingredients, adjusting the quantities to taste. Pour into 4 individual bowls.

Heat the oil in a deep-fat frier or deep frying pan to 180°C/350°F. Gently slide in the pork pieces one at a time. Deep-fry in batches for 3–5 minutes until golden brown, then remove with a perforated spoon and drain on a wire rack. When all the pork has been cooked, arrange the slices on the plates with the cabbage. Serve immediately, with the tonkatsu sauce for dipping.

JAPAN & KOREA
FISH DISHES

Japan's most important harvest is that which it reaps from the seas, and from its many rivers. Fish, shellfish and seaweed are plentiful, and the varieties available numerous, so it is not surprising that these foods play a dominant role in Japanese Cookery.

Many of the fish eaten in Japan are not available in the West, but alternative salt or freshwater fish, round or flat fish can be substituted. There are almost as many types of seaweed as there are fish, and packets of dried seaweed can be purchased from Japanese supermarkets or oriental stores. Dried seaweed is easily rehydrated for use in cooked dishes and salads.

The Japanese are perhaps best known for their love of raw fish, and Sashimi (below) is one of the most famous dishes. For Sashimi only the freshest fish can be used, and the greatest care is taken over its preparation and presentation. Korea, too, has an abundance of seafoods, as well as freshwater fish from the country's many rivers. Unlike their Japanese neighbours, the Koreans do not eat raw fish, but prefer it cooked in a variety of ways – even mixing it with meat or poultry in the same dish.

Sashimi

Assorted Raw Fish / Japan

Sashimi is a general term for prepared raw fish, *sashi* meaning to stab or cut, and *mi* meaning body or meat. It can be served as a starter but this recipe is served with rice for a main course. You can use tuna, salmon, lemon sole, Dover sole, sea bass, sea bream, mackerel, prawns, squid, cuttlefish, bonito, carp, trout or even salmon roe. Whichever fish you choose, it must be very fresh, and you need to serve at least 3 different types to make an interesting main-course Sashimi.

Simply choose whichever fish you are going to serve, looking for the freshest kinds available on the day. The fish should have clear, bright eyes and scales; avoid any squid or cuttlefish that is reddish in colour.

SERVES 4

750 g (1½ lb) mixed fresh fish
1 teaspoon wasabi powder
soy sauce
5 cm (2 inch) piece daikon (Japanese radish), peeled and shredded
plain boiled Japanese rice, to serve

Gut the fish, then wash it well. (In the case of squid, clean it and remove the ink sac, as if ready for cooking.) You can ask the fishmonger to skin and fillet the fish for you, or do this yourself. Do not wash the fish again after it has been filleted, or it will be too wet and not have a good texture for serving raw; simply pat the fillets dry with paper towels before slicing and serving.

Slice the fish with a very sharp knife. Fish such as sole or plaice should be paper thin, sea bass and bream 1 cm (½ inch) thick. Tuna needs to be cut into bite-sized pieces 5 mm–1 cm (¼–½ inch) thick. Skin squid, octopus and cuttlefish, then cut into strips 5 cm (2 inches) long and 5 mm (¼ inch) wide.

Put the wasabi powder in an egg cup, add 1 teaspoon cold water and stir; the consistency should be firm, but not lumpy. Keep the egg cup well covered until serving time, or the pungency of the wasabi will be lost. Pour the soy sauce into individual shallow dishes.

To serve: arrange the different fish decoratively on a large serving platter or board and garnish with the shredded daikon. Mould the wasabi into a small mound and place on the serving platter or board. Guests should mix a little of the wasabi with soy sauce, then dip a slice of sashimi into this 'sauce' before eating. Boiled rice is eaten between mouthfuls of sashami to cool down the palate – the combination of wasabi and soy sauce is quite hot and salty.

Kareino Kara-Age

Plain Fried Plaice / Japan
To make momiji-oroshi/grated 'autumn leaves',
pierce a hole lengthways in a daikon with a
hashi (chopstick). Insert red chillies into the
daikon so that, when grated, the daikon is
reddish in colour, like autumn leaves.

SERVES 4

4 small plaice, scaled and gutted
salt
2–3 teaspoons sake (rice wine)
plain flour, for coating
vegetable oil, for deep-frying
momiji-oroshi (above), to garnish
4 lemon wedges

Wash the fish and remove the heads. Cut 2 crosses in the
skin on each side of the fish, then place on a wire rack.
Sprinkle with salt and sake and leave for 10 minutes.

Coat the fish thoroughly in flour. Heat the oil in a deep
frying pan to about 160°C/325°F. Deep-fry the plaice
until the slits in the skin open up, then increase the heat
to crisp up the fish. Remove and drain. To serve, garnish
with momiji-oroshi and lemon wedges.

Hana Tarako

Cod's Roe Flower / Japan
Crisp mangetout peas form the 'leaves' of these
delicate and soft cod's roe flowers.

SERVES 4

225 g (8 oz) fresh cod's roe
salt
200 ml (7 fl oz) Dashi / Soup Stock (page 105)
100 ml (3½ fl oz) sake (rice wine)
50 ml (2 fl oz) mirin (sweet rice wine)
3 tablespoons sugar
1 tablespoon soy sauce
100 g (4 oz) mangetout, lightly cooked

Wash the cod's roe in lightly salted water. Make a slit in
the skin. Mix the dashi in a saucepan with the sake,
mirin, sugar, soy sauce and ⅔ teaspoon salt. Bring to the
boil, add the roe and cook for a few minutes. Lower the
heat and simmer for about 20 minutes. Leave to cool.

Drain the cod's roe, discarding the cooking liquid, then
cut the row into 'flower' shapes, 2.5 cm (1 inch) thick.
Divide the cod's roe 'flowers' and mangetout equally
between 4 individual plates, sprinkling the mangetout
lightly with salt. Serve cold.

Tempura

Deep-fried Fish and Vegetables/Japan

Tempura is a famous Japanese fish dish, sometimes described as the Japanese answer to fish and chips! Take care not to overmix the ingredients for the batter – the idea is to make a very light, lumpy batter, not a sticky, runny one. If you can manage to mix the batter with 2 pairs of hashi (chopsticks), you will find this gives you exactly the right consistency. Do not deep-fry the ingredients for longer than stated in the recipe as they will continue to cook after they have been removed from the oil.

SERVES 4

8 headless uncooked prawns, defrosted if frozen
1 medium squid, cleaned
1 large red pepper
8 button mushrooms
1 large carrot, peeled
100 g (4 oz) French beans, trimmed
1 small aubergine, trimmed and sliced
100 g (4 oz) mangetout, trimmed
vegetable oil, for deep-frying
plain flour, for coating
Batter:
1 egg
75 g (3 oz) plain flour
25 g (1 oz) cornflour
Tentsuyu sauce:
200 ml (7 fl oz) Dashi/Soup Stock (page 105)
50 ml (2 fl oz) soy sauce
50 ml (2 fl oz) mirin (sweet rice wine)
To serve:
2.5 cm (1 inch) piece fresh root ginger, peeled and grated
5 cm (2 inch) piece daikon/Japanese Radish, peeled and grated
1 lime, cut into wedges

Wash and shell the prawns, retaining the tail shell. Take the black vein out of the back of the prawns, then make a slit along the belly to prevent the prawns curling during cooking. Skin the squid and cut in half. With a sharp knife, make fine diagonal slits on the outside to prevent curling during cooking. Cut the body into 5 × 4 cm (2 × 1½ inch) pieces. Cut the pepper lengthways into quarters; remove the seeds, then halve each piece of pepper to make 8 bite-sized pieces. Halve the mushrooms. Cut the carrot into 5 cm (2 inch) pieces, then cut each piece lengthways into slices. Make a cut at both ends of each slice almost to the opposite end, then twist the strips in opposite directions to make a decorative triangle.

Make the batter immediately before frying: mix the egg and 100 ml (3½ fl oz) ice-cold water in a bowl, then sift in the plain flour and cornflour. Mix very briefly, using 2 pairs of hashi (chopsticks) or a fork. Do not overmix: there should still be lumps in the flour.

Put a wire rack over a roasting tin and place by the side of the cooker. Heat the oil in a deep-fat frier or deep frying pan to about 160°C/325°F. Dip the pieces of pepper in the batter so that only the inside is coated, then deep-fry skin side up for about 30 seconds. Transfer to the wire rack with a perforated spoon. Dip the mushrooms in the batter, deep-fry in the hot oil for 30 seconds, then drain. Repeat with the carrot, clusters of French beans, slices of aubergine and the mangetout.

Increase the temperature of the oil to about 180°C/350°F. Hold the prawns by their tails and dip them into the batter one at a time (do not batter the tail shell). Deep-fry for about 1 minute, then remove and drain. Coat the squid pieces with flour, dip them in the batter and deep-fry in the hot oil for 1 minute. Remove and drain.

Make the sauce: bring the dashi to the boil in a small saucepan with the soy sauce and mirin, then pour into 4 small bowls. Arrange the fish and vegetables on a bamboo dish or serving platter with the grated ginger and daikon. Garnish with lime wedges and serve immediately, with the bowls of sauce. Each person mixes ginger and daikon to taste with some of the sauce, then dips the tempura into the sauce before eating.

OPPOSITE: *Assorted Raw Fish (page 113), served with plain boiled rice.* **BELOW**: *Deep fried Fish and Vegetables.*

Tara-Chiri

Cod Cooked in Earthenware/Japan

At the end of the meal, season the liquid remaining in the pot with salt, soy sauce and lemon juice to taste, then add some boiled rice or noodles. Serve as a soup.

SERVES 4

750 g (1½ lb) cod fillet
225 g (8 oz) firm tofu (bean curd)
225 g (8 oz) spinach
7.5–10 cm (3–4 inch) square konbu (dried kelp)
2 thin leeks, washed and cut into ovals
To serve:
4 spring onions, finely chopped
momiji-oroshi (page 114)
4 lemon wedges
soy sauce
plain boiled Japanese rice

Cut the cod into chunky 5 cm (2 inch) squares, retaining the skin. Cut the tofu into bite-sized cubes. Wash and trim the spinach, then cut into 5 cm (2 inch) lengths.

Put the konbu in a donabe (earthenware pot) or flameproof casserole and fill two-thirds full with cold water. Bring to the boil and immediately remove the konbu. Transfer the donabe or casserole to a portable cooking stove on the dining table. Bring to the boil and add the cod, tofu, spinach and leeks.

Each diner makes a 'dip sauce' in his or her own bowl by mixing together spring onions, momiji-oroshi, a squeeze of lemon juice and soy sauce to taste. Pieces of food are then taken from the pot and dipped into the bowl of sauce before eating. Rice is served separately.

Iwashi no Nishiki-Age

Egg-battered Sardines/Japan

The Japanese word *nishiki* means colourful or glittering – the egg batter gives the fish a glittering effect.

SERVES 4

8 medium-sized fresh sardines
salt
2 parsley sprigs, finely chopped
2 eggs
1 teaspoon mirin (sweet rice wine)
plain flour, for coating
2 tablespoons vegetable oil
4 lemon wedges, to garnish

Cut the heads off the sardines, then gut the fish and wash thoroughly in lightly salted water. Open up the sardines and take out the bones with your fingers. Sprinkle salt very lightly over the fish.

Put the parsley in a shallow dish with the eggs, mirin and ¼ teaspoon salt. Beat well to mix. Coat the fish lightly with flour, then dip into the beaten egg mixture.

Heat the oil in a heavy-based frying pan, then add the fish and a little of the egg mixture remaining in the dish. Fry over low heat until lightly browned, then turn the fish over, cover the pan with a lid and continue cooking over the lowest possible heat for 2–3 minutes. Arrange the sardines on a warmed serving platter, garnish with lemon wedges and serve hot.

Tara no Teriyaki

Cod Teriyaki/Japan

Do not skin or bone the cod steaks, or they may fall apart during cooking. Serve with 450 g (1 lb) Brussels sprouts which have been cooked in lightly salted water for 3 minutes, then stir-fried in a little butter and sprinkled with salt – they should still be firm and crisp.

SERVES 4

4 cod steaks
Tare sauce:
2 tablespoons soy sauce
2 tablespoons mirin (sweet rice wine)
1 tablespoon sake (rice wine)
1 tablespoon sugar

First make the sauce: put the soy sauce, mirin, sake and sugar in a small saucepan and boil for 1 minute. Remove from the heat.

Thread each cod steak on to 2 lightly greased metal skewers, then cook the fish under a preheated hot grill until lightly browned on both sides. Remove from the grill and brush with some of the tare sauce. Return to the heat and cook until the tare dries. Repeat with more sauce until it is all used up. Turn the skewers in the fish each time you remove them from the grill, to prevent them sticking to the fish.

Remove the skewers from the fish, then place the fish on 4 warmed individual plates. Serve immediately.

Tatsuta-Age

Marinated Mackerel/Japan

Tatsuta-Age is a method of frying. In this recipe the fish is marinated before frying to give it extra flavour. Any type of fish, meat or poultry, can be used. To obtain ginger juice, grate fresh root ginger then squeeze out the juice.

SERVES 4

2 medium mackerel, total weight about
750 g (1½ lb), filleted
4 tablespoons soy sauce
2 tablespoons sake (rice wine)
1 teaspoon ginger juice
50 g (2 oz) cornflour
vegetable oil, for deep-frying
8 small button mushrooms, wiped and trimmed
To garnish:
4 lemon wedges
5 cm (2 inch) piece daikon (Japanese radish),
peeled and grated

Using tweezers, remove all the bones which are hidden in the centre of the mackerel fillets. Place the fillets skin side down on a board and cut slightly on the diagonal into slices about 2.5 cm (1 inch) thick. Put the soy sauce in a shallow dish with the sake and ginger juice and mix well. Add the mackerel slices, cover and leave to marinate for about 10 minutes, stirring occasionally to ensure the slices of fish are evenly coated.

Drain the mackerel thoroughly, then coat in some of the cornflour. Heat the oil in a deep-fat frier or deep frying pan to 160°C/325°F and deep-fry the mackerel slices until golden brown. Remove from the oil with a perforated spoon and drain on paper towels. Keep hot.

Coat the mushrooms in the remaining cornflour. Add to the hot oil and deep-fry for 1 minute. Remove and drain as for the mackerel slices. Arrange a few slices of mackerel and 2 mushrooms on each of 4 warmed individual plates. Garnish each serving with a lemon wedge, and some of the grated daikon. Serve immediately.

Uono Misoyaki

Miso Marinated Fish/Japan

Meat, especially beef, can be marinated in the same way as the fish used here, in which case use red rather than white miso, and add 2 tablespoons sugar to produce a stronger marinade. The miso can be used a second time if you add a small amount of fresh miso, and even after the second time it can still be used to make miso soup.

SERVES 4

4 fillets sea bream, haddock, whiting
or mackerel
salt
parsley sprigs, to garnish
Miso marinade:
450 g (1 lb) white miso (soy bean paste)
100 ml (3½ fl oz) mirin (sweet rice wine)

Place the fish fillets, skin side down, on a wire rack. Sprinkle with salt, then leave for at least 1 hour.

Put the miso and mirin in a bowl and mix with a wooden spoon. Spread half of this mixture evenly over the bottom of a medium-sized roasting tin and cover with a piece of fine cheesecloth. Lay the fish fillets directly on the material, then cover with another piece Spread the remaining miso over the material so that the fish fillets are sandwiched between layers of miso. Cover the tin and leave the fish to marinate overnight.

The next day, remove the fillets from the pieces of cheesecloth and pat dry with paper towels. Preheat the grill and the grill rack. Meanwhile, cut decorative slits in the skin of the fish, either on the diagonal or in the form

of a cross. Place the fish on the preheated grill rack and grill under moderate heat until light brown. Turn the fish over and grill on the other side. Serve hot, garnished with parsley sprigs.

Sabano Sashimi

Mackerel Sashimi/Japan
This dish is simple to make and serve; each person should mix ginger and soy sauce to taste in a small bowl, then dip a piece of mackerel into it before eating.

SERVES 4

1 large fresh mackerel
2 tablespoons rice vinegar
5 cm (2 inch) piece fresh root ginger, peeled and grated
soy sauce

Gut the mackerel and remove the head, then wash the fish thoroughly and carefully fillet it. Pat dry with paper towels, but do not wash again or the fish will lose its texture.

Using fingers and working from the tail end, remove the transparent skin, leaving the silver pattern intact. Using tweezers, remove all the bones which are hidden in the centre of the mackerel fillets. Cut diagonally into slices about 2.5 cm (1 inch) thick.

Arrange the mackerel slices on a serving platter and sprinkle with the rice vinegar. Serve the grated ginger and soy sauce separately.

Nanban-Zuke

'Pickled' Sardines/Korea
The sardines in this dish are first deep-fried to seal in their natural flavours, then marinated in a special sauce to add piquancy and spice.

SERVES 4

2 dried red chillies
100 ml (3½ fl oz) rice vinegar
100 ml (3½ fl oz) mirin (sweet rice wine)
100 ml (3½ fl oz) soy sauce
shredded rind of 1 orange
5 spring onions
20 small fresh sardines
vegetable oil, for deep-frying

Put the dried red chillies in a bowl, cover with water and leave to soak for 10 minutes. Drain the chillies and cut into rings, removing as many seeds as possible. Put the rice vinegar in a saucepan with the mirin, soy sauce and 100 ml (3½ fl oz) water. Add the chillies and bring to the boil. Lower the heat, then add half the shredded orange rind. Remove the saucepan from the heat.

Trim off the root ends of the spring onions. Cut 4 of the spring onions into 10 cm (4 inch) lengths, discarding the top green part. Put under a preheated hot grill for a few moments until lightly browned (this takes the raw 'edge' off the spring onions and gives them a smoky flavour). Finely shred the white part of the remaining spring onion, discarding all the green part. Place in a bowl of ice-cold water to crisp up.

Meanwhile, wash the sardines and pat dry with paper towels. Heat the oil in a deep-fat frier or deep frying pan to 160°C/325°F and deep-fry the sardines until crisp. Transfer immediately to the prepared chilli sauce, add the grilled spring onions and leave to marinate for about 20 minutes. Arrange 5 sardines and 2 spring onion sticks on each of 4 individual dishes. Drain the shredded spring onion and use as a garnish, with the remaining orange rind.

Sengsun Meuntang

Spicy Fish with Vegetables/Korea

This simple fish stew is quick to prepare. It is both warming and filling, and makes a colourful winter dish. Any combination of white fish and shellfish may be used.

SERVES 4

450 g (1 lb) cod fillets
4 scallops
20 shellfish (eg. cooked mussels, prawns, etc.)
1 medium onion
20 button mushrooms
1 red pepper
1 garlic clove
4 spring onions, trimmed
1 courgette
1 teaspoon chilli powder
1 tablespoon chilli sauce
1 teaspoon salt
To garnish:
cress
enokitake mushrooms (optional)

Cut the cod into bite-sized pieces, retaining the skin. Remove the scallops, mussels and prawns, etc., from their shells. Peel the onion and cut into eighths. Wipe and trim the mushrooms. Halve the red pepper and remove the seeds, then cut each pepper half into quarters to make 8 pieces altogether. Peel the garlic, then grate or crush it. Cut the spring onions into 2.5 cm (1 inch) pieces. Trim the courgette and cut into 8 equal pieces.

Bring 600 ml (1 pint) water to the boil in a large saucepan. Add the chilli powder, chilli sauce and salt, then all of the prepared fish and vegetables, except the spring onions and courgette. Bring the water back to the boil, add the spring onions and courgette, then simmer for 10 minutes or until the ingredients are just cooked. Be careful not to overcook the stew – the fish pieces should remain whole and the vegetables should retain their shape.

Divide the ingredients and liquid equally between 4 warmed individual bowls and serve immediately, garnished with little bunches of cress and enokitake mushrooms (if using).

BELOW: *Left, 'Pickled' Sardines (page 118).*
Right, Spicy Fish with Vegetables.

JAPAN & KOREA
SUSHI, RICE & NOODLES

Rice is more than just an accompaniment to other dishes, in fact the Japanese consider it to be the most important element of any meal. Rice is food itself; even its name, *gohan*, is the generic word for 'meal'. Most Japanese eat rice at every meal, including breakfast! A bowl of steaming white rice is served in individual bowls and savoured as a delicacy in its own right, or perhaps accompanied by side dishes of pickled vegetables and miso soup. Unlike Indian and Chinese rice, Japanese rice is a short grain variety. Japanese rice is normally boiled, and when cooked clings together. It is essential to eat every grain of rice that is served to you, as it would be considered unforgiveable to waste this revered food.

A selection of dishes made from Sumeshi/Vinegared Rice (below) go under the name *sushi*. In Japan, sushi-making is usually left to professionals, as sushi-bars, which prepare a wide variety of sushi, are found in every town. However, sushi are not difficult to make at home provided the freshest raw ingredients are used. Sushi are one of Japan's most popular snacks, although they can be served as an appetizer or main dish.

Noodles are considered to be country-style fare and are therefore never included in a formal Japanese meal. Never-the-less noodle dishes of every type are immensely popular, and in Japan there are more noodle shops than any other kind of restaurant. Noodles can be served either hot or cold, depending on the time of year. They come in many sizes and varieties and should be cooked *al dente*.

Rice is the staple food in Korea and is usually served plain, although it is sometimes mixed with barley, millet or beans. Noodles are also popular; they are generally stir-fried or served cold.

Sumeshi

Vinegared Rice/Japan

The term *sushi* is a corruption of Sumeshi, meaning vinegared rice, which is used for all sushi dishes. Nigiri-Zushi/Handfuls of Sushi (page 122), a small amount of compressed sumeshi with a piece of raw fish on top, is the most famous of all sushi. Specially-flavoured rice vinegar is available for making Sumeshi; called *Sushi-su*, it can be bought in oriental stores.

SERVES 4

350 g (12 oz) Japanese short grain rice
50 ml (2 fl oz) rice vinegar
1½ tablespoons sugar
1 teaspoon salt

Wash the rice very thoroughly, changing the water several times until it is clear. Drain on a bamboo dish or in a very fine sieve for about 1 hour.

When ready to cook, transfer the rice to a deep saucepan (the rice should not fill more than one-quarter of the pan). Add 450 ml (¾ pint) cold water and bring to the boil over high heat. Lower the heat, cover and simmer gently for about 15 minutes, until all the water has been absorbed by the rice. Try not to remove the lid more than once during cooking to check whether the water has been absorbed.

Remove the pan from the heat and leave tightly covered for 10–15 minutes. Put the rice vinegar, sugar and salt in a bowl and mix well until the sugar and salt have dissolved.

Transfer the rice to a large (non-metal) bowl and pour over the vinegar mixture. Using a wooden spatula or Japanese rice paddle, fold the vinegar into the rice; do not stir. Leave to cool to room temperature before using in a dish of your choice.

Gomoku-Zushi

Sushi with Five Ingredients/Japan

Gomoku means 'five kinds'. Although five kinds of ingredients are sufficient to make this dish, the Japanese do not normally limit themselves to this number. Rice cooked in this way is usually served for a special guest or occasion.

SERVES 4

1 small mackerel, filleted
salt
rice vinegar
3 dried shiitake mushrooms
1 medium carrot, peeled and shredded
5 tablespoons sugar
3 tablespoons soy sauce
2 tablespoons mirin (sweet rice wine)
50 g (2 oz) mangetout, cooked
2 eggs
1 tablespoon vegetable oil
Sumeshi/Vinegared Rice (page 120), made with
350 g (12 oz) rice
beni shoga (pickled ginger roots), shredded
1 sheet nori (dried lava paper) (optional)

Sprinkle the mackerel fillets with salt and leave for 3–4 hours. Wash the salt away with rice vinegar. Using your fingers and working from the tail end, remove the transparent skin from each fillet, leaving the silver pattern intact. Remove all the bones which are hidden in the centre of the mackerel fillets. Slice the flesh into thin strips, cover and set aside.

Soak the mushrooms in warm water for 25 minutes, then drain, reserving 120 ml (4 fl oz) of the soaking liquid. Squeeze the mushrooms dry, discard the hard stalks, then finely shred the mushrooms. Place both mushrooms and carrot in a saucepan with 3 tablespoons of the sugar, the soy sauce and mirin. Simmer until all the juice has been absorbed. Cut the mangetout into thin strips.

Beat the eggs in a small bowl, add the remaining sugar and a pinch of salt. Heat the oil in a heavy-based frying pan. Pour in half of the egg mixture, tilting the pan so that it spreads evenly over the base. Fry over the lowest possible heat for 30 seconds, or until the surface of the mixture is dry. Turn the omelette on to a board and leave to cool. Repeat with the remaining mixture, then cut the omelettes into thin strips 5 cm (2 inch) long.

Put the sumeshi in a large (non-metal) bowl. Add the mushrooms, carrot, mangetout, mackerel and shredded beni shoga. Using a wooden spatula, gently fold the ingredients into the rice; do not stir. Garnish with the omelette strips. If using nori, grill it under the lowest possible heat for only a second until crisp, then shred into 4 cm (1½ inch) strips with a sharp knife. Arrange the nori shreds on top of the rice before serving. Serve cold.

Ika Gohan

Squid Stuffed with Rice/Japan

This method of making Ika Gohan is the best, as the rice is cooked inside the squid so that it absorbs the delicious taste of the squid and the simmering sauce.

SERVES 4

175 g (6 oz) glutinous rice
4 small squid, cleaned, with tentacles separated
65 ml (2½ fl oz) soy sauce
65 ml (2½ fl oz) sake (rice wine)
65 ml (2½ fl oz) mirin (sweet rice wine)
2.5 cm (1 inch) fresh root ginger, peeled and sliced
parsley sprigs, to garnish

Wash the glutinous rice, place in a bowl and cover with water. Leave to soak overnight.

The next day, put the tentacles from the squid in a saucepan with the soy sauce, sake and mirin. Bring to the boil, cook for 2 minutes, then remove from the heat. Lift the tentacles out of the liquid with a perforated spoon and chop finely. Reserve the cooking liquid.

Drain the rice, mix with the chopped tentacles, then stuff the squid with this mixture. (Do not overstuff or the squid may burst during cooking.) Close the squid and secure with toothpicks.

Lay the stuffed squid side by side in a heavy-based saucepan or flameproof casserole. Pour in the reserved cooking liquid from the tentacles, add the sliced ginger and bring to the boil. Cover and simmer for about 40 minutes, or until the squid are tender. Remove from the heat and leave the squid to cool in the sauce.

Cut the squid into rings. Arrange on a large serving platter and garnish with parsley sprigs.

Hiyashi Somen

Fine Noodles and Prawns and Ham/Japan

This is very popular in the summer in Japan as it is a cooling meal to serve during the long and stifling months of hot weather. Hiyashi Somen is a very colourful dish and any ingredients can be used instead of ham: try shredded cooked breast of chicken, fried and crumbled bacon or chopped anchovies.

SERVES 4

450 g (1 lb) somen (dried fine noodles)
8–12 large, headless uncooked prawns, defrosted if frozen
4–5 dried shiitake mushrooms
2 tablespoons soy sauce
2 tablespoons mirin (sweet rice wine)
1 tablespoon sugar
Sauce:
15 cm (6 inch) square konbu (dried kelp)
25 g (1 oz) katsuo-bushi (dried bonito flakes)
65 ml (2½ fl oz) soy sauce
65 ml (2½ fl oz) mirin (sweet rice wine)
To serve:
2 small tomatoes, quartered
225 g (8 oz) boiled ham, finely shredded
½ cucumber, finely shredded
2.5 cm (1 inch) piece fresh root ginger, peeled and grated
2 shiso leaves or spring onions, finely chopped

Plunge the somen into a large saucepan of boiling water. Cook, uncovered, over moderate heat for 8–10 minutes until the somen is tender but still crisp. Drain in a colander and rinse under cold running water to remove excess starch.

Place the somen in a large glass bowl and cover with fresh cold water. Add a few ice cubes, then place the bowl in the refrigerator while preparing the remaining ingredients.

Wash and shell the prawns, retaining the shell on the end of the tail. Take the black vein out of the back of the prawns. Plunge the prawns into a saucepan of boiling water for 2 minutes, then drain thoroughly and rinse under cold running water until cool. Drain on paper towels and chill in the refrigerator until serving time.

Soak the mushrooms in warm water for 25 minutes, then drain and reserve 300 ml (½ pint) of the soaking liquid (if there is not enough, make up the quantity with water). Squeeze the mushrooms dry, discard the hard stalks, then shred the mushrooms finely. Place them in a saucepan with the soy sauce, mirin and sugar and cook until all the liquid has been absorbed. Remove from the heat and set aside.

Make the sauce: pour the reserved soaking liquid from the mushrooms into a saucepan. Add the konbu, katsuo-bushi, soy sauce and mirin and bring to the boil, taking out the konbu just before boiling. Cook for 5 minutes, then strain through a fine sieve lined with muslin or cheesecloth. Leave the sauce to cool, then chill in the refrigerator.

To serve: garnish the somen in cold water with quartered tomatoes. Arrange the ham, cucumber, mushrooms and chilled prawns in a serving dish. Divide the cold sauce equally between 4 individual bowls and stir in the grated ginger and chopped shiso leaves or spring onions. Each diner puts a little of the ham, cucumber, mushrooms and prawns into his or her bowl of sauce, then takes some cold somen with hashi (chopsticks) and dips this into the sauce before eating.

Nigiri-Zushi

Handfuls of Sushi/Japan

This is one of Japan's most popular snacks and originates from Tokyo. Fresh tuna or sea bass is used to top small handfuls of 'sticky' rice but almost any other type of fish or shellfish could be substituted.

MAKES 30

Sumeshi/Vinegared Rice (page 120), made with
350 g (12 oz) rice
and 450 ml (¾ pint) water
1 teaspoon wasabi powder
30 small slices raw fresh tuna or sea bass
soy sauce, to serve

With the hands, mould 2 tablespoons of the rice into a compact oval shape, about 5 cm (2 inch) long. Repeat with the remaining rice to make 30 ovals.

Put the wasabi powder into a small cup, add 1 teaspoon cold water and stir; the consistency should be firm but not lumpy. Spread a little wasabi on to the top of each rice ball then cover with a slice of fish, pressing it down firmly with the fingers.

Arrange the nigiri-zushi on a platter. Pour the soy sauce into small shallow bowls and serve separately with the nigiri-zushi.

OPPOSITE: *Right, Mackerel Sushi (page 123). Left, Three Colour Rice (page 125).*

Saba-Zushi

Mackerel Sushi/Japan

This combination of fresh mackerel and vinegared rice is well worth the time and effort it takes to prepare. Special wooden moulds can be purchased for preparing Saba-Zushi, although a loaf tin lined with cling film can be used successfully. Saba-Zushi makes a popular party starter or pre-dinner appetizer.

SERVES 4

1 large fresh mackerel, filleted
salt
rice vinegar
Sumeshi/Vinegared Rice (page 120), made with 350 g (12 oz) rice and 450 ml (¾ pint) water
To garnish:
beni shoga (pickled ginger roots), shredded chives

Put the mackerel fillets on a bed of salt, then pour over more salt to completely cover the fish. Leave for several hours or overnight. Remove the fillets from the salt and rub the salt off roughly with paper towels. Wash the remaining salt away with rice vinegar. Using your fingers and working from the tail end, remove the transparent skin from each fillet, leaving the silver pattern intact. Carefully remove all the bones which are hidden in the mackerel fillets.

Put the mackerel fillets, skin side down, on a board. Slice off the thick flesh from the centre to make the fillets even in thickness. Reserve these slices of flesh.

Place one of the mackerel fillets, skin side down, on the bottom of a wooden mould, or a loaf tin lined with a large sheet of cling film. Fill any gaps with some of the reserved slices of thick flesh. Press the sumeshi down firmly on top of the fish with your hands. Top with the remaining mackerel fillet, skin side up and fill in any gaps with the remaining slice of thick flesh. Place the wooden lid on top of the mould (or wrap in the sheet of cling film) and put a weight on top. Leave the saba-zushi wrapped in cling film in a cool place (not the refrigerator) for a few hours or overnight. Remove from the mould or tin, unwrap and slice into bite-sized pieces. Garnish with beni shoga and chives and serve cold.

Nori-Maki

Rolled Rice Wrapped in Nori/Japan

Sumeshi/Vinegared Rice (page 120) and other ingredients are rolled inside sheets of nori (dried lava paper) to make Nori-Maki, *maki* means rolling. You can use almost any ingredient you wish as long as it looks attractive: any colour goes well with the brilliant white of Sumeshi. Strips of cucumber look good, so too do strips of raw tuna, smoked cod's roe, ham, cheese and tsukemono (Japanese pickled vegetables), and you can even use canned sardines, tuna, salmon or anchovies.

SERVES 4

25 g (1 oz) packet kanpyo (dried shaved gourd strings), cut into 15 cm (6 inch) lengths
salt
6 tablespoons sugar
6 tablespoons soy sauce
5–6 sheets of nori (dried lava paper)
3 dried shiitake mushrooms
1 medium carrot, peeled
2 tablespoons mirin (sweet rice wine)
100 g (4 oz) fresh spinach leaves
Sumeshi/Vinegared Rice (page 120), made with 500 g (1 lb 2 oz) rice and 685 ml (23 fl oz) water
beni shoga (pickled ginger roots), shredded, to garnish (optional)
Thick egg omelette:
2 eggs
3 tablespoons Dashi/Soup Stock (page 105)
2 tablespoons sugar
1 tablespoon vegetable oil
Fish flakes:
1 white fish fillet (eg. cod, haddock or whiting)
$1\frac{1}{2}$ tablespoons sake (rice wine)
$1\frac{1}{2}$ tablespoons sugar
red food colouring

Put the kanpyo in a saucepan, add 1 teaspoon salt and a few drops of water, then squeeze with your fingers. Rinse the salt away, then add enough water to cover and soak for 20 minutes. Place the pan over heat and boil until the kanpyo becomes soft enough to break if pinched between the fingers, then drain. Add half of the sugar and soy sauce, then simmer until all the juice disappears. Remove from the heat and set aside.

Grill the nori sheets lightly on both sides, placing them on the lowest possible grill position; this is to bring out their flavour and make them crisp. Remove from the heat and set aside.

Make the omelette: beat the eggs in a bowl, add the dashi, sugar and $\frac{1}{4}$ teaspoon salt and beat well to mix.

Heat the oil in a heavy-based (preferably square) frying pan. Pour in one-third of the egg mixture, cook until it is set, then fold in half. Grease the empty half of the pan with a wad of paper towels dipped in oil. Pour the remaining egg mixture into the empty half of the pan and cook until set. Fold on to the previously cooked half, then remove this omelette 'sandwich' from the pan. Leave to cool, then cut into long strips about 5 mm ($\frac{1}{4}$ inch) thick.

Make the fish flakes: put the fish fillet in a saucepan, add just enough water to cover and bring to the boil. Drain thoroughly. Using 2 pairs of hashi (chopsticks) or a fork, mash the fish to make flakes. Put the sake in a shallow frying pan with the sugar, $\frac{1}{4}$ teaspoon salt and enough food colouring diluted with a little water to turn the mixture pink. Add the fish flakes, place over very low heat and cook for 2 minutes, stirring all the time. Remove from the heat and leave to cool.

Soak the mushrooms in warm water for 25 minutes, then drain and reserve 120 ml (4 fl oz) of the soaking liquid. Squeeze the mushrooms dry, discard the hard stalks, then finely shred the mushrooms. Finely shred the carrot, then place both mushrooms and carrot in a saucepan with the remaining sugar and soy sauce, the mirin and the reserved soaking liquid from the mushrooms. Simmer over very low heat until all the juice has been absorbed.

Wash and trim the spinach, then blanch in lightly salted water for 1 minute. Drain, then squeeze out the water with your hands.

Place a sheet of nori, shortest side closest to you, on a makisu (bamboo mat). Put half a sheet of nori crossways in the centre on top (this is not strictly necessary, but it does help to prevent the wrapper splitting). Spread 200–225 g (7–8 oz) sumeshi over the nori, leaving a 1 cm ($\frac{1}{2}$ inch) margin on the side nearest to you and on the opposite side. Using your fingers, press the sumeshi to the nori. Place one-quarter of the kanpyo and one-third of the omelette strips, fish flakes, mushrooms, carrots and spinach crossways to within 5 cm (2 inches) of the side furthest from you.

Roll up the makisu from the side nearest to you so that the ingredients are in the centre of the sumeshi. Lightly press the rolled makisu with your fingers. Repeat with more nori and the same filling ingredients to make 3 thick nori-maki altogether.

Use the remaining sumeshi, kanpyo and nori to make thinner nori-maki: place half a sheet of nori on a makisu, with the longest side nearest to you. Put a handful of sumeshi on the nori, then spread it with your fingers and press it to the nori, leaving a 5 mm ($\frac{1}{4}$ inch) margin on the side nearest to you and 1 cm ($\frac{1}{2}$ inch) on the opposite side. Put 1–2 kanpyo strips crossways in the centre and roll the makisu from the side nearest to you.

To serve: cut the thick nori-maki into 6–8 rings and the thinner ones into 4–6 pieces. Arrange them on a wooden or bamboo dish, or on a serving platter, then garnish with shredded beni shoga. Serve cold.

Sanshoku Gohan

Three Colour Rice/Japan

Sanshoku Gohan is a typical lunch dish, especially enjoyed by Japanese school children. It is traditionally made as a portable lunch to be carried in a beautiful lacquered box.

SERVES 4

500 g (1 lb 2 oz) Japanese short grain rice
Fish flakes as for Nori-Maki/Rolled Rice Wrapped in Nori (page 124)
Meat flakes:
2 tablespoons soy sauce
2 tablespoons Dashi/Soup Stock (page 105)
1½ tablespoons sugar
1 tablespoon sake (rice wine)
1 tablespoon mirin (sweet rice wine)
1 teaspoon finely chopped fresh root ginger
225 g (8 oz) minced chicken or beef
Egg flakes:
4 eggs
1½ tablespoons sugar
1 tablespoon sake (rice wine)
1 tablespoon vegetable oil
½ teaspoon soy sauce
⅓ teaspoon salt
To garnish:
4 large unpeeled cooked prawns
6 mangetout, cooked and halved
lemon slices

Make plain boiled rice as for Sumeshi/Vinegared Rice (page 120), using 685 ml (23 fl oz) water.

Make the meat flakes: put all the ingredients, except the meat, in a saucepan and bring to the boil. Add the meat and stir well. Cook over low heat, stirring all the time, until all the juice has been absorbed. Remove from the heat, cover and keep warm.

Make the egg flakes: beat the eggs in a saucepan, add the remaining ingredients and cook over moderate heat, stirring all the time until the eggs are very finely scrambled. Remove from the heat and stir for 30 seconds.

Put the hot rice in 3 individual bowls and garnish with the fish, meat and egg flakes, prawns, mangetout halves and lemon slices. Serve warm.

Chap-Chae

Vermicelli with Pork and Vegetables/Korea

This is one of the most popular dishes in Korea. It is easy to prepare, and the fine balance of varied ingredients makes it both nutritious and delicious. Chap-Chae is traditionally eaten as a main course, but it can also be served as a vegetable accompaniment or starter.

SERVES 4

4 dried shiitake mushrooms
100–175 g (4–6 oz) vermicelli
225 g (8 oz) lean boneless pork
1 courgette, topped and tailed
1 small carrot, peeled
1 green pepper, halved and seeded
2 small onions
3 tablespoons vegetable oil
2 garlic cloves, peeled and finely chopped
3 tablespoons soy sauce
1 teaspoon freshly ground black pepper
3–4 spring onions, finely chopped, to garnish

Soak the mushrooms in warm water for 20–25 minutes, then drain. Squeeze the mushrooms dry, discard the hard stalks, then cut each mushroom into 5–6 strips.

Put the vermicelli in a bowl, pour in boiling water to cover and leave to soak for 10 minutes. Drain well, then cut into 5 cm (2 inch) lengths.

Finely shred the pork into 5 cm (2 inch) lengths. Cut the courgette, carrot and green pepper into 5 cm (2 inch) lengths. Peel and thinly slice the onions.

Heat the oil in a heavy-based frying pan, add the garlic, then the pork. Stir-fry for about 5 minutes until the pork is cooked. Add the soy sauce and pepper, stir well to mix, then add the vegetables and vermicelli. Stir-fry for 2 minutes, or until the carrot is tender but still crisp. Transfer to 4 warmed individual plates or 1 large serving platter, sprinkle with the chopped spring onions and serve immediately.

Oyako Donburi

Parent-child Bowl/Japan

Parent-child bowl is a direct translation of
oyako, and the dish is so named because the
recipe combines both chicken and egg. *Donburi*
often refers to a large bowl of rice
topped with poultry, meat or fish.
In Japan a special Oyako Donburi frying
pan is used but a pancake pan can
be used successfully.

SERVES 4

500 g (1 lb 2 oz) Japanese short grain rice
2 medium onions
4 spring onions
225 g (8 oz) boneless chicken breast
meat, skinned
400 ml (14 fl oz) Dashi/Soup Stock (page 105)
5 tablespoons soy sauce
2 tablespoons sake (rice wine)
1 tablespoon mirin (sweet rice wine)
1 tablespoon sugar
4 eggs, beaten
watercress, roughly chopped, to garnish

Make plain boiled rice as for Sumeshi/Vinegared Rice
(page 120), using 685 ml (23 fl oz) water. Slice the onioins
thinly. Cut the spring onions in half lengthways, reserve
the green part, then slice the remainder into 5cm
(2inch) lengths. Chop the chicken into bite-sized pieces.
Mix the dashi with the soy sauce, sake, mirin and sugar
and stir well.

Pour one-quarter of the dashi mixture into a small,
heavy-based frying pan or pancake pan. Add one-quarter
of the thinly sliced onions and bring to the boil, then add
one-quarter of the chicken meat and cook for 2 minutes.
Add one-quarter of the spring onions, cook for a few
seconds, then pour over one-quarter of the beaten eggs.
Cook until only just set.

Remove the pan from the heat, sprinkle over a little
chopped watercress, then remove from the pan. Repeat
with the remaining ingredients to make 4 oyako donburi
altogether. Divide the hot rice equally between 4
individual plates, top with the oyako donburi and
garnish with the reserved spring onion and the
remaining watercress.

Asari Gohan

Rice with Cockles/Japan

This dish is served at lunchtime. Most Japanese
homes have cooked rice keeping warm in an
electric rice cooker from morning to night. For
lunch, a little rice is used with whatever fresh
ingredient is available on the day.

SERVES 4

500 g (1 lb 2 oz) Japanese short grain rice
225 g (8 oz) cockles
salt
5 cm (2 inch) piece fresh root ginger
3 tablespoons soy sauce
2 tablespoons mirin (sweet rice wine)
1 tablespoon sake (rice wine)
2 tablespoons sugar

Make plain boiled rice as for Sumeshi/Vinegared Rice
(page 120), using 685 ml (23 fl oz) water. Wash the cockles
in salted water and drain. Peel and slice the ginger. Put
the soy sauce, mirin, sake and sugar in a saucepan and
bring to the boil. Add the cockles and ginger slices, bring
back to the boil, then lower the heat. Skim, then cook
gently until all the juice has soaked into the cockles.

Divide the hot rice equally between 4 individual
noodle bowls, arrange the cooked cockles on top and
serve immediately.

Keikitamo-Udon

Noodles in Egg Soup/Japan

The garnish of finely chopped spring onions complements the soup well, the grated ginger and shichimi pepper can be added at the table.

SERVES 4

450 g (1 lb) udon (thick dried noodles)
salt
1 litre (1¾ pints) Dashi/Soup Stock (page 105)
50 ml (2 fl oz) soy sauce
2 tablespoons mirin (sweet rice wine)
3 tablespoons cornflour
4 eggs, beaten
To serve:
3 spring onions, finely chopped
2.5 cm (1 inch) piece fresh root ginger, peeled and grated
shichimi pepper

OPPOSITE: Rolled Rice Wrapped in Nori (page 124).
ABOVE: Right, Noodles in Egg Soup.
Left, Parent-child Bowl (page 126).

Plunge the udon into a large saucepan of lightly salted boiling water. Bring back to the boil, then lower the heat and simmer, uncovered, for about 10 minutes until they are soft but not soggy. Drain well in a colander and rinse under cold running water, to remove excess starch.

Bring the dashi to the boil in a saucepan with the soy sauce, mirin and ½ teaspoon salt. Mix the cornflour to a smooth paste with a little water, add to the pan and stir until the soup thickens slightly. Slowly add the eggs to the soup, then cook over low heat until threads of egg float to the surface. Remove the pan from the heat.

Put the cooked udon in a bowl of hot water for a few seconds to reheat them. Drain, then divide equally between 4 individual noodle bowls. Pour the egg soup over the noodles, then sprinkle over the chopped spring onions. Place a little grated ginger in a small dish. Serve hot, with shichimi pepper and ginger handed separately at the table.

127

JAPAN & KOREA
VEGETABLE DISHES

Meat is a relatively recent innovation in the Japanese diet, due to the predominant Buddhist faith. Vegetables, therefore, have always played an important role in Japanese Cookery. As is the rule with most Japanese food, vegetables must be young, tender and absolutely fresh. Most Japanese cooks shop daily for the best ingredients and will throw away any vegetables that are even slightly sub-standard. There is an enormous variety of vegetables available in Japan. Daikon (Japanese radish) is often cooked, but is particularly popular when shredded raw and used as an attractive garnish. Mushrooms are also popular; especially the shiitake mushroom which imparts a strong flavour and has an appealing texture.

Many Japanese vegetables may not be found in the West, although they are often available canned or dried, and indeed the increasing numbers of oriental stores stock some of the more unusual varieties, such as burdock and daikon. Many large supermarkets are also expanding their product lines and now carry vegetables such as Chinese leaves and ginger although fresh shiso leaves, a delicious leaf vegetable, may still be a little difficult to obtain. Vegetables are often salted and parboiled even when used in salads, for example, Sunomono/Vinegar Cucumber (page 129), the traditional vinegared salad, which is so popular in Japan.

Soboro Ankake

Hot Daikon with Sauce/Japan
Daikon is usually associated with salads or garnishes, when it is grated or cut into shapes. In this recipe the daikon is cooked slowly over low heat to make a warming winter dish, but it still retains its characteristic crispness.

SERVES 4

1 large daikon (Japanese Radish)
salt
400 ml (14 fl oz) Dashi/Soup Stock (page 105)
2 tablespoons soy sauce
4 teaspoons mirin (sweet rice wine)
1 tablespoon vegetable oil
100 g (4 oz) minced beef
1 teaspoon sugar
1½ tablespoons cornflour

Peel the daikon and cut into rounds about 4 cm (1½ inch) thick. Plunge into a saucepan of gently simmering lightly salted water, cover with an otoshi-buta (small wooden lid) or small upturned plate and cook very gently for about 45 minutes. Drain and set aside.

Pour the dashi into the rinsed-out pan, then add half of the soy sauce, 1 teaspoon of the mirin and ½ teaspoon salt. Bring to the boil, add the drained daikon and cover with an otoshi-buta or a sheet of greaseproof paper (the plate would be too heavy at this stage). Simmer over very low heat for a further 30 minutes, then remove from the heat and keep warm.

Heat the oil in a separate saucepan, add the minced beef and fry until it changes colour, stirring all the time to remove any lumps. Add the remaining soy sauce and mirin, the sugar and salt to taste. Pour in the liquid from the daikon, cook over high heat for 2 minutes, then taste and adjust seasoning – it should be slightly salty. Mix the cornflour to a smooth paste with 3 tablespoons cold water. Add to the pan of meat and stir until the mixture thickens. Arrange 2 daikon pieces in each of 4 warmed individual bowls and pour the meat sauce over them. Serve hot.

Sunomono

Vinegared Cucumber / Japan

This classic Japanese vinegared salad of finely sliced cucumber and soft wakame (seaweed) can be served as an hors d'oeuvre or as a refreshing accompaniment to a main meal.

SERVES 4

1 large or 2 small cucumbers
1 teaspoon salt
15 g ($\frac{1}{2}$ oz) wakame (dried young seaweed)
2.5–4 cm (1–$1\frac{1}{2}$ inch) piece fresh root ginger
Saubaizu sauce:
3 tablespoons rice vinegar
1 tablespoon soy sauce
1 tablespoon sugar
$\frac{1}{4}$–$\frac{1}{2}$ teaspoon salt

Halve the cucumber(s) lengthways; remove the seeds with a sharp-edged teaspoon. Slice the cucumber very thinly and sprinkle with the salt. Using your hands, squeeze the cucumber slices a few times, then rinse under cold running water in a bamboo strainer or sieve.

Put the wakame in a bowl and cover with cold water. Leave to soak for 5–10 minutes, or until it becomes fully expanded and soft. Drain in a sieve, rinse with boiling water, then rinse under cold running water. Drain well and squeeze out any excess water with your hands. Cut the wakame into 2.5 cm (1 inch) lengths if it is not already chopped.

Peel and shred the ginger, then place in a bowl of ice-cold water to crisp up. Put all the ingredients for the sauce in a bowl, mix well together, then add the sliced cucumber and wakame. Toss well.

Transfer the salad to individual salad bowls, shaping it into neat mounds. Drain the shredded ginger and sprinkle over the top. Serve cold.

Kaki-Age

Vegetable Tempura / Japan

Kaki-Age is often made with leftover batter from fish Tempura (page 115). The trimmings from the fish are sometimes mixed with the vegetables and deep-fried in the batter.

SERVES 4

$\frac{1}{2}$ medium carrot
50 g (2 oz) French beans
2 potatoes, peeled
1 egg
50 g (2 oz) plain flour, plus extra for sprinkling
vegetable oil, for deep-frying
To serve:
Tentsuyu sauce as for Tempura / Deep-fried Fish and Vegetables (page 115)
2.5 cm (1 inch) piece fresh root ginger, peeled and grated
5 cm (2 inch) piece daikon (Japanese Radish), peeled and grated

Peel the carrot and shred finely into 5 cm (2 inch) lengths. Slice the French beans in half lengthways, then cut into 5 cm (2 inch) lengths. Cut the potatoes into matchsticks.

Put the egg in a bowl, stir in 50 ml (2 fl oz) ice-cold water, then sift in the 50 g (2 oz) flour. Using 2 pairs of hashi (chopsticks) or 2 forks, mix to a lumpy batter.

Put some of the prepared vegetables in a ladle and sprinkle them with a little flour. Add 1–2 tablespoons of the batter and mix well in the ladle.

Heat the oil in a deep-fat frier or deep frying pan to about 160°C/325°F. Deep-fry the vegetables a ladleful at a time for about 2 minutes until they are golden and crisp.

Remove from the hot oil with a perforated spoon and drain on paper towels.

To serve: pour the tentsuyu sauce into 4 small bowls. Put the grated ginger and daikon in separate bowls. Fold a large paper towel in half and place on a bamboo dish or serving platter. Arrange the vegetables on the paper and serve immediately, with the bowls of sauce, ginger and daikon. Each diner should mix grated ginger and daikon to taste with some of the sauce, then dip the Kaki-Age into the sauce before eating.

Wafu Salada

Japanese Salad/Japan

The key to making this salad look authentic is to shred the vegetables as thin as a needle.

SERVES 4

½ *medium carrot, peeled*
1 cucumber
½ *bunch spring onions*
100 g (4 oz) boneless chicken breast meat
1 tablespoon sake (rice wine)
15 g (½ oz) wakame (dried young seaweed)
shiso or lettuce leaves, to serve

Gomadare dressing:
4 tablespoons sesame seeds, toasted and pounded, or 2 tablespoons sesame paste (tahini)
1 small garlic clove, peeled and grated
5 tablespoons rice vinegar
3 tablespoons Dashi/Soup Stock (page 105)
1 tablespoon soy sauce
1 tablespoon mayonnaise
pinch of chilli powder
salt

First make the gomadare dressing: mix all the ingredients together in a bowl with 1 teaspoon salt. Set aside.

Finely shred the carrot, cucumber and spring onions and place them in separate bowls of ice-cold water to crisp up, while preparing the remaining ingredients.

Skin the chicken and lay on a plate, sprinkle with sake and a little salt, then place in a steamer and steam for 12 minutes or until tender. Remove from the steamer and leave to cool, then shred the chicken finely with your fingers. Return to the juices on the plate.

Put the wakame in a bowl and cover with cold water. Leave to soak for 5–10 minutes, or until it becomes fully expanded and soft. Drain in a sieve, rinse with boiling water, then rinse under cold running water. Drain well and squeeze out any excess water with your hands. Cut the wakame into 2.5 cm (1 inch) lengths if it is not already chopped.

Line a large plate with shiso or lettuce leaves; place the bowl of gomadare dressing in the centre and arrange all the shredded ingredients around it.

OPPOSITE: *Spinach with Cockles in Mustard Sauce (page 131).* BELOW: *Left, Vegetables in Tofu Dressing (page 131). Right, Japanese Salad.*

Shira-Ae

Vegetables in Tofu Dressing / Japan

Vegetables are rarely used raw in Japan, but are often part-cooked in a little stock. This combination of vegetables is dressed with a creamy tofu dressing that has been flavoured with 'nutty' toasted sesame seeds.

SERVES 4

3 dried shiitake mushrooms
½ cake kon-nyaku (arum root), or ½ fennel bulb
15–25 g (½–1 oz) abura-age (deep-fried bean curd), or 2 slices boiled ham
1 small carrot, peeled
50 g (2 oz) French beans, topped and tailed
400 ml (14 fl oz) Dashi/Soup Stock (page 105)
1 tablespoon soy sauce
2 teaspoons sugar
Shira-ae dressing:
100 g (4 oz) silken tofu (bean curd)
4 tablespoons sesame seeds, toasted and pounded, or 2 tablespoons sesame paste (tahini)
2½ tablespoons sugar
1 teaspoon salt

Soak the mushrooms in warm water for 20–25 minutes, then drain. Squeeze the mushrooms dry, discard the hard stalks, then cut the caps into thin strips.

Cut the kon-nyaku (if using) into strips about 4 cm (1½ inch) long and 5 mm (¼ inch) thick. Blanch in boiling water for a few seconds. If using abura-age, place in a bowl and pour over boiling water to cover. Drain and cut into strips 5 mm (¼ inch) wide. Cut the fennel and ham (if using) and the carrot and French beans into strips about the same size as the abura-age.

Bring the dashi to the boil in a saucepan with the soy sauce and sugar. Add the prepared ingredients (except the ham, if used) and simmer gently for 10 minutes. Remove from the heat and leave to cool.

Meanwhile, make the dressing: drop the tofu into a saucepan of boiling water, bring back to the boil, then drain. Put the tofu on a board, place a flat plate or another board on top and press down to squeeze out excess moisture.

Force the tofu through a sieve into a bowl, pressing it with a wooden spatula. Add the sesame paste, sugar and salt and mix well. Drain the cooled vegetables, reserving the juice. Add the vegetables to the dressing, with the ham, if used. Mix well, adding a little of the reserved juice from the vegetables if the dressing is too thick. Transfer to a salad bowl and serve cold.

Karashi-Ae

Spinach with Cockles in Mustard Sauce / Japan

Many Japanese salads are very quick and easy to prepare. This recipe is one of the simplest.

SERVES 4

1 tablespoon sake (rice wine)
225 g (8 oz) cockles, cleaned
3 tablespoons soy sauce, plus 1 teaspoon
1 teaspoon Japanese or other hot mustard
450 g (1 lb) spinach leaves, washed and trimmed
salt
1 teaspoon sesame seeds

Heat the sake in a small saucepan, add the cockles and heat through. Drain the cockles, reserving the juice.

Put 3 tablespoons soy sauce and the mustard in a bowl and mix together. Add the cockles. Cook the leaves in lightly salted boiling water for 30 seconds, then drain and plunge immediately into a bowl of ice-cold water. Drain again and squeeze out any excess water, pour over the 1 teaspoon soy sauce.

Add the cockle juice to the cockle mixture. Arrange the spinach in a serving bowl. Place the cockle mixture in the centre and garnish with sesame seeds.

Negi no Karashi-Ae

Spring Onions with Mustard Miso Sauce/Japan
Mustard Miso Sauce is a very traditional Japanese dressing, which complements the strong taste of the spring onions used in this recipe. When spring onions are not in season, use another vegetable such as lightly cooked leeks or fennel.

SERVES 4

2 bunches thin spring onions
15 g ($\frac{1}{2}$ oz) wakame (dried young seaweed)
Mustard miso sauce:
3 tablespoons white miso (soy bean paste)
3 tablespoons sugar
1 teaspoon Japanese or other hot mustard
1 teaspoon soy sauce
1 teaspoon mirin (sweet rice wine)

Trim the spring onions, then plunge into a saucepan of boiling water for 2 minutes. Drain in a colander and hold under cold running water until cool. Drain thoroughly.

Hold 2 spring onions together side by side and fold them 3-4 times, until about 4 cm (1½ inches) long. Tie each pair together at the centre, using the soft green part.

Put the wakame in a bowl and cover with cold water. Leave to soak for 5–10 minutes, or until it becomes fully expanded and soft. Drain in a sieve, rinse with boiling water, then rinse under cold running water. Drain well and squeeze out any excess water. Cut the wakame into 2.5 cm (1 inch) lengths if it is not already chopped.

Place the wakame on a large serving plate, then arrange the spring onion bunches on top. Put all the ingredients for the mustard miso sauce in a small bowl and stir well to mix. Pour the sauce over the vegetables and serve immediately.

Horenso no Ohitashi

Spinach with Bonito Flakes/Japan
This is one of the simplest but most nutritious vegetable dishes as the high iron content of the spinach complement the protein in the bonito flakes.

SERVES 4

450 g (1 lb) fresh young spinach leaves
salt
2½ tablespoons soy sauce
4–5 tablespoons Dashi/Soup Stock (page 105)
4 tablespoons katsuo-bushi (dried bonito flakes), to garnish

Trim the spinach, discarding any thick stalks. Blanch in a large saucepan of lightly salted boiling water for 2 minutes. Drain, plunge into a bowl of ice-cold water to prevent further cooking, then drain again thoroughly. Squeeze out the water from the spinach with your hands, then spread out on a board or large plate. Sprinkle ½ tablespoon of the soy sauce over the spinach, then squeeze out more liquid.

Put the dashi and remaining soy sauce in a wide, shallow tin. Add the spinach and soak in the sauce for about 5 minutes, then return to the board, arranging all the leaves side by side. Gently squeeze the sauce out of the spinach into the tin and reserve. Cut the spinach into 4–5 cm (1½–2 inch) pieces. Place the flavoured spinach in a bowl. Garnish with the dried bonito flakes and sprinkle over the reserved dashi sauce. Serve cold.

Agedashi Dofu

Tofu in Dashi Sauce/Japan
If using Japanese silken tofu (bean curd) it is essential to boil it before frying, as this makes it firmer. Chinese tofu is already firm and does not need to be boiled first.

SERVES 4

225 g (8 oz) silken or firm tofu (bean curd)
cornflour, for coating
vegetable oil, for deep-frying
Dashi sauce:
200 ml (7 fl oz) Dashi/Soup Stock (page 105)
4 tablespoons mirin (sweet rice wine)
4 tablespoons soy sauce
To serve:
5 cm (2 inch) piece daikon (Japanese Radish), peeled and grated
4 shiso or lettuce leaves, finely shredded

If using silken tofu (bean curd) drop the pieces into a saucepan of boiling water for 1 minute to make them firm. Drain well, then cut the tofu into 6–8 squares. Roll each piece in cornflour until evenly coated, shaking off any excess.

Heat the oil in a deep-fat frier or deep frying pan to 160°C/325°F, add the tofu and deep-fry until golden brown. Remove from the oil with a perforated spoon and drain on paper towels.

Make the sauce: pour the dashi into a saucepan, add the mirin and soy sauce and bring to the boil. Divide the sauce equally between 4 warmed individual bowls. Place 3–4 pieces of fried tofu in each bowl then garnish with grated daikon and shredded shiso or lettuce leaves. Serve immediately.

Nimame | Tsukemono

Simmered Soya Beans/Japan

This dish was created to cook slowly over a charcoal fire (hibachi) which traditional Japanese homes would have had burning throughout the day. It is still a popular dish, although nowadays it is usually cooked on a modern hob.

SERVES 4

200 g (7 oz) soya beans
salt
150 g (5 oz) can renkon (lotus root) or water
chestnuts, drained (optional)
200 g (7 oz) can gobo (burdock root), drained
½ medium carrot
½ cake kon-nyaku (arum root)
10 cm (4 inch) square konbu (dried kelp)
25 g (1 oz) sugar
5 tablespoons soy sauce

Wash the soya beans, then place in a bowl and cover with lightly salted water, allowing 3 times as much water as the volume of soya beans. Leave to soak overnight.

Put the beans and their soaking liquid in a saucepan and bring to the boil. Add 200 ml (7 fl oz) cold water, place an otoshi-buta (small wooden lid) or upturned plate directly on top of the beans and cover with a lid. Simmer for about 1 hour, or until the beans become soft.

Meanwhile cut the renkon or water chestnuts (if using) and the gobo into small cubes, about 1 cm (½ inch) square. Peel the carrot and cut into 1 cm (½ inch) squares. Tear the kon-nyaku into similar-sized pieces with your hands. Cut the konbu into 1 cm (½ inch) squares.

When the beans are cooked, add the renkon or water chestnuts, the drained gobo and the kon-nyaku. Cover again with the otoshi-buta or plate and simmer for about 10 minutes until the gobo is cooked. Add the squares of carrot and konbu and half of the sugar. Continue cooking for a further 10 minutes until the carrots are tender, then add the remaining sugar and the soy sauce. Simmer until almost all of the juice has been absorbed. Transfer to a bowl and serve either hot or cold.

Pressed Salad/Japan

Like rice and soup, Tsukemono is part of almost every Japanese meal. It is eaten with simple, everyday food, and is even served at the most formal of banquets. For a simple end to a meal, serve this salad with a bowl of plain boiled rice.

SERVES 4

15 cm (6 inch) piece daikon (Japanese Radish)
2 medium carrots
225 g (8 oz) French beans
salt
To serve:
Saubaizu sauce as for Sunomono/Vinegared
Cucumber (page 129)
1 tablespoon sesame seeds, toasted

Peel the daikon and carrots and cut into 5–7.5 cm (2–3 inch) lengths. Slice them into matchstick-size pieces. Top and tail the French beans and cut into 5–7.5 cm (2–3 inch) pieces, depending on their length, then slice lengthways in half. Mix the vegetables together and place one-quarter in a large bowl. Sprinkle over about ½ teaspoon salt. Repeat with more vegetables and salt until all the shredded vegetables are placed in the bowl. Cover the vegetables with an upturned plate (a little smaller than the bowl), place a heavy weight on top and leave for at least 1 hour, preferably overnight.

When ready to eat the salad, remove the weight and pour off any excess water from the vegetables, pressing the plate firmly to extract as much liquid as possible. Remove the plate and mix the vegetables well, then add the saubaizu sauce and mix well again. Transfer to individual salad bowls and sprinkle over the sesame seeds. Serve the pressed salad cold.

133

JAPAN & KOREA
MENUS & CUSTOMS

Unlike most Western cuisines, Japanese cooking does not aim to 'create' something by mixing together different ingredients, spices and seasonings, but rather to allow the natural taste and flavour of each individual ingredient to emerge and to be enjoyed for its own sake. To this end, cooking and seasoning is kept to an absolute minimum. To the Japanese cook it is the freshness, quality and flavour of the ingredients which are of prime importance rather than the way in which they are cooked. Food is bought daily, and the cook chooses only foods that are in season and in peak condition.

Kaiseki Ryori

This formal style of cooking developed from food served at the original Japanese tea ceremony, about three hundred years ago. Food is presented in a particular order determined by the cooking method, and the four seasons are followed rigidly in the selection of ingredients to be served. In a formal kaiseki meal, the courses follow one another in a set order: clear soup, hors d'oeuvre, simmered dish, grilled dish, meat dish, vegetables, large fried dish, boiled rice and sunomono (vinegared vegetables), miso soup and green tea.

Nowadays, kaiseki dishes are only served in first-class Japanese restaurants called *ryotei*, although at special parties and on ceremonial occasions such as New Year's Day, Children's Day and the Equinox, meals at home are traditionally served with a little more formality.

Home Cooking

For the Westerner it is quite simple to prepare a meal as it would be served in a Japanese home. When it comes to home cooking, most Japanese mealtimes are rather casual; all the dishes are placed on the table at the same time and everyone helps themselves.

Presentation and Garnishing

When planning a Japanese meal, thought should be given to pleasing the eye and the spirit as well as the palate, as presentation and atmosphere are both considered as important as the food itself. In most modern homes, meals are eaten around a conventional dining table, but in a traditional Japanese home, diners are barefoot and either kneel or sit cross-legged around a dining table that is as low as a Western coffee table.

Each person has a bowl of boiled rice on their left hand side and a bowl of soup on their right. Hashi (chopsticks) are placed immediately in front of each place setting. One or two dishes are served in individual bowls, immediately behind the rice and soup, while the remainder are served on larger dishes in the centre of the table.

Because the look of the table is so important, dishes, bowls and plates are chosen to harmonize with the shape and colour of the food they contain and with the season of the year, rather than to match each other. Considerable care is given to the garnishing of the food itself to enhance its visual appeal.

Etiquette There are few formal rules of etiquette to follow, but certain traditions are kept. It is customary, for example, to offer your guests rolled towels with which to wipe their hands (and face if wished) before eating. In winter these towels are dampened with very hot water, in summer with ice-cold water. Cutlery and serving utensils are not used, simply because all food is cut meticulously into small, bite-sized pieces before it is brought to the table. Hashi (chopsticks) must always be placed immediately in front of each person on a special hashi rest, with the points facing to the left, and they should always be returned to this rest if they are put down during a meal. Hashi should not be placed across a bowl or stuck into rice (this is a sign of mourning), and they should never be used to pierce or stab food, which should always be lifted to the mouth between the hashi.

Selecting the Dishes Harmony of colour, flavour and texture, and the reflection of the seasons, are the keynotes to planning an authentic Japanese meal.

Whatever the occasion, rice is almost always served, although in summer, cold noodle dishes are popular, together with tsukemono (pickled vegetables) which most Japanese housewives buy ready-made. Soup, too, is always served. In addition to these three basic dishes, a family meal usually consists of three or five other dishes. The method of cooking for each dish should be different to provide balance and variety, and to make up an harmonious whole.

Desserts are not normally served with everyday meals. Seasonal fresh fruits are preferred, and these are always in prime condition and beautifully presented. Most dishes are served at room temperature, and therefore it is quite in order to prepare and cook some of the dishes several hours in advance.

Green tea goes well with most Japanese food, but for a special meal, serve warmed sake (rice wine).

KOREA

Korean meals are similar to Japanese in that the accent is on harmony and balance. Visual appeal and flavour are equally important to the Koreans, and this must be borne in mind when menu planning. As with Japanese meals, there are no separate courses as everything is placed on the table together. Rice and soup are common to all meals, whatever the occasion, and for everyday family meals there are usually a few other dishes, plus an array of sauces and dips. Kimchee/Marinated Chinese Leaves (page 139) is served with absolutely everything. Desserts are not normally served with everyday meals as many of the savoury dishes include sweet flavours, but decoratively cut fresh fruit can be offered at the end of a meal to refresh the palate.

Koreans eat with chokkara (chopsticks); traditionally, these should be made of silver, although nowadays other metal, plastic and wooden chokkara are more common.

Korean 'tea', made by steeping roast barley in boiling water, is usually drunk with meals, and sometimes has a little ginseng added to it. Roast barley for making Korean tea can be bought at most oriental stores.

— Sample Menus —

JAPANESE BREAKFAST
Boiled Rice
Rolled Rice Wrapped in Nori
Bean Soup
Pressed Salad
Marinated Fish
Green Tea

JAPANESE PICNIC LUNCH
Rolled Rice Wrapped in Nori
Chicken Teriyaki
Three Colour Rice
'Pickled' Sardines
Pressed Salad
Fresh Fruits

JAPANESE FAMILY DINNER
Boiled Rice
Pickled Vegetables
Chicken Cooked with Vegetables
Cod Cooked in Earthenware
Boiled Spinach with Bonito Flakes
Bean Soup
Green Tea
Fresh Fruits

JAPANESE DINNER PARTY
Mackerel Sushi
Thick Egg Soup
Japanese 'Roast' Beef
Vinegared Cucumber
Vegetables in Tofu Dressing
Boiled Rice
Bean Soup
Fruit Salad
Green Tea

KOREAN DINNER PARTY
Fan-shaped Prawns in Egg Batter
Marinated Beef with Sweet Sauce
Boiled Rice
Vermicelli with Pork and Vegetables
Marinated Chinese Leaves
Korean Roast Barley Tea
Fresh Fruits

NOTE: Adjust quantities of individual dishes according to the number of people being served.

—KOREAN NEW YEAR'S DAY FEAST—

New Year's Day is celebrated in Korea as it is in Japan: it is the major celebration of the year, equivalent to Christmas Day in Christian societies. In Japan, New Year's Day is celebrated on the 1st of January, but the Koreans still retain the calendar of the old moon (as do the Chinese) and celebrate the New Year some time in early February. The following menu is made up of the type of party dishes that would be served at a New Year feast, but it is not essential to make all of them.

FOR 10 PEOPLE
Skewered Meat and Vegetables
Fan-shaped Prawns in Egg Batter
Celebration Firepot
Korean 'Pizza'
Rice Cake Soup
Marinated Chinese Leaves
Dried Persimmons in Cinnamon Syrup

San-Jeok

Skewered Meat and Vegetables
The egg batter on the meat and vegetables is very light so that the different colours of the ingredients show through.

SERVES 6 as an individual dish

450 g (1 lb) beef steak (sirloin, rump or fillet)
salt
freshly ground black pepper
2 carrots, peeled
1 bunch spring onions, washed and trimmed
12 Japanese bamboo skewers
plain flour, for coating
4 eggs, lightly beaten
vegetable oil, for shallow-frying

Cut the beef into 2.5 cm (1 inch) pieces, about 1 cm ($\frac{1}{2}$ inch) thick and season with salt and pepper. Cut the carrots into quarters, lengthways, then into 5 cm (2 inch) lengths. Cut the spring onions into 5 cm (2 inch) lengths, discarding the green parts.

Thread the beef, carrots and spring onion pieces on to the bamboo skewers, then coat lightly with flour. Dip the skewers into the beaten eggs.

Heat the oil in a heavy-based frying pan. Fry the skewered meat and vegetables over low heat for about 7–8 minutes or until cooked, turning them frequently. Drain well, then transfer to a warmed dish for serving.

Sae-Woo-Jeon

Fan-shaped Prawns in Egg Batter
The prawns should be served with a sauce made from soy sauce, finely chopped fresh chillies, garlic and spring onion to taste.

SERVES 6 as an individual dish

24 headless uncooked prawns, defrosted if frozen
salt
freshly ground black pepper
1 spring onion, trimmed and very finely chopped
$\frac{1}{4}$ onion, peeled and very finely chopped
plain flour, for coating
4 eggs
vegetable oil, for shallow-frying

Wash and shell the prawns, retaining the shell on the end of the tail. Take the black vein out of the back of the prawns, pat dry with paper towels. Cut each prawn lengthways into 3, keeping them attached at the tail end. Sprinkle with salt and pepper to taste, then with the spring onion and chopped onion. Coat lightly with flour. Beat the eggs in a bowl and dip in the prawns.

Heat 1 tablespoon oil in a small heavy-based frying pan. Fry the prawns, 3 at a time, in the pan and cook over moderate heat until they open up like fans. Drain well before serving.

Sin-Sol-Lo

Celebration Firepot

Sin-Sol-Lo was originally a royal dish made with many different kinds of meat and fish, and served only in the King's household. Nowadays, this more humble version is served on special occasions, especially New Year.

Sin-Sol-Lo is traditionally cooked at the table in a special firepot. This has a central chimney which contains glowing coals to keep the stock boiling hot. Firepots are not easy to obtain, but if you have an electric wok, this can be used with equal success.

SERVES 6 as an individual dish

450 g (1 lb) fillet steak
salt
freshly ground black pepper
4–5 tablespoons sake (rice wine)
450 g (1 lb) daikon (Japanese radish)
200 g (7 oz) cod fillets
plain flour, for coating
3 large eggs
vegetable oil, for shallow-frying
2 courgettes, trimmed
2 carrots, peeled
200 g (7 oz) minced beef
200 g (7 oz) prepared squid
10 Mediterranean or 'king' prawns, peeled
100 g (4 oz) gingko nuts
100 g (4 oz) pine nuts
about 1 litre (1¾ pints) beef stock
soy sauce
sugar
garlic

Freeze the fillet steak for 45 minutes, leave for 10 minutes on a board, then cut into wafer-thin slices with a very sharp knife. Put the slices in a bowl and sprinkle with salt and pepper to taste. Pour over 2–3 tablespoons of the sake and stir well to mix, then cover and leave to marinate while preparing the other ingredients.

Cook the daikon in boiling salted water for 20 minutes. Meanwhile, thinly slice the cod and sprinkle with salt and pepper to taste. Coat lightly in flour. Beat the eggs in a bowl. Dip the slices of cod into the beaten eggs. Heat 2–3 tablespoons of oil in a heavy-based frying pan, add the slices of cod and fry until golden brown. Remove from the pan with a perforated spoon and drain on paper towels.

Cut the courgettes and carrots into 2 cm (¾ inch) slices, then season and coat lightly in flour. Dip in the beaten eggs, fry in hot oil and drain as before.

Season the minced beef with salt and pepper to taste, then form into small balls. Coat lightly in flour, then dip in the beaten eggs. Fry in hot oil and drain as before.

Sprinkle the squid and prawns with salt and pepper to taste, coat lightly in flour, then dip in the beaten eggs. Fry in hot oil and drain as before.

Drain the daikon, slice thinly and arrange in the firepot or electric wok. Place the beef on top, then the cod, courgettes, carrots, meatballs, squid, prawns, gingko and pine nuts.

Add the remaining sake to the beef stock, then add soy sauce, sugar and garlic to taste. Pour the stock gently into the pot, taking care not to disturb the arranged ingredients. Ignite the charcoal or electric wok and heat for about 5 minutes before serving.

Bin-Dae-Tok

Korean 'Pizza'

In Korea, Bin-Dae-Tok are often eaten as a snack between meals, or even as a tea-time accompaniment. Traditionally, the mung beans are ground in a stone grinder, but nowadays electric machines are used to make grinding quicker and easier. Dried mung beans can be bought at most health food shops, but if you find them difficult to obtain, use split peas instead.

If liked, Bin-Dae-Tok can be served with a dipping sauce made by mixing together soy sauce, finely chopped fresh chillies, garlic and spring onion to taste.

MAKES 5

225 g (8 oz) dried mung beans, soaked in cold water overnight
225 g (8 oz) lean pork
½ bunch spring onions, trimmed
1 small onion, peeled
1 carrot, peeled
3 eggs, beaten
salt
vegetable oil, for greasing

Drain the mung beans, then work in batches in a blender or food processor until mashed, adding enough water to moisten. Slice the pork very thinly, then cut into strips. Finely chop the spring onions, onion and carrot.

Put all the ingredients in a large bowl and add the beaten eggs and salt to taste. Mix well together. Grease the base of a heavy-based frying pan with a little oil, then place the pan over moderate heat until hot. Add one-fifth of the mixture and fry over low heat, turning once, until a golden-brown 'pancake' is formed. Remove from the pan, then repeat with the remaining mixture to make 5 pancakes altogether. Cut each fried 'pancake' into quarters and arrange on a large serving dish. Serve at room temperature.

Tok Kuk

Rice Cake Soup

Rice Cake Soup is traditionally served on New Year's Day. Rice cake itself is made by pounding glutinous rice in big tubs to produce a chewy white mixture, which is then shaped into squares or balls. Today rice cake is commercially produced and sold in packets. Korean rice cake is difficult to obtain, but Japanese rice cake, available from oriental stores, can be used.

SERVES 10 as an individual dish

1 large beef bone, or 1.75 litres (3 pints) boiling
beef stock
450 g (1 lb) sirloin beef
5 spring onions, trimmed
1 onion, peeled
vegetable oil, for shallow-frying
10 eggs
225 g (8 oz) firm tofu (bean curd), chopped
1 sheet of nori (dried lava paper)
5 rice cakes
soy sauce
freshly ground black pepper
2 tablespoons sesame seed oil

If making beef stock, chop the bone into small pieces (or get your butcher to do this for you), place in a saucepan and cover with 2 litres (3½ pints) cold water. Bring to the boil, then lower the heat and simmer for 5 hours. Remove the bones and simmer for 30 minutes.

Finely slice the beef, spring onions and onion. Heat 2–3 tablespoons of oil in a heavy-based frying pan, add the finely sliced ingredients and fry for 3–4 minutes, or until the beef is well done. Beat 5 of the eggs in a bowl and pour into the frying pan. Scatter the chopped bean curd on top and cook for a further 2–3 minutes, or until the eggs are set. Remove from the heat and cut into small pieces.

Roast the nori under a preheated hot grill, then crumble on to a plate. Place the rice cakes under the grill and brown each side. Remove from the grill, and using a fork, pierce each cake in several places, then cut each one in half. Beat the remaining 5 eggs and stir into the stock, to create a 'marbled' effect. Season with soy sauce, salt and pepper.

To serve: divide the stock equally between 10 warmed soup bowls, then add a piece of rice cake and some beef, onion and egg mixture. Sprinkle with the roasted nori and sesame seed oil and serve immediately.

BELOW: *Clockwise from top left, Celebration Firepot (page 137), Rice Cake Soup, Skewered Meat and Vegetables (page 136), Korean 'Pizza' (page 137).*

Kimchee | Su-Jung-Ga

Kimchee

Marinated Chinese Leaves
Kimchee is served at most meals and could almost be called Korea's 'National' dish.

MAKES ABOUT 450 g (1 lb)

450 g (1 lb) Chinese leaves, sliced
3 tablespoons salt
100 g (4 oz) daikon (Japanese radish)
1 teaspoon chilli powder
2 teaspoons crushed garlic
1 teaspoon sugar
4 spring onions, finely chopped
2.5 cm (1 inch) piece fresh root ginger, peeled and grated

Wash the Chinese leaves and drain well. Place in a bowl and sprinkle with the salt, then cover with a plate and place heavy weights on top. Leave for 2–3 days then rinse and drain the leaves.

Peel and shred the daikon. Place the Chinese leaves and daikon in a large bowl and stir in the chilli powder, garlic, sugar, spring onions and ginger. Cover with a weighted plate and leave for 1–2 days before using.

Su-Jung-Ga

Dried Persimmons in Cinnamon Syrup
There are very few Korean desserts, as fresh fruit is usually served at the end of a meal, but for a special occasion these stuffed dried persimmons are considered a real delicacy.

This dessert is very simple to make, and because dried persimmons are naturally very sweet, there is little need for extra sweetening to be added. The cinnamon syrup used to pour over the persimmons takes the juicy flavour and sweet taste from the fruit and makes a most refreshing dessert. Dried persimmons are available from most oriental stores.

SERVES 10 as an individual dish

10 cm (4 inch) piece fresh root ginger, peeled and sliced
4 tablespoons soft brown sugar
4 tablespoons clear honey
2 tablespoons ground cinnamon
10 dried persimmons, soaked overnight in cold water
2 tablespoons shelled walnuts, roughly chopped
2 tablespoons pine nuts

Put the sliced ginger in a medium-sized saucepan, pour in 1.2 litres (2 pints) cold water and bring to the boil. Add the soft brown sugar, clear honey and cinnamon and continue boiling for 10 minutes. Remove the saucepan from the heat and leave to cool. Pour the syrup into a large bowl and chill in the refrigerator for 2 hours.

Drain the persimmons and pat dry with paper towels. Gently squeeze each persimmon to open it and, using a teaspoon, carefully scoop out the flesh. Mix the persimmon flesh with half of the walnuts and half of the pine nuts, then use to fill the persimmons, making sure that the filling is well enclosed.

Place the persimmons in a serving bowl. Pour over the cold sugar syrup, then sprinkle the remaining walnuts and pine nuts on top. Serve well chilled.

JAPANESE GIRLS' DAY PARTY

Girls' day is traditionally celebrated each year on the 3rd of March — the significance of this date being the association between the Japanese words for 'three' and 'beauty', the sound *mi* meaning both. Traditionally, the maternal grandparents of a baby girl should present her with a set of dolls at birth. Called *ohina-sama*, these dolls are arranged on a kind of staircase, and are kept safely in boxes during the year, but brought out and displayed on girls' day, which is also called 'doll festival' or *hinamatsuri*. Food is chosen for its beauty and colour on girls' day, and the following menu is typical, centred around the three-coloured rice dish called Sanshoku Gohan.

FOR 10 PEOPLE
Three Colour Rice (page 125)
Saffron Soup with Chicken (page 105)
Japanese Salad (page 130)
Peach Flowers
Sardine Balls
Fried Tofu Stuffed with Sushi

Inari Zushi

Fried Tofu Stuffed with Sushi

To make this dish look more attractive, turn half of the abura-age (deep-fried tofu) inside out after cutting them in half. The texture of the outside is like smooth leather, whereas the inside looks like a sponge, which gives an interesting contrast in both colour and texture. Bamboo leaves can be bought at some oriental shops; if you cannot obtain them, use any other long green leaves instead, such as Cos lettuce.

SERVES 4–6 as an individual dish

350 g (12 oz) Japanese short grain rice
1½ tablespoons mirin (sweet rice wine)
20 g (¾ oz) kanpyo (dried shaved gourd strings)
salt
135 ml (4½ fl oz) Dashi/Soup Stock (page 105)
1½ tablespoons soy sauce
4 teaspoons sugar
50 ml (2 fl oz) rice vinegar
50 g (2 oz) tsukemono (pickled vegetables), finely chopped
10 pieces abura-age (deep-fried tofu)
bamboo leaves, to serve

Wash the rice in at least 3 changes of water, until the water becomes clear. Drain well, then place in a large saucepan. Pour in 400 ml (14 fl oz) fresh cold water and leave the rice to soak for 2 hours.

Add the mirin to the pan, cover with the lid and place over high heat. Bring to the boil and simmer for 10–15 minutes, until all the water has been absorbed. Remove from the heat and leave to stand, covered, for 15 minutes.

Wet the kanpyo a little and, using your hands, rub it with a lot of salt. Wash well to remove the surface salt, then place the kanpyo in a small saucepan, cover with cold water and bring to the boil. Simmer for 5 minutes until the kanpyo becomes soft, then drain off the water. Add the dashi to the kanpyo together with the soy sauce and half of the sugar. Simmer gently for a further 5 minutes, then remove from the heat and set aside.

Turn the cooked rice into a large bowl. Mix together the rice vinegar, remaining sugar and ⅔ teaspoon salt. Add the tsukemono and fold into the rice with a wooden rice paddle or spatula; do not stir.

Cut each piece of abura-age in half and open up with your fingers to make a pocket. Stuff the pockets with the rice mixture until two-thirds full.

Tie each Inari Zushi pocket with a 15 cm (6 inch) string of cooked kanpyo. Arrange on a bed of bamboo leaves and serve.

Momo no Hana

Peach Flowers

In Japan, turnips are used to make flowers, but Japanese turnips are closer to red radishes than they are to Western turnips, which is why red radishes are used here, with equally good effect. The 'flowers' should be prepared well in advance and the 'leaves' cooked on the day. Girls' Day is sometimes referred to as Peach Celebration, and these flowers are said to resemble peach blossom.

SERVES 10

1 bunch large red radishes
1 tablespoon salt
100 ml (3½ fl oz) rice vinegar
2 tablespoons sugar
100 g (4 oz) mangetout

Wash the radishes and trim off the stems. Place a radish, trimmed side down, on a board between a pair of parallel hashi (chopsticks). Using a sharp knife and holding the radish steady with your other hand, finely slice the radish, making sure that the knife does not go all the way to the bottom (the hashi will help prevent this). Turn the radish 90° so that the incisions are parallel to the hashi. Again, finely slice the radish, creating a criss-cross effect. Repeat with the remaining radishes.

Place the radishes in a large bowl and sprinkle the salt all over them, mixing well. Put a small plate over the radishes, place heavy weights on top and leave pressed down overnight.

Drain off the water from the radishes then mix together the vinegar and sugar and pour over the radishes. Cover again with the plate and weights and leave again overnight.

The following day, cook the mangetout in a saucepan of lightly salted boiling water for 2–3 minutes. Drain and rinse under cold running water to prevent further cooking.

Arrange the pickled radish 'flowers' on a plate and surround with the mangetout to resemble 'leaves'. Serve cold.

Tsukune

Sardine Balls

Speared on to bamboo skewers, these sardine balls are very easy for little girls to eat with their fingers. If you find the texture of the mixture too soft to form into balls (which is quite likely if you are using frozen sardines), add 1–2 teaspoons cornflour to thicken the mixture and make it more manageable.

SERVES 4 as an individual dish

450 g (1 lb) sardines, defrosted if frozen
2 spring onions, finely chopped
1 egg
1½ tablespoons sake (rice wine)
½ teaspoon ginger juice (see page 117)
pinch of salt
2 tablespoons vegetable oil
1½ tablespoons soy sauce
1½ tablespoons mirin (sweet rice wine)
10 Japanese bamboo skewers

Scale and gut the sardines and chop off the heads. Using your fingers, remove the bones from the belly. Place the sardines on a board, skin side down. With a sharp pointed knife, separate the meat from the skin. Finely chop the meat, or work in a food processor for a few seconds, then place in a bowl.

Add the spring onions, egg, sake, ginger juice and salt to the sardines, then mix well together. Using your hands, form the mixture into 20 small balls.

Heat the oil in a heavy-based frying pan, add the sardine balls and fry over high heat until golden brown on all sides. Lower the heat, mix together the soy sauce and mirin and pour over the balls. Remove from the heat and cool slightly, then arrange 2 balls on each bamboo skewer. Serve at room temperature.

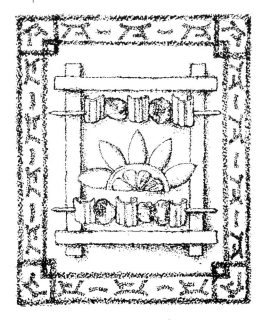

— SOUTH-EAST ASIA —

Each of the countries that make up South-East Asia – Indonesia, Malaysia, Singapore, Thailand, Burma, Cambodia, Laos, Vietnam and the Philippines – is very different in terms of peoples, cultures, religions and traditions. Yet the cuisines are inextricably linked, as rice is the staple food throughout South-East Asia, and most meals are centred around it. Almost every country in South-East Asia has miles of coastline, and the seas of this area yield plentiful supplies of fish, as do the many rivers. Meat plays a less important part, since most of the terrain in this part of the world is not suitable for grazing animals. But, for special occasions, there are many superb meat dishes to be had and both pork and chicken are popular. Fresh fruits and vegetables also play a vital role in the everyday diet.

There are many ingredients which are common to all countries – coconut milk, shrimp paste, fish sauce, chillies, garlic, fresh root ginger, coriander and lemon grass to name but a few. Yet each country has retained its own special culinary identity. To some extent this has been shaped by history, as many of these countries became the home of foreigners and traders who settled in this area; for example the Spanish in the Philippines and the Chinese in Malaysia and Singapore.

Whatever the country, the food of South-East Asia is varied and exciting, and as you become familiar with the cuisine of this area, you will be able to distinguish between the different flavours of individual countries and to enjoy each one in its own right.

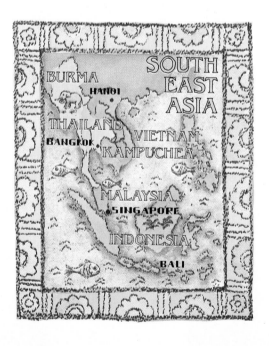

SOUTH-EAST ASIA
INDONESIA

Indonesian food has a strong affinity with that of Malaysia: both countries share a tropical monsoon climate and so are extremely fertile. The cuisine of Indonesia is, however, as diverse as the number of cultures which have come to the islands over the centuries. Buddhists and Hindus from India, Arab and Indian Muslim traders, the Portuguese and the Dutch and last, but not least, the Chinese. Each of these has made their mark, and influenced the cooking throughout the region.

Saté Kambing

Lamb Saté

Ask the butcher not to trim away the fat from the leg of lamb when he is preparing it for you; the fat adds to the flavour and keeps the meat moist during cooking. When the spice mixture for the marinade has been added to the meat, mix well with your fingers to make sure that the pieces of lamb are thoroughly coated. The soy and chilli sauce used here makes a change from the peanut sauce so often associated with saté, and the result is equally delicious.

MAKES 25–30 STICKS

1 kg (2–2¼ lb) boned lamb from the leg
3 garlic cloves, peeled and crushed
4–6 tablespoons kecap manis (sweet soy sauce)
1–2 tablespoons sambal ulek (chilli paste), or 1–2 teaspoons chilli powder
juice of 1 lemon
salt
freshly ground black pepper
peanut or vegetable oil, for brushing
Sauce:
6 garlic cloves, peeled and crushed
6 tablespoons kecap manis (sweet soy sauce)
1½ tablespoons lemon juice
1 tablespoon sambal ulek (chilli paste), or 1 teaspoon chilli powder
To serve:
rings of onion
wedges of cucumber
Lontong/Compressed Rice (page 145)

Cut the lamb into slices, then into neat 1 cm (½ inch) cubes. Do not trim off any fat. Put the garlic in a bowl with the kecap manis, sambal ulek or chilli powder, lemon juice and salt and pepper to taste. Mix them well then put the lamb in a bowl and pour over the chilli marinade. Mix well with your fingers until the lamb is thoroughly coated in the marinade, then cover and leave to marinate in a cool place for 6 hours, turning the lamb in the marinade during this time.

Meanwhile, soak 25–30 bamboo skewers in a bowl of water (so that they do not burn when under the grill or on the barbecue). Put all the ingredients for the sauce in a bowl and stir well to mix. Set aside.

Drain the skewers and thread about 4–5 pieces of meat on to the lower third of each one. Place the skewers on a lightly oiled grill or barbecue rack with the unfilled part away from the heat. Cook for about 5–8 minutes, turning frequently until tender. Arrange the skewers on a serving platter with the onion, cucumber and Lontong. Hand the bowl of sauce separately. Each person takes a few skewers of meat and a little of the sauce for dipping, together with a few onion rings, cucumber wedges and cubes of Lontong.

Krupuk

Prawn Crackers

Indonesian *kroepoek* are similar to the more familiar Krupuk, or prawn crackers, except that they are larger and made from nuts.

SERVES 6–12

vegetable oil, for deep-frying
225 g (8 oz) prawn crackers, or 225 g (8 oz)
large Indonesian kroepoek

Heat the oil in a wok or deep-fat frier to 190°C/375°F. Deep-fry 8–10 prawn crackers at a time, or 2–3 large kroepoek, until they become puffy. Do not allow them to colour. Remove from the oil and drain on paper towels.

Lontong

Compressed Rice

This is the traditional accompaniment to Saté Kambing/Lamb Saté (page 144). In Indonesia, banana leaves are used to wrap the rice.

SERVES 8

two 100 g (4 oz) packets 'boil-in-the-bag' rice
salt

Place the bags of rice in a large saucepan of boiling salted water and cook for 1¼ hours, or until the rice is cooked and fills the bags like a plump cushion. The bags must be covered with water throughout the cooking time, and a saucer or plate may be used to weight them down, if necessary.

Lift the bags out of the water and leave until completely cold. Strip off the plastic bags, cut the rice into neat slices, then cut into diamond shapes or cubes.

Serudeng

Coconut and Peanut Accompaniment

Serudeng is a traditional Indonesian accompaniment. With its crisp texture and nutty flavour, it combines well with most main course and rice dishes. If stored in a cool place, it will keep fresh for up to 1 week.

MAKES ABOUT 350 g (12 oz)

100 g (4 oz) grated fresh coconut
or desiccated coconut
175 g (6 oz) roasted salted peanuts
5 mm (¼ inch) cube terasi (shrimp paste),
dry-fried
1 small onion, peeled and roughly chopped
2–3 garlic cloves, peeled
3 tablespoons peanut or vegetable oil
1 teaspoon coriander seeds, dry-fried
and pounded
½ teaspoon cumin seeds, dry-fried and pounded
½ teaspoon tamarind, soaked in 2 tablespoons
warm water for 10 minutes
1 teaspoon dark brown sugar
salt

Put the coconut in a hot wok or large, heavy-based frying pan and dry-fry over moderate heat, turning all the time until crisp and rich golden in colour. Remove from the pan and leave to cool. Turn half of the coconut into a bowl, add the peanuts and mix together.

Pound the terasi, onion and garlic to a paste in a mortar and pestle, or work in a food processor. Heat the oil in a clean hot wok or heavy-based frying pan. Add the paste, coriander and cumin, strain in the juice from the tamarind, then add the sugar and cook for 2–3 minutes, stirring all the time. Stir in salt to taste and the remaining dry-fried coconut and remove from the heat. Leave until cold, then stir into the peanut and coconut mixture. Cover the bowl if not using immediately.

Nasi Kuning

Turmeric Rice

This festive dish is served with a myriad of accompaniments; prepare them first, so they are ready when the rice is cooked.

SERVES 8

4 tablespoons peanut or vegetable oil
2 medium onions, peeled and thinly sliced
2 garlic cloves, peeled and crushed
450 g (1 lb) long grain rice
1 teaspoon turmeric
300 ml ($\frac{1}{2}$ pint) coconut milk (page 184)
1–2 stems lemon grass, bruised,
or $\frac{1}{2}$–1 teaspoon serai powder
salt
Garnish:
1 chilli flower
Accompaniments:
omelette strips, as in Nasi Goreng/Indonesian
Fried Rice (page 148)
crisp deep-fried onions (page 186)
Serudeng/Coconut and Peanuts (page 145)
Krupuk/Prawn Crackers (page 145)
Rempayak Kacang/Peanut Fritters (page 148)
$\frac{1}{4}$–$\frac{1}{2}$ cucumber, cut into chunks

Heat the oil in a hot wok or large, heavy-based saucepan, add the onions and garlic and fry gently until soft and transparent but not coloured. Stir in the rice and turmeric and turn in the pan to make sure that all the grains are glossy. Add the coconut milk and 900 ml ($1\frac{1}{2}$ pints) cold water, then the lemon grass or serai powder and salt to taste.

Stir well and bring to the boil, then cover and cook over gentle heat for 15–20 minutes, until all the liquid has been absorbed. Remove from the heat and leave to stand in a warm place for 15 minutes.

Turn the rice on to a warmed serving platter and, using oiled hands, form into a mound. Arrange the omelette strips and cucumber chunks attractively around the edge of the platter and top the rice with the chilli flower garnish. Serve with the remaining accompaniments handed separately in individual bowls.

BELOW: *Clockwise from top; Prawn Crackers (page 145), Peanut Fritters (page 148), Coconut and Peanut Accompaniment (page 145), crisp deep-fried onions (page 186) Turmeric Rice. OPPOSITE: Vegetable Salad with Peanut Sauce.*

Gado Gado

Vegetable Salad with Peanut Sauce

The vegetables can be blanched, cooked, or left uncooked, depending on which ingredients are selected. The ingredients can either be arranged in piles on a platter or in layers in a bowl, although the platter makes it easier for guests to select what they like. Using peanut butter for the sauce cuts down on preparation time. *Emping*, crackers made from pounded nuts, may be served as an accompaniment instead of the Krupuk/Prawn Crackers suggested here. They are slightly bitter in flavour and do not swell up quite so much when deep-fried.

SERVES 4

100 g (4 oz) deep-fried bean curd
1 large potato, peeled and boiled
100 g (4 oz) cauliflower
175–225 g (6–8 oz) Chinese leaves
100 g (4 oz) green beans
salt
1–2 carrots
¼ cucumber
100 g (4 oz) bean-sprouts
2 hard-boiled eggs, shelled
Garnish:
crisp deep-fried onions (page 186)
Krupuk/Prawn Crackers (page 145)
Peanut sauce:
175–225 g (6–8 oz) roasted salted peanuts,
or 100 g (4 oz) crunchy peanut butter
1 garlic clove, peeled
1 medium onion, peeled
2–3 fresh red chillies, seeded
3–4 tablespoons peanut or vegetable oil
1 teaspoon tamarind, soaked in 50 ml (2 fl oz)
warm water for 10 minutes
150 ml (¼ pint) coconut milk (page 184)
brown sugar
salt

Pour boiling water over the bean curd and leave for 30 seconds. Drain and leave until cool enough to handle, then squeeze dry in paper towels, to remove any fattiness from the bean curd. Cut each cube into 2–3 slices. Slice or dice the potato. Divide the cauliflower into small florets. Shred the Chinese leaves. Top and tail the green beans.

Bring a large saucepan of salted water to the boil. Add the cauliflower and cook for 2–3 minutes, then remove. Add the Chinese leaves and cook for 30 seconds, then remove. Add the beans and cook for 2–3 minutes, then remove. Lift each batch of vegetables out of the water with a perforated spoon and plunge into a bowl of ice-cold water to prevent further cooking and to keep their colour. Drain and dry each vegetable on paper towels.

Peel the carrots and cut them into matchstick strips. Cut the cucumber into chunks. Remove the brown tails from the bean-sprouts, if liked. Cut each egg into quarters or slices and have the garnishes ready.

Arrange the prepared ingredients attractively in separate piles on a large serving platter, or in layers in a bowl. Cover and set aside while preparing the sauce.

To prepare the sauce: if using peanuts, pound them to a coarse-textured paste in a mortar and pestle, or work in a food processor. Remove and set aside, then pound the garlic, onion and chillies to a paste. Heat the oil in a hot wok or heavy-based saucepan. Add the paste and fry gently without browning, stirring constantly, until it gives off a rich aroma. Strain in the tamarind juice, add the pounded peanuts or peanut butter, then the coconut milk, sugar and salt to taste. Simmer for a few minutes, then pour into a sauceboat.

To serve: uncover the salad platter or bowl and garnish with the crisp deep-fried onions and Krupuk. Serve immediately, with the hot peanut sauce handed separately.

Nasi Goreng | Rempayak Kacang

Indonesian Fried Rice

This is one of the best-known Indonesian recipes, and a marvellous way to use up leftover cooked meat such as beef, pork or chicken.

SERVES 4–6

2 eggs
salt
freshly ground black pepper
8 tablespoons peanut or vegetable oil
3–4 fresh red chillies, seeded
1 cm ($\frac{1}{2}$ inch) cube terasi (shrimp paste), dry-fried
1 medium onion, peeled and roughly chopped
2 garlic cloves, peeled and roughly chopped
225 g (8 oz) pork or beef fillet, cut into strips
100 g (4 oz) peeled cooked prawns
225 g (8 oz) cooked chicken, diced
225 g (8 oz) long grain rice, cooked and cooled
2 tablespoons kecap manis (sweet soy sauce)
Garnish:
crisp deep-fried onions (page 186)
Krupuk/Prawn Crackers (page 145)
fresh coriander leaves

Put the eggs in a bowl with 2 tablespoons water and salt and pepper to taste. Whisk gently to mix. Heat 1–2 drops of the oil in an omelette pan or small, heavy-based frying pan. Make 2–3 omelettes with the whisked eggs. Leave until cold, then roll up each omelette and cut into slices.

Slice 2–3 chillies, finely shred the remainder and reserve for the garnish. Pound the sliced chillies to a fine paste in a mortar and pestle with the terasi, onion and garlic, or work to a paste in a food processor.

Heat the remaining oil in a hot wok or large, heavy-based saucepan. Add the paste and fry gently without browning, stirring constantly, until it gives off a rich aroma. Add the pork or beef and cook for 2 minutes, tossing the meat all the time to seal in the juices. Add the prawns and cook for a further 2 minutes, then add the chicken, rice, kecap manis and salt and pepper to taste. Continue cooking until the chicken and rice are heated through, stirring all the time to prevent sticking. Turn on to a warmed serving platter and garnish with the omelette strips, crisp deep-fried onions, Krupuk, reserved shredded chilli and coriander leaves. Serve immediately.

Peanut Fritters

Brown rice flour, available at health food shops, has a slightly grainy texture, and is ideal for these fritters; white rice flour, which looks like cornflour, is not suitable. Peanut Fritters are traditionally served with Nasi Kuning/Turmeric Rice (page 146), and as part of the Rijsttafel/Rice Table (page 180). They can be made in advance and reheated just before serving – they crisp up beautifully. Lay the fritters on a large baking sheet and reheat, uncovered, in a preheated moderate oven (180°C/350°F, Gas Mark 4) for about 10 minutes.

MAKES 20–25

50 g (2 oz) brown rice flour
$\frac{1}{2}$ teaspoon baking powder
salt
1 garlic clove, peeled and crushed
$\frac{1}{2}$ teaspoon ground coriander
$\frac{1}{2}$ teaspoon turmeric
$\frac{1}{4}$ teaspoon ground cumin
50 g (2 oz) roasted salted peanuts, crushed
about 150 ml ($\frac{1}{4}$ pint) coconut milk (page 184) or water
peanut or vegetable oil, for shallow-frying

Put the rice flour, baking powder and a pinch of salt in a bowl and stir well to mix. Add the garlic, coriander, turmeric and cumin with the peanuts. Gradually add the coconut milk or water and beat with a wooden spoon to make a smooth, slightly runny batter.

Heat the oil in a deep, heavy-based frying pan. Add a few dessertspoonfuls of the batter to make individual fritters, and shallow-fry until they become lacy and begin to look crisp. Turn them over and fry the other side, then remove from the oil with a perforated spoon. Drain well on paper towels while frying the remaining batter in the same way. Serve immediately, or leave to cool and store in an airtight tin.

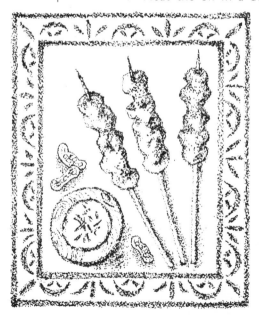

SOUTH-EAST ASIA
MALAYSIA & SINGAPORE

The cuisine of Malaysia is immensely rich and exciting. The Malays themselves are devout Muslims and do not eat pork, but Indian and Chinese settlers have brought their own cooking styles, resulting in a fascinating intermingling of all three cuisines. In Singapore – the culinary melting pot of the East – the cuisine is predominantly Chinese, but includes the Nonya style of cooking, a mixture of Chinese and Malay which uses pork.

Poh Pia

Nonya Spring Rolls

This recipe was created by Malay (Nonya) women for their Chinese husbands.

MAKES 20–24

225 g (8 oz) plain flour
25 g (1 oz) cornflour
salt
6 eggs, beaten
a little vegetable oil, for frying
Cooked filling:
3 tablespoons coconut or vegetable oil
1 onion, peeled and finely chopped
2 garlic cloves, peeled and crushed
100 g (4 oz) cooked pork, chopped
100 g (4 oz) peeled cooked prawns or crab meat
100 g (4 oz) bamboo shoots, drained and chopped
8 water chestnuts, chopped
1–2 tablespoons yellow salted beans, crushed
2 tablespoons light soy sauce
Fresh fillings:
25 g (1 oz) deep-fried bean curd, sliced
2 Chinese sausages, steamed and sliced (optional)
2 hard-boiled eggs, shelled and chopped
175 g (6 oz) peeled cooked prawns or crab meat
100–175 g (4–6 oz) bean-sprouts
½ cucumber, coarsely grated
1 bunch spring onions, chopped
20–24 lettuce leaves, or half this quantity if large
fresh coriander leaves
Sauces:
6 garlic cloves, peeled and pounded
6 fresh red chillies, seeded and pounded
8 tablespoons hoisin (barbecue) sauce

Make the pancakes: sift the plain flour and cornflour into a bowl with a pinch of salt. Add the eggs and whisk in about 450 ml ($\frac{3}{4}$ pint) cold water to make a smooth batter.

Brush the base of an omelette pan or small, heavy-based frying pan with oil and place over moderate heat until hot. Using a measuring jug or ladle, pour in just enough of the batter to cover the base. Cook for 1–2 minutes until set, then turn the pancake over and cook the other side. Transfer to a plate and repeat with the remaining batter to make 20–24 pancakes altogether, adding more oil as necessary. Pile the pancakes on top of each other as they are made, with a sheet of greaseproof paper between each one; wrap the stack loosely in foil.

Prepare the cooked filling: heat the oil in a hot wok or heavy-based saucepan, add the onion and garlic and fry gently without browning. Add the pork, prawns or crab, bamboo shoots and water chestnuts. Toss gently for 2–3 minutes. Add the crushed yellow beans, the soy sauce and salt to taste, then cook for a further 3–5 minutes, adding a little stock or water if the mixture becomes dry. Turn into a bowl, cover and leave to cool.

Make the fresh fillings: arrange the ingredients in separate piles on a large serving platter or in individual bowls. Arrange the lettuce leaves on a separate platter, tearing them in half if they are large. Arrange the coriander leaves with the lettuce. Put the 3 sauces in individual bowls. Cover the platters and bowls to keep the ingredients as fresh as possible.

When ready to serve, reheat the pancakes in the foil parcel in a preheated moderately hot oven (200°C/400°F, Gas Mark 6) for 10 minutes.

Each guest assembles their own Poh Pia by spreading a pancake with the minutest amount of garlic or chilli paste (or both) and a little of the hoisin sauce. This is then topped with a lettuce leaf, a little of the cold cooked filling and a selection of the fresh fillings. The edges of the pancakes should be tucked in, the pancake rolled up and eaten at once. Advise your guests not to overfill their pancakes, or they will not roll up neatly.

Kepiting Pedas

Chilli Crabs

In Kuala Lumpur, these crabs are served in seafood restaurants in a large pot, which is placed steaming hot in the centre of the table for people to help themselves – there are no plates, just warm cloths to wipe the hands and face! Chunks of cucumber are served to help counteract the hotness of the crabs.

SERVES 4–6

2 cooked crabs, each weighing 750 g (1½ lb)
6 fresh red chillies
2.5 cm (1 inch) piece fresh root ginger, peeled and sliced
2–3 garlic cloves, peeled and crushed
6–8 tablespoons coconut or vegetable oil
300 ml (½ pint) tomato ketchup
1½–2 tablespoons brown sugar
salt
1 egg, beaten (optional)
fresh coriander leaves, to garnish
Accompaniments:
1 cucumber, cut into chunks
slices of toast or French bread

Remove the large claws from each crab and crack at the joints. Using a hammer or the end of a rolling pin, crack the broadest part of the claws cleanly, taking care not to splinter the shell. Turn each crab on its back with the tail flap towards you. Tap around the fault line with a hammer, then use the thumbs to push the body out of each shell. Discard the stomach sac and lungs (dead men's fingers).

Leave the creamy brown meat in the shell and break in half. Cut the body in half and crack the smaller claws.

Pound the fresh chillies, ginger and garlic to a fine paste in a mortar and pestle, or work in a food processor. Heat the oil in a hot wok or heavy-based saucepan, add the paste and fry gently without browning until the mixture gives off a spicy aroma. Add the tomato ketchup, brown sugar, 150 ml (¼ pint) boiling water and salt to taste. When the sauce is bubbling, toss in the crabs and stir to coat in the sauce. Add the beaten egg, if liked – it becomes almost scrambled in the sauce. Turn out on to a warmed serving platter and sprinkle with coriander leaves. Serve immediately, with the cucumber and toast or French bread handed separately.

BELOW: *Left, Nonya Spring Rolls (page 149). Right, Chilli Crabs*

Acar

Vegetable Pickle

This popular vegetable pickle, served as an accompaniment to main course dishes, is a distant relation of piccalilli, but without the mustard content. If stored in the refrigerator, Acar will keep for several weeks, although the keeping quality will be improved if the peanuts are not included until the time of serving.

MAKES 1 kg (2–2¼ lb)

100 g (4 oz) whole shelled peanuts,
or roasted salted peanuts
4 shallots or small red-skinned onions, peeled
4 garlic cloves, peeled
4–6 tablespoons coconut or vegetable oil
100 g (4 oz) dried shrimps, pounded (optional)
1½ tablespoons turmeric
300 ml (½ pint) white vinegar
3 tablespoons light brown sugar
salt
750 g (1½ lb) mixed vegetables and fruit, peeled and sliced (e.g. cauliflower, cabbage, cucumber, carrots, green beans, red and green chillies, small onions, mango, pineapple)

If using whole peanuts, spread them out on a baking sheet and roast in a preheated moderately hot oven (200°C/400°F, Gas Mark 6) for 10 minutes. Turn into a clean, dry teatowel, fold into a loose parcel and rub vigorously to remove the skins. Crush lightly in a mortar and pestle and set aside. If using salted peanuts, simply crush them lightly.

Pound the shallots or onions to a fine paste in a mortar and pestle with the garlic cloves, or work in a food processor. Heat the oil in a hot wok or large, heavy-based saucepan, add the spice paste and fry gently without browning until it gives off a spicy aroma. Stir in the dried shrimps (if using) and the turmeric, then pour in the vinegar. Add the sugar and salt to taste, then bring to the boil and simmer for 3–4 minutes. Add the prepared vegetables and fruit, bring back to the boil, then immediately turn off the heat.

Leave the pickle to cool, turning the vegetables and fruit over in the liquid once or twice, to ensure that they become submerged. Stir in the crushed peanuts and transfer to clean glass jars. Cover closely with cling film, then seal with screw-topped lids.

Roti Jala

Coconut Pancakes

These pancakes are traditionally served with Penang Ayam Kapitan/Penang-style Chicken Curry (page 177). If liked, you can make them in advance. Layer them up on a plate with a sheet of greaseproof paper between each one, then wrap in foil. Reheat in the foil in a preheated moderately hot oven (200°C/400°F, Gas Mark 6) for 10 minutes, then fold into quarters.

MAKES 8–10

175 g (6 oz) plain flour
½ teaspoon salt
2 eggs, beaten
300 ml (½ pint) coconut milk (page 184)
a little vegetable oil, for frying

Sift the flour and salt into a bowl. Make a well in the centre and pour in the beaten eggs and a little of the coconut milk. Stir with a wooden spoon, gradually incorporating the flour and adding more coconut milk and about 150 ml (¼ pint) cold water to make a batter.

Brush the base of an omelette pan or small, heavy-based frying pan with oil and place over moderate heat until hot. Using a measuring jug or ladle, pour in just enough of the batter to cover the base. Cook for 1–2 minutes until set, then turn the pancake over and cook the other side. Remove from the pan and fold in half, then fold into quarters. Make 8–10 pancakes altogether, adding more oil as necessary.

Rojak | Mee Rebus

Singapore Chinese Salad

This salad has a very interesting sweet and sour dressing, which can be poured over the salad just before serving, or drizzled over each portion before eating. If liked, you can buy deep-fried bean curd. Prepare according to the instructions on page 147.

SERVES 6–8

100–225 g (4–8 oz) firm bean curd (tofu)
vegetable oil, for deep-frying
$\frac{1}{2}$ bangkwang (Chinese turnip),
or 6–8 water chestnuts
100 g (4 oz) spinach, or other green leaves
175 g (6 oz) bean-sprouts
$\frac{1}{2}$ cucumber
1 onion
1 small pineapple
1 fresh red chilli, seeded and thinly sliced
Sauce:
1 fresh red chilli, seeded
1 cm ($\frac{1}{2}$ inch) cube blachan (shrimp paste), dry-fried
2 teaspoons sambal rojak (soya and shrimp paste)
1 tablespoon dark brown sugar
1 teaspoon dark soy sauce
juice of 1 lime or lemon
1 tablespoon tamarind, soaked in 85 ml (3 fl oz) warm water
50 g (2 oz) roasted salted peanuts, crushed

First prepare the sauce: pound the chilli in a mortar and pestle with the blachan, sambal rojak, sugar, soy sauce and lime or lemon juice. Strain in the tamarind juice and stir in the peanuts. Taste and adjust flavourings, if necessary, then set aside.

Dry the bean curd on paper towels. Heat the oil in a hot wok or deep, heavy-based frying pan. Add the bean curd and fry for 2–3 minutes until golden and crisp. Remove from the oil with a perforated spoon, drain and cut into 4–6 slices. Peel the bangkwang (if using) and cut into bite-sized pieces. If using water chestnuts, slice them thinly.

Place the spinach or other green leaves in a bowl and pour over boiling water. Immediately drain and rinse in cold water, to prevent the leaves from cooking and to retain colour. Remove the brown tails from the bean-sprouts and blanch in the same way as the spinach. Cut the cucumber into small pieces. Peel the onion and slice thinly. Peel the pineapple, cut in half and remove the centre core, then slice the flesh.

Arrange the vegetables and fruit in a salad bowl, then sprinkle the sliced chilli over the top. Drizzle over the sauce and serve immediately, or hand the sauce separately in a small bowl.

Noodles with Beef and Spicy Sauce

This unusual-textured dish is made by shredding a piece of tender cooked beef, then adding it to a rich, spicy sauce. It is a perfect lunch dish.

SERVES 8

450 g (1 lb) topside of beef
1 small onion, peeled
2 celery sticks, chopped, with leaves reserved
salt
4–6 fresh red chillies, seeded,
or 1 teaspoon chilli powder
75 g (3 oz) shallots, peeled and roughly chopped
2.5 cm (1 inch) lengkuas (laos root),
or 2 teaspoons laos powder
2 garlic cloves, peeled and roughly chopped
25 g (1 oz) dried shrimps
1 teaspoon turmeric
3–4 tablespoons yellow salted beans, crushed
1 sweet potato, peeled, boiled and mashed
fresh coriander leaves, to garnish
Accompaniments:
225 g (8 oz) bean-sprouts, brown tails removed
2 limes, cut into wedges
2 hard-boiled eggs, shelled and cut into wedges
crisp deep-fried onions (page 186)
750 g ($1\frac{1}{2}$ lb) mee (egg noodles), cooked

Put the beef in a large saucepan with the onion, chopped celery and salt to taste. Cover with cold water and bring to the boil. Skim, then cover and cook for 1 hour, or until the meat is tender. Remove the meat from the cooking liquid and dice coarsely, using a food processor if available. Strain the stock and reserve 750 ml ($1\frac{1}{4}$ pints).

Pound the chillies or chilli powder to a paste in a mortar and pestle with the shallots, lengkuas or laos powder, garlic, dried shrimps and turmeric, or work in a food processor. Heat the oil in a hot wok or heavy-based saucepan, add the paste and fry gently without browning until the mixture gives off a spicy aroma. Add the salted beans and cook for 2 minutes, then add the sweet potato and beef. Pour in enough reserved stock to make a sauce. Cook for 2–3 minutes, then remove from the heat.

Prepare the accompaniments: plunge the bean-sprouts into a large saucepan of boiling water. Blanch for 30 seconds, drain, then toss into ice-cold water and drain again. Put the lime and egg wedges and the deep-fried onions in separate serving bowls.

To serve: place a helping of bean-sprouts and noodles in individual bowls. Reheat the meat sauce and pour into the bowls. Garnish with coriander leaves and the reserved leaves from the celery. Serve immediately, with the accompaniments handed separately for guests to help themselves.

Ikan Moolie

Fish in Coconut Milk with Chillies

This is a delicious fish curry to which coconut milk is added to make a rich, creamy sauce. Boiled rice is the usual accompaniment.

SERVES 4–6

750 g (1½ lb) firm white fish fillets (e.g. monkfish, halibut or thick end of haddock)
salt
75 g (3 oz) shallots or small red-skinned onions, peeled
6 macadamia nuts
3 garlic cloves, peeled
2 stems lemon grass, or 1 teaspoon serai powder
2.5 cm (1 inch) fresh root ginger, peeled and bruised
6 tablespoons coconut or vegetable oil
1 tablespoon turmeric
just over 600 ml (1 pint) coconut milk (page 184)
50 g (2 oz) desiccated coconut, dry-fried and pounded to a paste
3 fresh red chillies, seeded and shredded

Skin the fish, then cut the flesh into 2.5 cm (1 inch) cubes and place in a bowl. Sprinkle with a little salt and set aside. Put the shallots or onions in a hot wok or heavy-based saucepan with the macadamia nuts, garlic, lemon grass (if using) and ginger. Dry-fry for a few minutes, stirring constantly, to bring out the flavour, then transfer to a mortar and pestle and pound to a paste. Alternatively, work in a food processor.

Heat the oil in the wok or saucepan, add the paste and fry gently without browning until the mixture gives off a spicy aroma. Add the turmeric and serai powder (if using).

Spoon off the cream which has risen to the top of the coconut milk and reserve. Add the coconut milk to the spices in the pan. Bring just to the boil, then add the cubes of fish and cook gently for 3–4 minutes only.

Mix the coconut paste in a bowl with the reserved coconut cream, then blend in a little of the hot cooking liquid. Stir this mixture back into the pan, cook for a further minute, then taste and add salt if necessary. Add the shredded red chillies and serve immediately.

Dangang Semur

Malay Beef Stew

Marinating beef in spices and two different kinds of soy sauce gives this stew a wonderful richness, both in colour and flavour. The addition of potato helps thicken the stew – you could use sweet potato if you prefer. Freshly boiled rice is the usual accompaniment.

SERVES 8

1.5 kg (3 lb) best stewing steak
2 teaspoons black peppercorns, lightly crushed
3 tablespoons vinegar
3 tablespoons light soy sauce
1½ tablespoons dark soy sauce
8 tablespoons coconut or vegetable oil
450 g (1 lb) medium onions, peeled and thinly sliced
3 garlic cloves, peeled and crushed
4 cardamom pods, bruised
4 cloves
5 cm (2 inch) cinnamon stick
½ teaspoon grated nutmeg
450 ml (¾ pint) beef stock or water
500 g (1¼ lb) large potatoes, peeled and cubed
salt

Cut the meat into 4 cm (1½ inch) pieces, trimming off any gristle and excess fat. Place the pieces in a bowl with the peppercorns, vinegar and the soy sauces. Leave to marinate for 1 hour.

Heat the oil in a hot wok or large, heavy-based saucepan, add the onions and garlic and fry gently over a low heat until soft and transparent, but not brown.

Add the beef to the pan, reserving the marinade. Fry the beef on all sides to seal in the juices, then add the bruised cardamom pods, the cloves, cinnamon and nutmeg. Pour in the reserved marinade and the stock or water and bring to the boil. Cover and simmer for 1¼–1½ hours or until the beef is tender. Add the potatoes and salt to taste and cook for a further 30 minutes, or until the potatoes are tender. Serve hot.

Pisang Goreng

Banana Fritters

If possible, buy very small bananas for these fritters; they look better than the large ones, and are usually sweeter in flavour.

SERVES 8

100 g (4 oz) self-raising flour
40 g (1½ oz) rice flour
½ teaspoon salt
finely grated rind of 1 lime (optional)
vegetable oil, for deep-frying
8 small bananas
To serve:
2 limes, cut into quarters
caster sugar, to taste

Sift the flours and salt into a bowl. Add about 200 ml (7 fl oz) cold water to make a smooth, coating batter, then stir in the grated lime rind (if using).

Heat the oil in a hot wok or deep-fat frier. Meanwhile, peel the bananas, spear them one at a time with a skewer and dip into the batter until evenly coated. Deep-fry the bananas in batches in the hot oil until they are crisp and golden. Remove with a perforated spoon and drain on paper towels. Serve hot, with the lime wedges and sugar for sprinkling.

Bubor Pulot Hitam

Black Glutinous Rice Pudding

Black glutinous rice still retains its husk and has a nutty texture, while the coconut topping provides a creamy contrast.

SERVES 6

100 g (4 oz) black glutinous rice
1 cm (½ inch) fresh root ginger, peeled and bruised
50 g (2 oz) dark brown sugar
50 g (2 oz) granulated sugar
300 ml (½ pint) coconut milk or cream (page 184)

Wash the rice and place in a large saucepan with 450 ml (¾ pint) water. Bring to the boil, cover and cook gently for 30 minutes. Add the ginger and sugars and cook for a further 15 minutes, until the rice has the consistency of porridge, adding a little more water if necessary.

Serve warm in individual bowls, topped with coconut milk or cream.

BELOW: Right, Black Glutinous Rice Pudding served with coconut cream. Left, Banana Fritters.

SOUTH-EAST ASIA
THAILAND

The cooking of Thailand is unique, as it is the only country in
South-East Asia which has never been colonized, therefore outside influences
have hardly affected the local cuisine. Infinite care and skill is
taken in the preparation of food, which should please the eye and the nose as well
as the tastebuds, although specific quantities of ingredients are rarely adhered
to. The 'uniqueness' of Thai food lies in the predominant flavours of hot
chillies, garlic, shrimp paste, lemon grass, fresh coriander, laos root and,
most important, fish sauce.

Tom Yam Kung

Prawn Soup

This hot and sour clear broth is eaten
throughout the meal in Thailand. If you prefer,
you can use 225 g (8 oz) peeled cooked prawns
and make the fish stock with fish bones, water,
1 small onion and 2.5 cm (1 inch) piece fresh
root ginger, peeled and bruised. Bring to the
boil, skim and simmer for 20 minutes only.

SERVES 8

450 g (1 lb) headless uncooked prawns
1 tablespoon vegetable oil
2 stems lemon grass, bruised, or 2 teaspoons
serai powder
3 citrus leaves, torn (optional)
1–2 fresh chillies, halved lengthways and seeded
1 tablespoon fish sauce, or to taste
juice of 2 lemons or limes, or to taste
fresh coriander leaves, to garnish

Peel and rinse the prawns, reserving the shells. Heat the
oil in a large saucepan, add the shells and fry until they
turn pink. Stir in 1.75 litres (3 pints) cold water, the
lemon grass or serai powder, the citrus leaves (if using)
and the chillies. Bring to the boil and simmer for 15
minutes, then remove from the heat and leave to cool.

Strain the stock into a clean saucepan and bring to the
boil. Add the prawns and simmer for 3 minutes, then add
the fish sauce and lemon or lime juice. Serve hot,
sprinkled with coriander leaves.

Sawn Tham

Thai-style Salad
This is a typical Thai salad, combining sharp,
sweet and fish flavours, the latter being enhanced
by the lemon or lime juice in the dressing.

SERVES 8

225 g (8 oz) green beans, topped and tailed and
cut into 2.5 cm (1 inch) pieces
salt
225 g (8 oz) white cabbage, finely shredded
2 tomatoes, skinned, seeded and diced
100 g (4 oz) peeled cooked prawns
1 papaya, peeled, seeded and diced
50 g (2 oz) roasted salted peanuts, crushed
1–2 fresh red chillies, seeded and shredded
a few lettuce or spinach leaves
fresh coriander leaves, to garnish
Dressing:
4 tablespoons lemon or lime juice
2 tablespoons fish sauce
sugar, to taste

Boil the beans in salted water for 3 minutes, then drain
and cool. Toss in a bowl with the cabbage, tomatoes,
prawns and most of the papaya, peanuts and chillies.

Line a serving platter with lettuce or spinach leaves
and pile the salad in the centre. Mix together the
ingredients for the dressing, adding sugar to taste, then
pour over the salad. Garnish with coriander leaves and
the remaining papaya, peanuts and chillies. Serve
immediately.

Mee Krob | Nam Prik

Fried Noodles

Do not be tempted to fry too many of the rice noodles at once, or you will not be able to remove them from the pan as they puff up.

SERVES 6–8

vegetable oil, for frying
1 large onion, peeled and finely chopped
3 garlic cloves, peeled and crushed
100–175 g (4–6 oz) boneless chicken breast,
skinned and finely sliced
225 g (8 oz) pork fillet, thinly sliced
100 g (4 oz) firm bean curd (tofu), cubed
2–3 tablespoons salted yellow beans
100 g (4 oz) peeled cooked prawns
3 eggs, beaten
2–3 tablespoons rice or cider vinegar
3–4 tablespoons caster sugar
1–2 tablespoons fish sauce
225 g (8 oz) lai fan (rice vermicelli)
a little chilli powder, to taste
Garnish:
100 g (4 oz) bean-sprouts
2 fresh red chillies, seeded and shredded
1 strip of lime rind, finely shredded
½ bunch spring onions, trimmed and shredded
fresh coriander leaves
1 red chilli flower

Heat 6 tablespoons oil in a hot wok or large, heavy-based saucepan, add the onion and garlic and fry gently for 4–5 minutes until soft. Add the chicken and pork and fry over fairly high heat for 2–3 minutes, tossing the ingredients all the time. Add the bean curd, then the salted beans, which may be crushed lightly first to release their flavour. Add the prawns and beaten eggs, turning the mixture all the time and adding 1–2 more tablespoons of oil if necessary. Stir in the vinegar, sugar and fish sauce to taste – the flavour should be sweet, sharp and salty. Transfer the mixture to a bowl.

Clean the wok or pan, then pour in enough oil for deep-frying and heat to 190°C (375°F). Deep-fry the lai fan a handful at a time straight from the packet, removing them from the oil as they puff up – do not allow them to colour. Remove from the oil and drain on paper towels while frying the remainder.

When ready to serve, put half of the savoury mixture in a clean hot wok or pan with a little chilli powder and half of the lai fan. Toss together over high heat, then turn on to a warmed serving platter. Repeat with the remaining savoury mixture, lai fan and chilli powder. Garnish attractively with the bean-sprouts, shredded chillies, lime rind, spring onions and coriander. Top with the chilli flower and serve.

Crudités with Thai Shrimp Sauce

Thai shrimp, or Nam Prik, sauce is served in every Thai house at every meal, and each family will have their own favourite recipe. To make it even more potent, crushed dried chillies (with or without a few seeds) may be added, but try the following recipe first.

Nam Prik sauce is best made a day ahead of serving, and will keep for several weeks in the refrigerator if stored in an airtight jar.

Hard-boiled quail's eggs are often added to the platter of fruit and vegetables and they make a most attractive garnish.

SERVES 6

750 g (1½ lb) prepared raw fruit and vegetables
(e.g. celery, cucumber, green and red peppers,
pineapple, green apples, broccoli, cauliflower)
fresh coriander leaves, to garnish
Sauce:
1 cm (½ inch) cube kapi (shrimp paste), dry-fried
50 g (2 oz) whole dried shrimps, soaked in warm
water for 10 minutes and drained
3 garlic cloves, peeled and roughly chopped
4–6 fresh red chillies, seeded and
roughly chopped
6 stems fresh coriander
fish sauce, to taste
brown sugar, to taste
juice of 1–2 lemons or limes, to taste

Make the sauce: pound the kapi to a paste in a mortar and pestle with the drained shrimps and the chopped garlic. Add the chopped chillies and pound again, then repeat with the coriander stems. (A food processor can be used instead of a mortar and pestle, but do not blend too smooth.)

Turn the mixture into a serving bowl and add the fish sauce, brown sugar and lemon or lime juice to taste. Cover the bowl closely with cling film, then chill in the refrigerator until required, preferably for 24 hours.

To serve: arrange the fruit and vegetables on a large serving platter and garnish with coriander leaves. Hand the sauce separately in the serving bowl, for guests to help themselves.

Kaeng Mus Sa Man

Muslim Beef Curry

This is a famous Thai Muslim curry. Cubes of fresh pineapple or daikon can be substituted for the potato; they should be added to the curry when the onions are half cooked.

SERVES 8

1 kg (2–2¼ lb) best stewing steak
1 litre (1¾ pints) coconut milk (page 184)
9–12 tablespoons vegetable oil
2 large potatoes, peeled and diced
450 g (1 lb) shallots, peeled
4–6 tablespoons Mus Sa Man/Red Curry Paste (right)
2 tablespoons tamarind, soaked in 200 ml (7 fl oz) warm water for 10 minutes
25–50 g (1–2 oz) dark brown sugar
Garnish:
1 fresh red chilli, seeded
fresh coriander leaves
25 g (1 oz) roasted salted peanuts, crushed

Cut the meat into 4 cm (1½ inch) pieces, trimming off any gristle and fat. Spoon off the cream which has risen to the top of the coconut milk and reserve. Heat 6–8 table-spoons of the oil in a hot wok or large, heavy-based saucepan, add the meat and fry quickly until browned on all sides. Pour the coconut milk over the beef and cook for 1 hour, or until the meat is tender.

Meanwhile, heat the remaining 3–4 tablespoons oil in a separate pan, add the potatoes and shallots and fry until just golden. Lift out with a perforated spoon and reserve. Add 150 ml (¼ pint) of the cooking liquid from the meat to the pan with the curry paste. Cook over high heat for 2–3 minutes, stirring all the time to bring out the full flavour of the spices. Slowly stir in the remaining cooking liquid, then add the meat and return the potatoes and onions to the pan. Strain in the tamarind juice, then add sugar to taste. Simmer for 15–20 minutes, or until the vegetables are tender. Pour in the reserved coconut cream and stir until it comes to the boil. Transfer to a warmed large serving bowl and garnish with the chilli, coriander leaves and crushed peanuts. Serve immediately.

Mus Sa Man

Red Curry Paste

This paste will keep in a tightly covered glass jar in the refrigerator for 2–3 weeks, or in a sealed container in the freezer for 3 months.

MAKES 8–12 TABLESPOONS

1 tablespoon coriander seeds
1 tablespoon cumin seeds
3 cardamom pods, bruised
½ teaspoon ground mace
½ teaspoon grated nutmeg
½ teaspoon ground cloves
½ teaspoon ground cinnamon
6–8 tablespoons vegetable oil
12 shallots, or 2 onions, peeled and chopped
6 garlic cloves, peeled
10 fresh red chillies, seeded, or 1 tablespoon chilli powder
6 stems coriander
2 stems lemon grass, or 1 teaspoon serai powder
1 cm (½ inch) lengkuas (laos root), or 1 teaspoon laos powder
1 teaspoon finely grated magrut, lime or grapefruit rind
1 cm (½ inch) cube kapi (shrimp paste), dry-fried
salt

Put the coriander and cumin seeds and the bruised cardamom pods in a heavy-based frying pan. Dry-fry over gentle heat until they give off a rich aroma, moving the spices in the pan all the time. Remove the seeds from the cardamom pods and pound in a mortar and pestle with the coriander and cumin. Add the mace, nutmeg, cloves and cinnamon, stir well to mix and set the mixture aside.

Heat the oil in the pan, add the chopped shallots or onions, garlic, fresh chillies, coriander stems, lemon grass and lengkuas (if using). Fry over moderate heat for 3–4 minutes, tossing frequently, then pound to a fine paste in a mortar and pestle, or work in a food processor. Add the magrut, lime or grapefruit rind, the kapi and about 1 tablespoon salt, or to taste. Work again, then add the spice mixture and the chilli, serai and laos powders (if using). Work again until evenly mixed.

Tom Kha Kai

ABOVE: *Chicken in Coconut Milk, served with boiled rice*

Chicken in Coconut Milk

The subtle blend of flavours in this dish is in marked contrast to the Kaeng Mus Sa Man/Muslim Beef Curry (page 157). For a party of 8 people, serve both dishes to accommodate the tastes of all your guests. Steamed or boiled rice is the ideal accompaniment.

SERVES 4

1.5 kg (3–3½ lb) chicken, cut into 8 pieces
900 ml (1½ pints) coconut milk (page 184)
5 cm (2 inch) piece lengkuas (laos root), or 4 teaspoons laos powder
3 fresh green chillies, seeded
8 stems coriander
4 citrus leaves (optional)
a few black peppercorns, crushed
1 teaspoon finely grated magrut, lime or grapefruit rind
salt
2 tablespoons fish sauce
1 tablespoon magrut, lime or grapefruit juice
fresh coriander leaves, to garnish

Skin the chicken and place in a wok or heavy-based saucepan. Spoon off about 150 ml (¼ pint) of the cream which has risen to the top of the coconut milk and reserve. Pour the remaining coconut milk over the chicken in the pan.

Using a knife or a food processor, finely chop the lengkuas (if using) with the chillies and coriander stems. Add to the pan with the laos powder and citrus leaves (if using), the crushed peppercorns, grated magrut, lime or grapefruit rind and salt to taste. Bring to the boil, then reduce the heat and simmer, uncovered, for 35–40 minutes, or until the chicken is tender and about half of the liquid has evaporated.

About 5 minutes before serving, pour in the reserved coconut cream and stir until it comes to the boil. Add the fish sauce and magrut, lime or grapefruit juice. Transfer to a warmed large serving bowl, sprinkle with coriander leaves and serve immediately.

SOUTH-EAST ASIA
INDO-CHINA

The three countries that make up Indo-China retain their separate identities in their cuisines. The cooking of *Cambodia* has many similarities to that of Thailand and Laos. Herbs and spices are used freely to provide rich, full flavours, most meals are centred around rice and fish, vegetables and fruit, and precise amounts of ingredients are seldom used. In *Laos*, a landlocked country, sea fish is not so prolific as in Cambodia. However, freshwater fish are plentiful enough and together with meat and top-quality fruit and vegetables, it makes a varied, though simple, diet. The interesting feature of the Laotian cuisine is a great love of glutinous rice – in Laos it is eaten with every meal. The cooking of *Vietnam* is closely linked to that of China, especially in the north where the two countries share a border, but this is not to say that Vietnam does not have a cuisine with its own character. The Vietnamese use fish sauce as extensively as the Chinese use soy sauce, and in central and southern Vietnam, the food is more heavily spiced.

Canh Cua

Crab Soup/Vietnam

It is important to use a well-flavoured homemade chicken stock for this soup. In this recipe, the stock is given extra flavour by the addition of Chinese dried mushrooms.

SERVES 8–10

1 kg (2–2¼ lb) cooked crab
2 litres (3½ pints) well-flavoured chicken stock, strained
3 Chinese dried mushrooms, soaked in warm water for 20 minutes
225 g (8 oz) fresh spinach or other green leaves
2–3 tablespoons vegetable oil
1 moolie (Japanese radish), peeled and coarsely grated
1 piece canned bamboo shoot, cut into fine strips
1 tablespoon cornflour
2 egg whites
salt
Garnish:
3–4 spring onions, finely shredded
sprigs of fresh coriander

Remove the large claws from the crab and crack at the joints. Using a hammer or the end of a rolling pin, crack the broadest part of the claws cleanly and remove the flesh, taking care not to splinter the shell. Put the flesh in a bowl. Turn the crab on its back with its head furthest away from you. Tap round the fault line with a hammer, then use the thumbs to push the body out of the main shell. Discard the stomach sac and lungs (dead men's fingers). Cut the body in half. With a skewer, pick out all the white flesh, then remove the brown meat. Add to the bowl of flesh from the large claws. Crack the smaller claws, remove the flesh and add to the bowl. Set aside while making the soup.

Skim any excess fat off the chicken stock. Drain and slice the mushrooms. Finely shred the spinach or other green leaves, with the stems, into 5 cm (2 inch) lengths. Heat the oil in a hot wok or large, heavy-based saucepan. Toss in the grated moolie, strips of bamboo shoot and sliced mushrooms. Pour in the stock and bring to the boil, then simmer, uncovered, for 5–10 minutes.

Just before serving, mix the cornflour to a smooth paste with a little cold water. Stir into the soup to thicken it a little, then add the shredded leaves and stems. Cook for a further minute. Add the crab meat to the soup, then whisk in the egg whites to form white threads. Taste and add salt if necessary. Serve hot in individual bowls, garnished with shredded spring onions and the sprigs of coriander.

Cha Gio

Crab Rolls/Vietnam

To serve Cha Gio, each guest takes a piece of lettuce, mint and coriander, places a crab roll on top, then wraps the lettuce around it. This 'parcel' is then dipped in a little of the sauce on the side of the plate.

MAKES ABOUT 18

18 rice paper wrappers, measuring 21 cm
(8½ inches) in diameter
soy sauce
1 egg, beaten
vegetable oil, for deep-frying
Filling:
10 dried wood ears (black fungus), soaked in
warm water for 25 minutes
25 g (1 oz) mien (cellophane noodles), soaked in
warm water for 5 minutes
225 g (8 oz) lean belly pork, minced
225 g (8 oz) cooked crab meat, shredded, or
peeled cooked prawns, coarsely chopped
3 spring onions, finely chopped
2 teaspoons fish sauce
1 teaspoon brown sugar
salt
freshly ground black pepper
1 egg, beaten
Dipping Sauce:
2–3 fresh red chillies, seeded
2 garlic cloves, peeled and crushed
1 tablespoon brown sugar
about 3 tablespoons fish sauce
about 2 tablespoons lime or lemon juice
1 carrot, peeled and grated or cut into
julienne strips
To serve:
crisp lettuce leaves
mint leaves
coriander leaves

First make the filling: drain the soaked wood ears and chop finely, then place in a bowl. Drain the noodles and, using kitchen scissors, snip them in 2.5 cm (1 inch) lengths into the bowl. Add the pork with the shredded crab or chopped prawns and mix well. Stir in the spring onions, fish sauce, sugar and salt and pepper to taste. Bind with the beaten egg.

Spread 2 damp teatowels out on a flat work surface. Place 2 of the brittle rice paper wrappers on each tea-towel. Mix 3 tablespoons soy sauce with 1 tablespoon cold water, then brush the wrappers lightly on each side. After a few minutes, they will become soft.

Spoon a little of the filling on 1 of the wrappers, placing it just off centre, towards the edge which is nearest to you. Fold the wrapper over the filling, working away from you, then roll once. Brush the ends of the roll and the round part of the wrapper with the beaten egg. Fold the ends in towards the centre just a little, then continue to roll up. Repeat with the remaining 3 softened wrappers and more filling. Spread more brittle wrappers out on the damp teatowels and brush with the soy sauce and water mixture, making up more if necessary. Continue until all the wrappers and filling are used.

If the Cha Gio are not to be cooked immediately, arrange them in a single layer on a tray (do not stack them up as this will spoil their shape and they may stick together). Cover with a clean, dry cloth and leave in a cool place; they will keep for several hours.

To prepare the sauce: pound the chillies, garlic and sugar in a mortar and pestle, or work in a food processor. Add the fish sauce and lime or lemon juice to taste, and a little water if the sauce seems too strong in flavour. Transfer to small serving bowls and sprinkle with the carrot. Set aside in a cool place.

When ready to cook, brush the wrappers with a little soy sauce if a deeper golden-brown colour is required. Heat the oil in a wok or deep-fat frier and deep-fry 4–5 rolls at a time, for about 8 minutes. Drain on paper towels while frying the remainder.

To serve: arrange the lettuce, mint and coriander leaves on 1 serving platter and the crab rolls on another. Hand the bowls of dipping sauce round separately.

Xoi

Festive Glutinous Rice/Vietnam

The cooking time for the rice will vary according to the exact length of the soaking time. Test a few grains of rice after 30 minutes in the steamer; if the rice has been soaked for a full 12 hours, it may well be tender at this stage.

SERVES 8

450 g (1 lb) white glutinous rice
225 g (8 oz) black glutinous rice
6–8 tablespoons vegetable oil
1 tablespoon soy sauce

Soak the white and black rice in separate bowls of cold water overnight. Drain and rinse well. Heat the oil in a hot wok or large, heavy-based saucepan, add the rice and toss together for a few minutes until the grains are thoroughly coated with oil. Sprinkle over the soy sauce and remove from the heat.

Turn the rice into a muslin-lined steamer and cover with a lid. Steam for 10 minutes, then make several 'steam' holes in the rice with the handle of a wooden spoon. Cover again and steam for 30–50 minutes, or until al dente (tender but firm to the bite). Serve hot.

Phlea Sach Ko | Ca Hap

Beef and Vegetable Salad/Cambodia

Do not omit the tripe from this dish as it combines well with the other ingredients.

SERVES 6

225 g (8 oz) rump steak, cut into thin slices
150 ml (¼ pint) wine or cider vinegar
225 g (8 oz) tripe
450 ml (¾ pint) milk and water mixed
½ moolie (Japanese radish), peeled and cut into julienne strips
100 g (4 oz) bean-sprouts, brown tails removed
2 stems lemon grass, thinly sliced
I red pepper, seeded and cut into thin strips
I small onion, peeled and sliced
few leaves crisp lettuce, shredded
Sauce:
3 garlic cloves, unpeeled
3 shallots, unpeeled
I cm (½ inch) lengkuas (laos root), or I teaspoon laos powder
6–8 coriander stems, with leaves reserved
I–2 tablespoons fish sauce
brown sugar
lime juice
175 g (6 oz) roasted salted peanuts, crushed

Place the beef in a shallow dish; cover with the vinegar. Marinate for 30 minutes then squeeze the meat and reserve the marinade. Cook the tripe in the milk and water for 45 minutes. Drain and cut into thin slices.

Make the sauce: grill the garlic, shallots and lengkuas (if using). Cool, then peel. Pound the coriander stems, garlic, shallots, lengkuas or laos powder in a mortar and pestle. Mix the reserved marinade and the pounded mixture and heat for 2 minutes. Add the fish sauce and sugar, lime juice and salt to taste. Stir in most of the peanuts, then thin down with a little water.

Mix the beef and tripe with the moolie, bean-sprouts and lemon grass. Season to taste, then arrange on a platter. Sprinkle with the remaining peanuts, the red pepper and onion. Arrange the lettuce around the edge with the reserved coriander leaves. Serve immediately, with the sauce handed separately.

Steamed Grey Mullet with Stuffing/Vietnam

Cut the mullet into thin portions when serving, and hand round a bowl of Xoi/Festive Glutinous Rice (page 160) for guests to help themselves.

SERVES 4

1 kg (2–2¼ lb) grey mullet, scaled, gutted and central spine removed – head and tail left on
Stuffing:
3 dried wood ears (black fungus), soaked in warm water for 15 minutes
15 g (½ oz) mien (cellophane noodles), soaked in warm water for 5 minutes
50 g (2 oz) belly pork, minced
I garlic clove, peeled and crushed
I cm (½ inch) piece fresh root ginger, peeled and finely grated
50–75 g (2–3 oz) cooked crab meat, or peeled cooked prawns
I spring onion, chopped
I teaspoon cornflour
I egg white
I teaspoon fish sauce
2 teaspoons rice wine
salt
freshly ground black pepper
Garnish:
I red chilli flower
fresh coriander leaves

Make the stuffing: drain the soaked wood ears, chop finely, then place in a bowl. Drain the noodles and, using kitchen scissors, snip them in I cm (½ inch) lengths into the bowl. Add the pork, garlic, ginger, crab meat or prawns, spring onion, cornflour, egg white, fish sauce, rice wine and salt and pepper to taste. Mix well, then fill the cavity of the fish.

Lay the fish on a serving plate suitable for steaming (there is no need to sew or skewer the fish). Place in a bamboo steamer over a wok and steam for 35–45 minutes, or until the fish is cooked through. But do not overcook. Serve immediately, garnished with spring onions, a chilli flower and coriander leaves.

Kari Bangkang

Prawn Curry/Cambodia

Salting the cucumber strips is an essential stage of the method because it draws out excess moisture. If the cucumber is not salted, it will dilute the coconut sauce, making it thin and watery and lacking in flavour.

SERVES 2–3

1 cucumber
salt
1 garlic clove, peeled
1 small onion, peeled and sliced
1 stem lemon grass, or 1 teaspoon serai powder
1 tablespoon ground coriander
1 teaspoon turmeric
1 teaspoon chilli powder
3–4 tablespoons vegetable oil
450 ml (¾ pint) coconut milk (page 184)
1 teaspoon brown sugar
fish sauce
lime or lemon juice
225 g (8 oz) peeled cooked prawns
fresh coriander leaves, to garnish

Cut the cucumber into matchstick strips and place on a plate. Sprinkle with salt, leave for 15 minutes, then transfer to a colander and rinse thoroughly under cold running water. Drain on paper towels.

Pound the garlic and onion to a paste in a mortar and pestle with the lower stem of the lemon grass (if using), or work in a food processor. Add the coriander, turmeric, chilli powder and serai powder (if using). Mix well until the spices are evenly blended.

Heat the oil in a hot wok or large heavy-based saucepan. Add the paste and fry gently without browning, stirring constantly, until it gives off a spicy aroma. Add the coconut milk, sugar, fish sauce and lime or lemon juice to taste. Bring to the boil, simmer for 5 minutes, then add the cucumber and prawns. Simmer for a further 5 minutes, or until the cucumber is just tender. Transfer to a warmed serving dish and sprinkle with coriander leaves. Serve hot.

BELOW: *Top, Festive Glutinous Rice (page 160). Centre, Steamed Grey Mullet with Stuffing (page 161). Bottom, Prawn Curry.* OPPOSITE: *Turkey Soup, Turkey with Rice and Hot Dipping Sauce.*

Keng Som, Lap, Tcheo

Turkey Soup, Turkey with Rice and Hot Dipping Sauce/Laos

These three dishes are served together as a celebration meal in Laos, on very special occasions such as weddings and birthdays. All three dishes are placed on the table at the same time, together with a platter of vegetables such as carrots, cucumber, cauliflower, green and red peppers, tomatoes, radishes and celery. Everyone helps themselves, drinking the soup throughout the meal and dipping the vegetables into the hot sauce.

SERVES 8

2.25 kg (5–5¼ lb) turkey or chicken
Keng Som:
6 spring onions
salt
freshly ground black pepper
2 tablespoons tamarind, soaked in 300 ml
(½ pint) warm water for 10 minutes
3 green or unripe tomatoes, chopped
1 stem lemon grass, bruised,
or 1 teaspoon serai powder
2–3 tablespoons fish sauce, to taste
a little brown sugar
Lap:
100 g (4 oz) white glutinous rice
4 tablespoons vegetable oil
juice of 1 large lemon
2–3 tablespoons bagoong (shrimp paste)
4–8 dried red chillies, pounded
of 1–1½ tablespoons chilli powder
1 stem lemon grass, bruised,
or 1 teaspoon serai powder
1 cm (½ inch) lengkuas (laos root),
or 1 teaspoon laos powder
1 small onion, peeled and finely chopped
2 tablespoons fish sauce
a little sugar
Tcheo:
6 fresh red or green chillies, seeded
2 garlic cloves, peeled
about 2 tablespoons fish sauce, to taste
2 tablespoons chopped coriander

First make the Keng Som: slit the skin of the bird in several places with a sharp knife or kitchen scissors, then slip the hand underneath, remove the skin and reserve. Cut away the flesh from the bones and reserve for the Lap. Wash the giblets. Place the skin, bones and giblets in a large saucepan. Add 2 litres (3½ pints) cold water and the bulb part of the spring onions, reserving the tops for the garnish. Bring to the boil, skim, bring to the boil again, then add salt and pepper to taste. Reduce the heat and simmer for 45 minutes. Lift out the skin, bones and giblets. Discard the skin and bones, and slice the liver and gizzard finely and reserve.

Strain in the tamarind juice, then add the tomatoes and lemon grass or serai powder. Bring to the boil and simmer for a further 30 minutes. Just before serving, add the reserved sliced liver and gizzard, the fish sauce and sugar. Taste and adjust seasoning, then skim. Transfer to a serving bowl and garnish with the reserved spring onion tops, shredded.

Make the Lap: dry-fry the glutinous rice in a hot wok or large, heavy-based frying pan, stirring all the time until it becomes golden. Transfer to a mortar and pestle and pound until fine-textured, or work in a food processor. Mince the reserved turkey or chicken flesh, or chop in a food processor.

Heat the oil in a hot wok or heavy-based saucepan. Add the meat and fry, stirring all the time, until it begins to change colour. Add the lemon juice, bagoong, chillies or chilli powder and the dry-fried rice. Mix well, then add the lemon grass or serai powder, lengkuas or laos powder, onion, fish sauce, sugar and salt and pepper to taste. Moisten with a little of the hot soup if necessary. Turn into a serving bowl and serve hot.

Make the Tcheo: pound the chillies and garlic together, then add about 2 tablespoons of fish sauce, or to taste. Stir in half of the coriander leaves. Transfer to a small bowl for serving and garnish with the remaining chopped coriander.

Dia Rau Song

Salad with Three Sauces/Vietnam

This salad, which is served as an accompaniment, is always made with the very freshest vegetables from the market, and so varies from season to season. The salad ingredients listed here are only a suggestion; you can use whatever is freshest and best on the day. The chilli sauce needs to be made 3 days in advance, to allow time for it to mature.

SERVES 8

1 lettuce
½ cucumber
2 carrots
½ head celery
fresh coriander leaves
fresh mint leaves (optional)
Chilli sauce:
4 fresh red chillies (or 2 red and 2 green),
seeded and finely sliced
1 tablespoon brown sugar
2–3 tablespoons rice wine
salt
Bean sauce:
2 tablespoons black salted beans, drained
4 tablespoons yellow salted beans
1 cm (½ inch) fresh root ginger, peeled and
roughly chopped
2 garlic cloves, peeled
2½ tablespoons brown sugar
1 tablespoon rice wine
1 tablespoon soy sauce
1 teaspoon sesame seed oil
1 fresh chilli, seeded and chopped (optional)
1 tablespoon sesame seeds, toasted and pounded
25 g (1 oz) roasted salted peanuts, finely crushed
Fish sauce:
2–3 fresh red chillies, seeded
2 garlic cloves, peeled
1 tablespoon brown sugar
about 3 tablespoons fish sauce
about 2 tablespoons lime or lemon juice
1 carrot, peeled and grated or cut into
julienne strips

First prepare the chilli sauce: put all the ingredients in a bowl, adding salt to taste. Mix well, then cover and store in a cool place for 3 days before using. Transfer to a small bowl for serving.

Prepare the bean sauce: pound the beans, ginger and garlic to a paste in a mortar and pestle, or work in a food processor. Add the sugar, rice wine and soy sauce, then stir in the sesame seed oil and chopped chilli (if using). Transfer to a small bowl for serving. Add the sesame seeds and peanuts at the last minute, so that they retain a crisp, crunchy texture.

Prepare the fish sauce: pound the chillies, garlic and sugar in a mortar and pestle, or work in a food processor. Add the fish sauce and lime or lemon juice to taste. Transfer the sauce to a small bowl for serving and top with the carrot.

When ready to serve, prepare the salad ingredients: separate the lettuce into leaves. Slice the cucumber. Peel the carrots and cut into flower shapes. Slice the celery sticks finely. Arrange the prepared salad ingredients attractively on a large serving platter and garnish with the coriander and mint leaves (if using). Serve immediately, with the three bowls of sauce handed separately for guests to help themselves.

Che Dau Xanh

Bean and Kiwi Fool/Vietnam

It is possible to buy mung beans with the husks removed, but the texture given by the mung bean skins is good in this pudding, and the colour looks pretty too.

SERVES 8

175 g (6 oz) mung beans, soaked in cold
water overnight
100 ml (3½ fl oz) milk
300 ml (½ pint) double cream
1½ tablespoons brown sugar
2 tablespoons rice wine
1 teaspoon vanilla flavouring
2 kiwi fruit, peeled and puréed, to decorate

Drain the beans, rinse thoroughly under cold running water, then place in a large saucepan and cover with fresh cold water. Bring to the boil, half cover the pan with a lid and simmer for 45 minutes to 1 hour, or until the beans are tender. Drain thoroughly.

Put the cooked beans in a blender or food processor and work to a purée. Add the milk and 100 ml (3½ fl oz) of the cream to make a thick, batter-like consistency, then add the sugar, rice wine and vanilla. Pour into 8 individual glasses or bowls, cover and chill in the refrigerator for at least 2 hours.

To serve: pour a little of the kiwi fruit purée on top of each pudding. Whip the remaining cream until thick, then spoon on top. Serve well chilled.

SOUTH-EAST ASIA
BURMA

Burma has common borders with India and China, and both of these countries have made their mark on the cuisine of this beautiful country. The Burmese are very proud of their own cuisine, however, and claim that they have adapted the neighbouring cuisines to get the best of both worlds. Certainly the cooking of Burma contains a wide range of complementary and contrasting flavours. Curries are popular, mostly fairly mild in flavour and coconut milk is a favourite ingredient. Fish, fresh fruits and vegetables play an important part in every Burmese meal, along with rice and Balachaung, a relish made from dried shrimps, onions and garlic.

Hincho

Clear Soup with Shrimps
This clear soup flavoured with dried shrimps is typically Burmese. The green vegetable can be varied according to what is available on the day. Pumpkin or marrow can be used if they are in season.

SERVES 8

50 g (2 oz) powdered dried shrimps, or whole dried shrimps pounded in a mortar and pestle
2–3 garlic cloves, peeled and crushed
1 tablespoon fish sauce
1 tablespoon soy sauce
salt
freshly ground black pepper
½ cucumber, coarsely grated
50 g (2 oz) spinach, sorrel or Chinese leaves, torn or finely shredded

Bring 1.75 litres (3 pints) water to the boil in a large saucepan. Add the shrimps, garlic, fish and soy sauces, and season to taste with salt and pepper. Lower the heat slightly and simmer for 5 minutes.

Add the cucumber to the pan and continue simmering for a further 3–4 minutes. Bring the liquid to a rapid boil and then add the torn or shredded leaves. Taste and adjust seasoning. Serve immediately, while the leaves are still a rich green colour.

Kyaw

Bean-sprout Fritters
These fritters are usually served as an accompaniment, but they can also be served on their own for a tasty snack. If liked, 50 g (2 oz) canned chick peas can be used instead of the bean-sprouts.

MAKES 25–30

peanut or vegetable oil, for frying
100 g (4 oz) bean-sprouts, brown tails removed
Batter:
40 g (1½ oz) besan (chick pea flour)
40 g (1½ oz) self-raising flour
½ teaspoon turmeric
¼ teaspoon salt
150 ml (¼ pint) coconut milk (page 184) or water
1 cm (½ inch) piece fresh root ginger, peeled
1 garlic clove, peeled and crushed

Make the batter: sift the flours into a bowl together with the turmeric and salt. Make a well in the centre and stir in enough coconut milk or water to make a creamy batter. Grate in the ginger, using the finest side of the grater, then add the garlic and beat well to mix.

When ready to cook the fritters, heat 2.5 cm (1 inch) oil in a hot wok or deep, heavy-based frying pan. Stir the bean-sprouts into the batter, then drop spoonfuls into the oil and fry until crisp. Remove with a perforated spoon, drain on paper towels and serve immediately.

Htamin Le Thoke

'Rice Mixed with the Fingers'
This curiously named dish is the Burmese answer to dealing with leftovers. All the ingredients are arranged attractively in piles on a large platter, then each person takes a small amount from each pile and spoons some of the tamarind juice over the top. Tamarind adds a sourness much loved by the Burmese; if it is too bitter for your taste, use lemon juice instead.

SERVES 6

450 g (1 lb) potatoes, peeled
salt
175 g (6 oz) long grain rice, boiled and cooled
1 small onion, peeled and thinly sliced
1–2 fresh red chillies, seeded and finely chopped
3–4 tablespoons peanut or vegetable oil
350 g (12 oz) spinach leaves, shredded
225 g (8 oz) bean-sprouts
2 teaspoons tamarind, soaked in 300 ml ($\frac{1}{2}$ pint) warm water for 10 minutes
225 g (8 oz) mee (egg noodles), cooked
225 g (8 oz) lai fan (rice vermicelli), cooked
Accompaniments:
Ng Yok Thee Kyaw/Chilli and Shrimps (right)
1 large onion, peeled and cut into thin rings
1 bunch spring onions, trimmed and shredded
crisp deep-fried noodles as for Mee Krob/Fried Noodles (page 156)
roasted chick peas, pounded
fish sauce, to taste
fresh coriander leaves
Kyaw/Bean-sprout Fritters (page 165)
3 hard-boiled eggs, chopped

Cook the potatoes in boiling salted water for about 20 minutes, or until tender. Meanwhile, put the rice in a bowl and fork through to separate the grains. Pound the onion and chillies together in a mortar and pestle. Heat the oil in a small frying pan, add the pounded mixture and fry gently for 2 minutes. Stir into the rice.

Drain the potatoes, leave until cool enough to handle, then cut into neat dice.

Blanch the spinach leaves and bean-sprouts in separate pans of boiling water for 30 seconds only. Drain, then plunge into iced water for 2 minutes to retain colour and prevent further cooking. Drain well again. Strain the tamarind juice into a small bowl.

To serve, arrange the chilli rice, diced potatoes, noodles, vermicelli, spinach and bean-sprouts on a large serving platter and arrange the accompaniments in separate small serving bowls. Each person helps themselves from the main platter and the accompaniments, then pours over a little of the tamarind juice.

Ng Yok Thee Kyaw

Chilli and Shrimps
This is a traditional accompaniment to many savoury stews and soups. Dried shrimps have been dried in the sun to give them a concentrated flavour.

SERVES 6–8

8 dried red chillies
2 tablespoons peanut or vegetable oil
1 teaspoon powdered dried shrimps, or whole dried shrimps pounded in a mortar and pestle

Remove the seeds from the chillies unless a fiercely hot taste is liked, then gently dry-fry the chillies in a hot wok or small frying pan, to heighten the flavour. Pound the chillies in a mortar and pestle. Heat the oil in the wok or frying pan, add the pounded chillies and fry gently. Stir in the powdered shrimps, fry for a few minutes, then turn into a small serving bowl and leave until cold.

Balachaung

Spicy Burmese Accompaniment

No self-respecting Burmese has a meal without Balachaung. It is forked into plain rice for a snack, used as an accompaniment to a host of main dishes, as well as being served on slices of bread for breakfast! Stored in a closely covered jar in a cool place, Balachaung will keep for several weeks.

MAKES ABOUT 450 g (1 lb)

1 whole head garlic, peeled
3 medium onions, peeled
300 ml ($\frac{1}{2}$ pint) peanut or sunflower oil
100 g (4 oz) powdered dried shrimps, or whole dried shrimps pounded in a mortar and pestle
2 teaspoons chilli powder
1 teaspoon turmeric
1 teaspoon tamarind, soaked in 50 ml (2 fl oz) warm water for 10 minutes
2.5 cm (1 inch) cube ngapi (shrimp paste), dry-fried

Slice the garlic and onions finely, using the fine slicer of a food processor if possible. Pat dry on plenty of paper towels, keeping the garlic and onions separate. Heat half of the oil in a wok or frying pan, add the garlic and fry until crisp and golden, turning all the time. Remove from the oil with a perforated spoon and drain on paper towels. Set aside while frying the onion slices, adding more oil as necessary.

Drain off most of the oil from the pan, then add the dried shrimps, chilli powder and turmeric. Fry, stirring, for a few minutes, then remove from the heat.

Strain the juice from the tamarind. Put the ngapi in a bowl and gradually blend in the tamarind juice to make a paste. Pour the mixture into the spices in the pan, stir well to mix, then leave to cool. Stir in the garlic and onion until evenly mixed.

BELOW: Left, Chicken Curry (page 168) with traditional accompaniments. Right, 'Rice Mixed with the Fingers' (page 166), with Spicy Burmese Accompaniment, Bean-sprout Fritters (page 165), Chilli and Shrimps (page 166), and other accompaniments.

Panthe Kaukswe

Chicken Curry

This is a mild chicken curry which illustrates the links between Chinese and Burmese cooking, with the use of noodles and curry flavours.

SERVES 6–8

1.5 kg (3–3½ lb) chicken, cut into 8 pieces
1 teaspoon salt
2 large onions, peeled and finely chopped
3 garlic cloves, peeled
4–6 fresh red chillies, seeded and shredded, or
1–1½ tablespoons chilli powder
2.5 cm (1 inch) piece fresh root ginger, peeled and sliced
2 teaspoons turmeric
3–4 tablespoons peanut or vegetable oil
750 ml (1¼ pints) coconut milk (page 184)
4 tablespoons besan (chick pea flour)
about 2 tablespoons fish sauce, to taste
accompaniments as for Htamin Le Thoke/ 'Rice Mixed with the Fingers' (page 166)
450 g (1 lb) mee (egg noodles), cooked
fresh coriander leaves, to garnish

Place the chicken pieces in a large saucepan with 2 litres (3½ pints) cold water and the salt. Bring to the boil, skim, then cover with a tight-fitting lid and cook for 35–45 minutes, or until the chicken flesh is tender. Leave the chicken to cool in the liquid, then lift out of the pan and remove the flesh from the bones. Cut the flesh into bite-sized pieces, discarding the skin. Set aside.

Return the bones to the pan and cook, uncovered, over high heat for 15 minutes, to concentrate the stock. Leave the stock to cool, then strain and skim off any fat. Measure 1.25 litres (2¼ pints) stock, making the volume up with water if necessary.

Pound the onions, garlic, chillies or chilli powder, ginger and turmeric to a paste in a mortar and pestle, or work in a food processor. Heat the oil in a hot wok, add the paste and fry gently without browning until the mixture gives off a spicy aroma. Reserve a few tablespoons of the measured stock, then stir the remainder into the spice paste. Add the coconut milk and cook, uncovered, for 15 minutes. Put the besan flour in a small bowl and mix to a smooth paste with the reserved stock. Ladle a little of the mixture from the pan into this paste, blend well, then pour back into the pan. Simmer until the mixture thickens, stirring all the time. Add the chicken and fish sauce; remove from the heat.

To serve: arrange the accompaniments in separate small serving bowls and reheat the curry. Divide the noodles equally between individual bowls. Pour over the hot curry and garnish with coriander leaves. Hand the accompaniments separately.

Mohinga

Curried Fish Soup with Noodles

Mohinga is a national favourite in Burma, and is sold by hawkers almost everywhere.

SERVES 6–8

750 g (1½ lb) huss (rock salmon) or mackerel
3 stems lemon grass, or 1½ teaspoons serai powder
5 cm (2 inch) piece fresh root ginger, peeled
2 tablespoons fish sauce
2 medium onions, peeled and finely chopped
3–4 garlic cloves, peeled
3–4 fresh chillies, seeded
1 teaspoon turmeric
3–4 tablespoons peanut or vegetable oil
900 ml (1½ pints) coconut milk (page 184)
1 rounded tablespoon rice flour
1 rounded tablespoon besan (chick pea flour)
540 g (1 lb 3 oz) can bamboo shoots, diced
salt
accompaniments as for Htamin Le Thoke/ 'Rice Mixed with the Fingers' (page 166)
450 g (1 lb) lai fan (rice vermicelli), cooked

If using huss, it should be left on the bone; mackerel should be gutted, head removed and well rinsed. Place the fish in a large saucepan and pour in enough cold water to cover. Bruise 2 of the lemon grass stems (if using) and add to the fish with half of the ginger. Bring to the boil, skim, then add the fish sauce and cook for about 10 minutes. Remove the fish from the pan and leave until cool enough to handle. Strain the stock into a large measuring bowl and set aside. Remove the skin and bones from the fish, then flake the flesh into large pieces.

Pound the lower part of the remaining lemon grass (if using) to a paste in a mortar and pestle with the remaining ginger, the onions, garlic and the chillies, or work in a food processor. Add the turmeric and serai powder (if using). Heat the oil in a wok or very large, heavy-based saucepan, add the paste and fry gently without browning until the mixture gives off a spicy aroma. Remove the pan from the heat and set aside.

Blend the coconut milk into the strained fish stock and stir in enough water to make the volume up to 2.4 litres (4 pints). Put the flours in a separate small bowl and mix to a smooth creamy paste with some of the stock and coconut milk. Stir this paste into the remaining liquid, then stir into the spice paste in the pan.

Bring the liquid slowly to the boil, stirring all the time. Stir in the bamboo shoots and fish pieces, with salt to taste. Simmer gently for 5 minutes only, then cover the pan with a tight-fitting lid and remove from the heat. Arrange the accompaniments in small serving bowls and serve with the soup and lai fan.

SOUTH-EAST ASIA

PHILIPPINES

The cuisine of the Philippines is the most 'international' of all the cuisines of South-East Asia. Foreign influences have been long and many in these islands – first traders from Malay, Indonesia and China were followed by 400 years of Spanish rule, then half a century of American occupation. Each of these nations has left an indelible mark on the cooking of the Philippines, but it is the Spanish influence which remains the strongest. One example of this is in the *adobo* style of cooking, in which pork fat is combined with meat, poultry or fish and pungently flavoured with vinegar, garlic and pepper. Puchero is a popular Spanish-style stew, in which many ingredients are cooked together yet served in separate parts, not unlike the French cassoulet. Pork is the favourite meat and bagoong (shrimp paste) and patis (fish sauce), two of the favourite flavours. The Philippinos are devout Catholics who love festivals and pageants – and the traditional feasts that accompany them. They are also more sweet-toothed than most of their oriental neighbours, and frequently indulge in sweet snacks. Many well-to-do Philippinos observe the Spanish custom of *Meriendas*, morning and afternoon breaks when sweet cakes, tarts and fritters are eaten alongside savoury dishes, and hot chocolate and coffee are drunk in true Spanish style.

Sinegang

Clear Soup with Prawns and Vegetables
Uncooked prawns are available at high-class fishmongers and are worth buying if you wish to make an authentic Sinegang. They are expensive, however, and you may prefer to use peeled cooked prawns, in which case you will have to make the stock with fish bones and trimmings from your fishmonger – see the introduction to Tom Yam Kung/Prawn Soup (page 155).

SERVES 4

*225 g (8 oz) headless uncooked prawns,
defrosted if frozen
225 g (8 oz) sweet potato, peeled and diced
100 g (4 oz) French beans, topped and tailed,
then cut small
1 tablespoon tamarind
225 g (8 oz) tomatoes, skinned and chopped
100 g (4 oz) spinach, including a few leaves of
sorrel if available, torn into small pieces
salt
freshly ground black pepper*

Put the uncooked prawns in a large saucepan and cover with 1.75 litres (3 pints) cold water. Bring to the boil, then cover and simmer for 5 minutes. Strain the stock into a clean saucepan. Allow the prawns to cool, then remove and discard the shells.

Add the diced sweet potato and the French beans to the fish stock. Bring to the boil, then lower the heat, cover and simmer for 10 minutes. While the soup is simmering, put the tamarind in a bowl and pour over 150 ml ($\frac{1}{4}$ pint) warm water. Leave the tamarind to soak for 10 minutes.

Just before serving, strain the tamarind juice into the soup, add the chopped tomatoes, spinach and salt and pepper to taste, then the prawns. Bring back to the boil, then immediately pour into warmed individual soup bowls. Serve immediately.

Puchero

Spanish-style Meat and Vegetable Stew

This is the Philippino answer to the French *pot-au-feu*, a hearty and filling one-pot meal. If liked, it can be eaten in two stages. The soup first, followed by the meat and vegetables as the main course.

SERVES 8

225 g (8 oz) chick peas, soaked in cold water overnight
1.5 kg (3–3½ lb) chicken, cut into 8 pieces
350 g (12 oz) pork fillet, cut into cubes
2 large onions, peeled and chopped
salt
2.25 litres (4 pints) half chicken stock and half water
4 tablespoons vegetable oil
2 garlic cloves, peeled and crushed
450 g (1 lb) tomatoes, skinned and chopped
1–2 tablespoons tomato purée
225 g (8 oz) chorizo sausage, skinned and sliced
350 g (12 oz) plantain (cooking banana), peeled and sliced
350 g (12 oz) sweet potato, peeled and cubed
350 g (12 oz) Chinese leaves, shredded
6 spring onions, sliced, to garnish
Aubergine Sauce:
500 g (1¼ lb) aubergines
a little vegetable oil, for brushing
1 small onion, peeled and roughly chopped
2–3 garlic cloves, peeled and roughly chopped
3–4 spring onions, trimmed
freshly ground black pepper

First make the aubergine sauce: brush the aubergines with a little oil and place under a hot grill, turning frequently until the skins are scorched on the outside and the flesh feels soft and tender. Peel, then place the flesh in a blender or food processor with the onion, garlic, spring onions and salt and pepper to taste. Work to a purée, then turn into a serving bowl.

Drain the chick peas, rinse and drain again. Place in a large saucepan with the chicken pieces and the pork. Add half of the chopped onions and salt and pepper to taste, then cover with the stock and water. Bring to the boil, skim, then cover and simmer for 40–45 minutes.

Heat the oil in a large, heavy-based saucepan, add the remaining onions and the garlic and fry gently until soft. Stir in the tomatoes and tomato purée, then add to the chicken with the chorizo, plantain and sweet potato. Simmer for 20–25 minutes or until the sweet potato is tender, stirring occasionally. Add the Chinese leaves and cook for 2–3 minutes. Garnish the stew and aubergine sauce with the sliced spring onions before serving.

Inihaw Na Bangus

Mackerel Philippino Style

In the Philippines, 'milk' fish would be used for this recipe. Mackerel or grey mullet are the most suitable alternatives. Boiled or steamed rice may be served as an accompaniment.

SERVES 4

two 450 g (1 lb) mackerel, gutted with heads removed
banana leaves or foil
a few fresh coriander leaves, to garnish (optional)
Stuffing:
1 small onion, peeled
2.5 cm (1 inch) piece fresh root ginger, peeled
225–350 g (8–12 oz) tomatoes, skinned and seeded
1–2 fresh red or green chillies, seeded
a little coriander
salt
freshly ground black pepper

With a sharp knife, cut the mackerel carefully through the belly from the head end to the tail. Turn the fish cut side down on to a board and rub the heel of the hand firmly along the spine of the fish. Turn the fish over and lift out the whole of the spine. Repeat with the other fish, then wash both fish under cold running water and pat dry with paper towels.

If using banana leaves, pour boiling water over them to make them pliable. Using kitchen scissors, cut the leaves into suitable shapes to make 2 parcels. Place 1 fish on each piece, or on foil if banana leaves are not available.

Make the stuffing: chop all the ingredients finely, or work in a food processor for 30 seconds. Add salt and pepper to taste. Spoon the stuffing inside the fish and sew up or secure the openings with long skewers. Fold the banana leaves or foil around the fish to make parcel shapes and tie with string.

Place the fish parcels in the top of a steamer and steam for 10–15 minutes. Open the parcels and garnish the fish with coriander leaves, if liked. Serve immediately.

OPPOSITE: *Left, Spanish-style Meat and Vegetable Stew, accompanied by Aubergine Sauce and boiled rice. Right, Caramel Custard with Lime.*

Leche Flan

Caramel Custards with Lime

This variation of crème caramel shows a glimpse of the Spanish influence on Philippino cuisine. It has a delicious bitter-sweet flavour that makes it an ideal dessert to serve after a robust or rich main course dish.

MAKES 8

225 g (8 oz) granulated sugar
Custard:
410 g (14½ oz) can evaporated milk
300 ml (½ pint) fresh milk
5 eggs
1 tablespoon caster sugar
finely grated rind of 2 limes

Put the sugar in a heavy-based saucepan, add 8 table-spoons cold water and stir over gentle heat until the sugar has dissolved. Increase the heat and boil, without stirring, to a rich caramel. Immediately pour a little caramel into 8 warmed 150 ml (¼ pint) ramekin or soufflé dishes, rotating each one quickly so that the caramel covers the base and sides.

Make the custard: warm the evaporated and fresh milks together in a saucepan, without boiling. Put the eggs and sugar in a bowl, whisk together, then slowly stir in the hot milk. Strain into a large pouring jug to remove the threads from the eggs. Stir in the grated lime rind, then pour into the ramekin dishes.

Stand the dishes in a roasting tin, then pour in enough cold water to come halfway up the sides of the dishes. Cook in a preheated moderate oven (160°C/325°F, Gas Mark 3) for about 45 minutes or until set. Remove the dishes from the water and leave the custards to cool. Chill in the refrigerator for at least 2 hours before serving. Serve in the ramekins, or turn out.

SOUTH-EAST ASIA
MENUS & CUSTOMS

Salamat makan or 'good eating' heralds the start of a meal in **Indonesia**. The meal itself might be simple boiled white rice moistened with a vegetable and coconut soup and served with a hot and spicy sambal, or it might be a buffet-style Rijsttafel (page 180) with as many as 20 different dishes, but the greeting is always the same.

Over the centuries, Indonesia has become the home of many different races, religions and cultures – Hindus and Buddhists from India, Arab and Indian Muslims, Portuguese, Dutch and Chinese. Each group has brought its own individual style of food and eating but most meals are centred around rice, the staple diet of all Indonesians. Lunch and dinner are the two main meals of the day, usually consisting of a large bowl of boiled rice and two or three vegetable dishes. A meat, chicken, or fish dish may also be served. One vegetable dish known as *sayur* is like a soup, and is intended to moisten the rice. Accompaniments and condiments based on hot chillies are an integral part of almost every Indonesian meal.

There is no such thing as a main course, all the food is placed on the table at the same time, except any dessert or fruit which is served at the end. Everyone helps themselves to as much or as little as they like. Small helpings of other dishes are placed around or on top of the rice, then a krupuk (prawn cracker) may be crumbled on top or served as a separate accompaniment. Care is always taken that dishes complement each other in spice content and colour and, above all, in texture.

Although many Indonesians eat with the tips of their fingers (using the right hand only), it is also acceptable to eat Indonesian food with a dessertspoon and fork. When entertaining Indonesian-style, chilled lager is probably the best alcoholic drink to serve.

In **Malaysia and Singapore** meals are eaten in a similar fashion to those in Indonesia. However, Chinese and Indian influences are more pronounced, giving the food even greater variety. Rice is still the staple food, and Malay families centre their meals around it. In traditional Malay homes all the food for the meal is placed on mats in the centre of the floor and everyone sits barefoot around it, with their feet tucked in so that the soles do not show (it is a sign of disrespect to show the soles of your feet).

The Chinese settlers centred themselves around the Malacca Straits, Penang and Singapore and so are named 'Straits Chinese'. These Chinese merchants began to marry Muslim Malay women, who, in order to please their husbands, broke the Muslim faith which forbade the handling and eating of pork. Their style of cooking is called *Nonya*, a unique mixture of Chinese and Malay. Nonya food is eaten in Chinese style with chopsticks, with one bowl for rice and another for soup, which is drunk throughout the meal from a porcelain spoon.

In **Thailand**, as with all countries in South-East Asia, meals are based on rice, which is the staple food of this

beautiful country – the Thai words for meal and rice are one and the same and the invitation to a meal is 'come and eat rice'. Rice is served at breakfast, lunch and dinner, the latter being the main meal of the day. To eat Thai style, set a large bowl of fluffy steamed or boiled white rice in the centre of the table, then surround this with the other dishes. One of these should be a soup, then there should be up to three *kaeng*, which are dishes such as curries with a sauce or gravy – these may be fish, meat, poultry or vegetables. Other essential dishes are a salad of crisp raw vegetables and nam prik sauce (page 156), a fiery hot sambal which is served at every Thai meal. Spoons and forks are used to eat Thai food. Weak China, chrysanthemum or ginger tea is the customary drink, or even iced water. Chilled lager is also suitable.

Meals in **Cambodia and Laos** are invariably simple, with rice being the most important ingredient; in Laos, this will be the sticky or glutinous rice. A clear soup is always served and drunk throughout the meal. Fish dishes are popular for everyday meals; other dishes of meat, poultry and vegetables may also be served, but this will depend on the income of the family and the occasion. In **Vietnam**, chopsticks are used and food is eaten from bowls, Chinese-style. Rice is the main dish of every meal and clear soup is always served, drunk throughout the meal from small bowls with metal, rather than porcelain, spoons. Fish, poultry and vegetables form the basis of other dishes, beef and lamb are rarely used. No meal in Indo-China is complete without fish sauce, which is placed on the table with every meal and eaten with just about everything. Tea is the usual drink, either green China, jasmine or chrysanthemum, although cold beer may be served; rice wine is traditional in Laos, served with fresh fruit at the end of the meal.

In **Burma**, meals are centred around a curried dish of meat, fish or vegetables, then other dishes are chosen to complement or contrast with it so that a wide range of flavours and textures can be enjoyed. Rice is always served; fresh vegetables and salads are an important feature, and accompaniments and sambals are served in small bowls and placed around the main dishes in the centre of the table. Desserts are rarely eaten, although fresh fruit is often served at the end of a meal. Food is served 'help yourself' style and is always taken a small portion at a time. Traditionally Burmese food is eaten with the fingers, although a spoon and fork are often used.

The main meals of the day in **The Philippines** are lunch and dinner, both of which are quite substantial for the well-to-do. Meals in most families are eaten buffet-style, with everyone helping themselves from an array of savoury dishes in the centre of the table. Provide dinner plates and soup bowls with your usual cutlery, and encourage guests to help themselves from a selection of such dishes as a stew or casserole made with meat or poultry, a fish dish, vegetables and salads, plus dishes of bagoong (shrimp paste) and patis (fish sauce), which are placed on the table at virtually every Philippino meal.

—— Sample Menus ——

INDONESIAN MID-DAY SNACK
Vegetable Salad with Peanut Dressing
Fresh Fruit Juice or Lager
Fresh Fruits

MALAYSIAN LUNCH
Pork Satay
Fish in Coconut Milk with Chillies
Boiled Rice
Vegetable Pickle
Banana Fritters

THAI DINNER PARTY
Crudités with Thai Shrimp Sauce
Prawn Soup
Boiled or Steamed Rice
Muslim Beef Curry
Chicken in Coconut Milk
Fresh Fruits

BURMESE FAMILY MEAL
Curried Fish Soup with Noodles
Bean-sprout Fritters
Spicy Burmese Accompaniment
Chilli and Shrimps
Rice Noodles
Fresh Fruit

PHILIPPINO SUNDAY LUNCH
Spanish-style Meat and Vegetable Stew
Boiled or Steamed Rice
Caramel Custard with Lime

SINGAPOREAN SUPPER
Chilli Crabs
Chunks of Cucumber
Slices of Toast or French Bread

PENANG ISLAND DINNER
Penang-style Chicken Curry
Coconut pancakes
Singapore Chinese Salad
Mixed Tropical Fruits

NOTE: Adjust quantities of individual dishes according to the number of people being served.

MOON YIT CELEBRATION

The Singaporean Moon Yit is a Straits Chinese or Nonya celebration. It takes place one
month after a baby is born, to mark the release of burden from
the mother. Friends and relations come to the baby's home and on departure
they are given dyed red eggs as a symbol of the new life.

FOR 10–12 PEOPLE
Pork Satay
Coconut Rice
Shrimp and Chilli Sambal
Pickled Chillies
Pumpkin in Coconut Milk
Turmeric Fish
Penang-style Chicken Curry

Satay Babi

Pork Satay
Cubes of pork are marinated in spices, then
threaded on to bamboo satay sticks and
cooked on the barbecue or under the grill.

MAKES 30 STICKS

750 g (1½ lb) pork fillet
450 g (1 lb) belly pork
1 tablespoon ground coriander
1 tablespoon turmeric
75 g (3 oz) soft brown sugar
salt
a little coconut or vegetable oil, for brushing
Satay sauce:
100 g (4 oz) shallots or small onions, peeled
2 garlic cloves, peeled
*4–6 fresh red chillies, seeded, or 1½
tablespoons chilli powder*
1 cm (½ inch) cube blachan (shrimp paste)
2 stems lemon grass, or 1 teaspoon serai powder
1 tablespoon ground coriander
4–6 tablespoons coconut or vegetable oil
175 g (6 oz) crunchy peanut butter
300 ml (½ pint) coconut milk (page 184)
soft brown sugar
100 g (4 oz) roasted salted peanuts, crushed
To serve:
1 pineapple, peeled and cut into chunks
1 cucumber, cut into chunks
Lontong/Compressed Rice (page 145)

Remove any skin or membrane from the pork fillet, then cut into cubes. Remove the rind and any bones from the belly of pork, then cut into cubes the same size as the pork fillet. Place the cubes of meat in a bowl, sprinkle over the coriander, turmeric, sugar and salt to taste. Mix well, cover and leave to marinate for at least 1½ hours.

Meanwhile, prepare the sauce: pound the shallots or onions to a paste in a mortar and pestle with the garlic, chillies or chilli powder, blachan, lemon grass or serai powder and the ground coriander, or work in a food processor. Heat the oil in a hot wok or heavy-based saucepan, add the paste and fry gently without browning until the mixture gives off a spicy aroma. Reduce the heat and work in the peanut butter, then the coconut milk. Bring to the boil, then simmer for 5 minutes, stirring occasionally, until the sauce has a thick, creamy consistency. Add brown sugar and salt to taste and remove from the heat.

When ready to cook, soak 30 satay sticks in water for about 30 minutes. Thread the pork fillet and belly alternately on the sticks. Brush with oil and cook over a charcoal barbecue or under a hot grill for 10–15 minutes or until tender, turning frequently. Meanwhile, reheat the sauce and stir in about two-thirds of the crushed peanuts. Transfer the sauce to a serving bowl and sprinkle with the remaining peanuts. Serve the satay sticks hot, with the pineapple, cucumber and Lontong. Hand the sauce separately for guests to help themselves.

RIGHT: *Clockwise from top; Coconut Rice (page 176), Pumpkin in Coconut Milk (page 176), Turmeric Fish (page 177), Pork Satay, Penang-style Chicken Curry (page 177), Coconut Pancakes (page 151).*

Nasi Lemak

Coconut Rice

Rice cooked in coconut milk has a rich, nutty flavour – the perfect foil for the hot spicy accompaniments which are served with it.

SERVES 4 as an individual dish

225 g (8 oz) long grain rice
600 ml (1 pint) coconut milk (page 184)
1 stem lemon grass, bruised, or ½ teaspoon serai powder
salt
Accompaniments:
deep-fried ikan bilis (dried fish)
chopped hard-boiled egg
Chabai Acar/Pickled Chillies (right)
Sambal Blachan/Shrimp and Chilli Sambal (below)
Garnish:
a little shredded chilli
fresh coriander leaves

Soak the rice in cold water for a few minutes, then drain and place in a sieve. Rinse under cold running water. Spoon off the cream which has risen to the top of the coconut milk and reserve. Rinse a heavy-based saucepan with water, pour in the coconut milk, then add the lemon grass or serai powder. Bring to the boil, remove from the heat and stir in the rice and salt to taste.

Return the pan to the heat and bring to the boil again, stirring constantly. Half cover the pan with a lid and cook gently for 12 minutes, then remove from the heat. Stir in the reserved coconut cream, cover and keep warm for 10 minutes. Arrange the accompaniments in small bowls.

Just before serving, return the pan to the lowest possible heat and cook for a further 5 minutes. Discard the lemon grass (if used), then turn the rice into a warmed bowl and garnish with the chilli and coriander.

Sambal Blachan

Shrimp and Chilli Sambal

6 fresh red chillies, seeded
¼ teaspoon salt
1 cm (½ inch) cube blachan (shrimp paste)
1 tablespoon lime or lemon juice, or to taste

Pound the chillies and salt in a mortar and pestle until smooth, then work in the blachan. Add lime or lemon juice to taste. Serve in a small bowl.

Chabai Acar

Pickled Chillies

8–10 fresh red or green chillies, seeded and sliced into rings
150 ml (¼ pint) white vinegar
salt
light soy sauce, to serve

Put the chillies in a glass jam jar. Pour in the vinegar, then 85 ml (3 fl oz) boiling water and salt to taste. Leave to cool, then cover closely with cling film and a screw-topped lid. Leave in a cool place for several days.

To serve: lift the chillies out of the liquid with a perforated spoon and place in a small serving bowl. Pour over a little soy sauce.

Masak Lemak

Pumpkin in Coconut Milk

Almost any vegetable can be cooked in coconut milk in this way: try using 3 chayote (a member of the squash family), peeled and sliced with 450 g (1 lb) Chinese leaves, shredded.

SERVES 6–8 as an individual dish

50 g (2 oz) shallots or small onions, peeled
1 cm (½ inch) cube blachan (shrimp paste)
2 fresh red chillies, seeded and chopped
4–6 tablespoons coconut or vegetable oil
50 g (2 oz) dried shrimps, soaked in warm water
450 ml (¾ pint) coconut milk (page 184)
225 g (8 oz) French beans, halved
450 g (1 lb) pumpkin, peeled and cut into chunks
salt
freshly ground black pepper

Pound the shallots or onions, blachan and chillies in a mortar and pestle, or work in a food processor, to form a rough paste.

Heat the oil in a hot wok or large, heavy-based saucepan. Add the pounded mixture and fry gently without browning until it gives off a spicy aroma. Drain the shrimps, add to the pan and cook for 2 minutes. Spoon off the cream which has risen to the top of the coconut milk and reserve. Pour the milk into the pan and bring to the boil, then add the beans. Cook for 3 minutes, then add the pumpkin and salt and pepper to taste. Cook for a further 5–8 minutes, then stir in the reserved coconut cream. Serve hot.

Ikan Doedoeh

Turmeric Fish

Any fish can be used instead of mackerel in this recipe, although mackerel gives the most authentic flavour. If mackerel is not in season, use haddock or cod fillets instead.

SERVES 6–8 as an individual dish

1 kg (2–2¼ lb) fresh mackerel fillets, skinned
salt
2 tablespoons tamarind, soaked in 200 ml (7 fl oz) warm water for 10 minutes
1 medium onion, peeled and roughly chopped
2 garlic cloves, peeled
1 cm (½ inch) piece lengkuas (laos root), peeled and sliced, or 1 teaspoon laos powder
1–2 fresh red chillies, seeded, or 1 teaspoon chilli powder
1 teaspoon ground coriander
1 teaspoon turmeric
½ teaspoon fennel seeds
1 tablespoon dark brown sugar
10–14 tablespoons peanut or vegetable oil
200 ml (7 fl oz) coconut cream or milk (page 184)
chilli flower, to garnish

Rinse the fish fillets and pat dry with paper towels. Place in a shallow dish, sprinkle with salt to taste, then strain over the tamarind juice. Leave to stand for 30 minutes.

Meanwhile, pound the onion to a paste in a mortar and pestle with the garlic, lengkuas and chillies (if using), or work in a food processor. Add the coriander, turmeric, fennel, sugar, laos and chilli powders (if using), mix well and set aside.

Heat 6–8 tablespoons of the oil in a hot wok or large, heavy-based saucepan. Lift the fish fillets out of the marinade and fry in the hot oil for 5 minutes, or until cooked through. Remove from the pan and set aside.

Wipe out the pan with paper towels, then pour in and heat the remaining oil. Add the spice paste and fry gently without browning until it gives off a spicy aroma, then add the coconut cream or milk and bring to the boil, stirring. Simmer gently for a few minutes, then return the fish to the pan and heat through. Add salt if necessary, then transfer carefully to a warmed serving dish. Garnish with the chilli flower before serving.

Penang Ayam Kapitan

Penang-style Chicken Curry

This recipe title literally means 'the curry made for the captain', and is said to have originated on Penang Island – the pearl of the Orient. Traditionally, this curry is served with Roti Jala/ Coconut Pancakes (page 151) to mop up the sauce, but if you prefer not to go to the trouble of making them, they are not absolutely essential.

SERVES 4–6 as an individual dish

1.5 kg (3–3½ lb) chicken
450 ml (¾ pint) coconut milk (page 184)
1 cm (½ inch) cube blachan (shrimp paste)
6 fresh red chillies, seeded, or 2 tablespoons chilli powder
175 g (6 oz) shallots or small onions, peeled
3 garlic cloves, peeled
2 stems lemon grass, or 1 teaspoon serai powder
2.5 cm (1 inch) piece lengkuas (laos root), peeled and sliced, or 1 teaspoon laos powder
4 macadamia nuts, shelled
1 teaspoon turmeric
1 teaspoon ground coriander
6–8 tablespoons coconut or vegetable oil
2 tablespoons tamarind, soaked in 8 tablespoons warm water for 10 minutes
brown sugar
salt
juice of ½–1 lime (optional)
crisp deep-fried onions (page 186), to garnish

Quarter the chicken, then, using a good sharp knife, cut into as many small pieces as possible or into 8 pieces if preferred. Spoon off the cream which has risen to the top of the coconut milk and reserve.

Put the blachan in a food processor with the chillies or chilli powder, shallots or onions, garlic, lemon grass or serai powder, lengkuas or laos powder and the nuts. Work to a fine paste, then add the turmeric and coriander. (Alternatively, pound the whole ingredients in a mortar and pestle, then stir in the ground spices.)

Heat the oil in a hot wok or heavy-based saucepan, add the spice paste and fry gently without browning until it gives off a spicy aroma. Add the chicken pieces and cook for 3–4 minutes to flavour the meat with the spices. Strain in the tamarind juice, then pour in the coconut milk, stirring all the time. Add a little brown sugar and salt to taste, then simmer, stirring occasionally, for 35–40 minutes or until the chicken pieces are tender. (If the pieces are quite small, the cooking time will be shorter.) Just before serving, stir in the reserved coconut cream and the lime juice (if using). Turn into a warmed serving bowl and top with crisp deep-fried onions to serve.

LUNAR NEW YEAR DINNER

The Vietnamese celebrate the Chinese lunar new year, which means that New Year's Day in Vietnam can fall any time between 21 January and 19 February. It is a double celebration, in that the new year also heralds the coming of spring; the house must be cleaned from top to bottom and new clothes and shoes worn. Candles are kept burning all night long on New Year's Eve, and sticks of sugar cane are placed behind doors to ensure that the family will have a long life 'sweet to the end'. This is a typical Vietnamese dinner menu for New Year's Day, which is celebrated in style.

FOR 8 PEOPLE

Crab Soup (page 159)
Duck with Bean Paste and Five Spices
Poached Chicken
Salad with Three Sauces (page 164)
Festive Glutinous Rice (page 160)
Bean and Kiwi Fool (page 164)

Vit Quay

Duck with Bean Paste and Five Spices
Try to use a fresh duckling for this recipe; frozen ducks tend to be watery and often have less tender flesh than the fresh birds. Let the duck go completely cold before slicing, so that the flesh cuts neatly.

SERVES 4 as an individual dish

2.5 kg (4¾–5 lb) young fresh duckling
3 tablespoons yellow bean paste
2 squares preserved bean curd with sesame oil, from a 140 g (5 oz) jar
1 garlic clove, peeled and crushed
1 cm (½ inch) piece fresh root ginger, peeled and pounded
1 tablespoon brown sugar
1 teaspoon five spice powder
1 tablespoon rice wine
salt
2 tablespoons rice vinegar
85 ml (3 fl oz) clear honey
bean sauce as for Dia Rau Song/Salad with Three Sauces (page 164), to serve
Garnish:
few Chinese leaves, shredded
½ cucumber, cut into matchstick strips
spring onion curls

Rinse the duck well under cold running water, then dry inside and out with paper towels. Seal up the neck opening with a trussing needle and fine string. Put the yellow bean paste and the bean curd in a bowl and blend together until creamy. Stir in the garlic, ginger, sugar, five spice powder, rice wine and salt to taste. Smear this mixture all over the inner cavity of the duck, then sew up the vent with string.

Stir half of the rice vinegar into about 1 litre (1¾ pints) boiling water and immediately pour over the duck to seal the pores. This also makes the duck look rigid. Cool, then brush with the remaining rice vinegar. Tie the legs firmly together and hang the duck up in a cool airy place until dry – this will take from 12 to 24 hours.

Just before cooking, brush all over the duck with clear honey. Place the duck on a rack or trivet in a roasting tin, breast side down. Roast in a preheated moderate oven (180°C/350°F, Gas Mark 4) for 45 minutes, then turn the duck breast side uppermost and roast for a further 45 minutes. Leave until cold.

Cut the duck into serving pieces and arrange on a serving platter with the poached chicken, interleaving the white and dark meat. Garnish with Chinese leaves, cucumber and spring onion curls. Serve cold, with the bean sauce handed separately in small serving bowls.

OPPOSITE: *Clockwise from top; Salad with Three Sauces (page 164), Festive Glutinous Rice (page 160), Duck with Bean Paste and Five Spices, shown with Poached Chicken (page 179), Crab Soup (page 159).*

Ga Luot

Poached Chicken
Use the stock from this chicken dish in soups; it goes well in Canh Cua/Crab Soup (page 159).

SERVES 4 as an individual dish

2 kg (4½ lb) chicken
2 litres (3½ pints) homemade chicken stock
10 lily buds or golden needles, soaked in warm water for 30 minutes
1–2 stems lemon grass, or ½–1 teaspoon serai powder
50 ml (2 fl oz) rice wine
2.5 cm (1 inch) piece fresh root ginger, peeled and bruised
3 Chinese dried mushrooms, stems discarded
Garnish:
few Chinese leaves, shredded
½ cucumber, cut into matchstick strips
spring onion curls

Rinse the chicken well under cold running water. Bring the chicken stock to the boil in a saucepan large enough to fit the chicken comfortably. Meanwhile, drain the soaked lily buds or golden needles. If using lemon grass, cut off and reserve the top ends of the stems; bruise the lower part. Add both parts to the stock, or add the serai powder (if using), then add the rice wine, fresh root ginger, lily buds or golden needles and the Chinese dried mushrooms.

Bring the stock back to the boil, carefully lower in the chicken and allow to boil for 3–4 minutes. Turn to the lowest possible heat and cook for 30 minutes. Bring up to boil again for 8–10 minutes, then turn off the heat, cover the pan with tight-fitting lid and leave the chicken to stand in the liquid for 2 hours. To test if the chicken is tender, carefully insert a fine skewer into the back of the leg – if the chicken is cooked, the juices will run clear.

With your hands, carefully lift the cooled chicken out of the liquid and drain. Cut the bird into pieces and arrange on a serving platter with the Duck with Bean Paste and Five Spices. Garnish with Chinese leaves, cucumber and spring onion curls. Serve cold.

RIJSTTAFEL FEAST

When the Dutch East Indies became Indonesia in 1945, the *rijsttafel*, a Dutch word meaning 'rice table', stayed on. Meals in these islands have always centred around rice, the staple food, but the Dutch turned rice into a true feast – a full-scale *rijsttafel* consists of literally dozens of different dishes. This menu gives a selection of typical *rijsttafel* dishes that complement each other well in terms of colour, flavour and texture. Although the whole feast is quite time-consuming to make, many of the dishes can be made in advance and either refrigerated or frozen. Serve the food in a casual style, providing broad-rimmed soup plates and spoons and forks for eating. Guests should help themselves to rice first, moisten it with broth, then put portions of the other dishes on top.

FOR 10–12 PEOPLE

Boiled Rice
Vegetable Broth from Bali
Chicken with Turmeric
Eggs in Hot Spicy Sauce
Spiced Beef in Coconut Milk
Corn Fritters
Peanut Fritters (page 148)
Prawn Crackers (page 145)

Sayur Oelih

Vegetable Broth from Bali
This vegetable broth is used to 'moisten' the rice on your plate before spooning on a selection of other dishes from the *rijsttafel*. The vegetables may be varied according to seasonal availability and personal taste.

SERVES 6 as an individual dish

225 g (8 oz) green beans
salt
600 ml (1 pint) coconut milk (page 184)
1 garlic clove, peeled
2 macadamia nuts
1 cm ($\frac{1}{2}$ inch) cube terasi (shrimp paste)
2–3 teaspoons coriander seeds, dry-fried
3–4 tablespoons peanut or vegetable oil
1 medium onion, peeled and thinly sliced
2 bay leaves
225 g (8 oz) bean-sprouts
2 tablespoons lemon juice
bay leaves, to garnish (optional)

Top and tail the green beans, then cut into 2.5 cm (1 inch) lengths. Cook in boiling salted water for 3–4 minutes. Drain and set aside, reserving the cooking water.

Spoon off 3–4 tablespoons of cream which has risen to the top of the coconut milk and reserve. Pound the garlic to a paste in a mortar and pestle with the macadamia nuts, terasi and coriander seeds, or work in a food processor.

Heat the oil in a hot wok or large, heavy-based saucepan, add the onion and fry gently until soft and transparent. Remove from the pan with a perforated spoon and set aside. Add the pounded mixture and fry gently, stirring constantly, until it gives off a spicy aroma.

Pour in the reserved cooking water from the beans and the coconut milk and bring to the boil. Add the bay leaves and cook, uncovered, for 15–20 minutes. Just before serving, add the beans, fried onion, bean-sprouts, reserved coconut cream and the lemon juice. Taste and add salt, if necessary. Pour into a warmed serving bowl and garnish with bay leaves, if liked. Serve hot.

Ayam Kuning

Chicken with Turmeric

The yellow turmeric gives this mild-flavoured chicken dish a wonderfully rich colour, which contrasts with the dark brown of the Rendang Dagang/Spiced Beef in Coconut Milk (page 182) and the deep red of the Sambal Goreng Telur/Eggs in Hot Spicy Sauce (opposite).

SERVES 4 as an individual dish

1.5 kg (3–3½ lb) chicken, cut into 10–12
small pieces
salt
3 macadamia nuts
2 garlic cloves, peeled
1 large onion, peeled and roughly chopped
2.5 cm (1 inch) lengkuas (laos root), peeled and
sliced, or 1 teaspoon laos powder
2 stems lemon grass, or 1 teaspoon serai powder
1 cm (½ inch) cube terasi (shrimp paste)
1 tablespoon turmeric
4–6 tablespoons peanut or vegetable oil
1 tablespoon tamarind, soaked in 150 ml (¼ pint)
warm water for 10 minutes
300 ml (½ pint) coconut milk (page 184)
1 stem lemon grass, to garnish (optional)

Rub the chicken pieces with a little salt and set aside. Pound together the macadamia nuts and garlic in a mortar and pestle or work in a food processor, then add the onion, lengkuas or laos powder, lemon grass or serai powder, terasi and the turmeric. Pound or work again until the ingredients are well blended.

Heat the oil in a hot wok or large, heavy-based frying pan, add the pounded ingredients and fry gently without browning until they give off a spicy aroma. Add the chicken pieces and toss well to coat in the spices, then strain in the tamarind juice. Spoon off the cream which has risen to the top of the coconut milk and reserve. Add the coconut milk to the pan, cover and cook gently for 35–40 minutes, or until the chicken is tender. Just before serving, stir in the reserved coconut cream and bring back to the boil. Taste and add salt if necessary. Transfer to a warmed serving dish and garnish with lemon grass, if liked.

Sambal Goreng Telur

Eggs in Hot Spicy Sauce

Sambal Goreng sauce is immensely useful as a base for other ingredients besides the hard-boiled eggs suggested here. Make double the quantity of sauce and store half in the refrigerator or freezer for another occasion. For a main course for 4 people, try it with 450 g (1 lb) green beans, blanched, or 350 g (12 oz) chicken livers. Or, use only 5–6 hard-boiled eggs, with 225 g (8 oz) peeled cooked prawns.

SERVES 4 as an individual dish

2.5 cm (1 inch) cube terasi (shrimp paste)
2 onions, peeled and roughly chopped
2 garlic cloves, peeled
2.5 cm (1 inch) lengkuas (laos root), peeled and
sliced, or 1 teaspoon laos powder
1–2 tablespoons sambal ulek
2–4 fresh chillies, seeded, or 2 teaspoons
chilli powder
4–6 tablespoons peanut or vegetable oil
3–4 tablespoons tomato purée
400 ml (14 fl oz) stock or water
2 teaspoons tamarind, soaked in 4 tablespoons
warm water for 10 minutes
2 teaspoons brown sugar
1–2 tablespoons coconut cream (page 184)
salt
8 hard-boiled eggs, shelled
1–2 spring onion tops, shredded, to garnish

Pound the terasi to a paste in a mortar and pestle with the onions, garlic, lengkuas or laos powder, sambal ulek, and chillies or chilli powder, or work in a food processor. Heat the oil in a hot wok or large, heavy-based saucepan, add the paste and fry gently without browning until it gives off a spicy aroma.

Stir in the tomato purée and stock or water until well mixed, then simmer, uncovered, for a few minutes to concentrate the sauce.

Just before serving, strain in the tamarind juice; add the sugar, coconut cream or milk and salt to taste. Leave the hard-boiled eggs whole or cut in half, add to the sauce and heat through for a few minutes. Transfer carefully to a warmed serving dish and garnish with the spring onions. Serve hot.

Rendang Dagang

Spiced Beef in Coconut Milk

This is best cooked a day or two in advance, so that the rich blend of flavours has time to mellow. Traditionally, the meat should be almost dry, but a greater amount of sauce is often preferred in the West.

SERVES 4–6 as an individual dish

1 kg (2–2¼ lb) chuck steak
2 stems lemon grass, or 1 teaspoon serai powder
8 fresh chillies, or to taste, or 1–2 tablespoons sambal ulek (chilli paste)
1 teaspoon coriander seeds
1 teaspoon cumin seeds
6 cardamom pods, bruised
¼ teaspoon ground cinnamon, or 1 cinnamon stick, broken in half
4–6 tablespoons peanut or vegetable oil
2 large onions, peeled and finely chopped
3–4 garlic cloves, peeled and crushed
900 ml (1½ pints) coconut milk (page 184)
1 tablespoon tamarind, soaked in 50 ml (2 fl oz) warm water for 10 minutes
salt
Garnish:
crisp deep-fried onions (page 186)
a little shredded fresh red chilli

Cut the beef into neat, even-sized cubes and place in a bowl. If using lemon grass, pound the lower half of the stems in a mortar and pestle with the chillies (if using). Add to the meat and stir well to mix.

Dry-fry the coriander, cumin and cardamoms in a hot wok or large, heavy-based frying pan to draw out their full flavour. Remove the seeds from the cardamoms and discard the pods. Pound the seeds in a mortar and pestle with the coriander and cumin, then add the serai powder, sambal ulek (if using) and ground cinnamon or the cinnamon stick. Add the spices to the meat with the top half of the lemon grass stems (if using), mix well so that the meat is evenly coated and set aside.

Heat the oil in a hot wok or large, heavy-based saucepan, add the onions and garlic and fry gently until soft and transparent. Remove from the heat. Spoon off 4 tablespoons of the cream which has risen to the top of the coconut milk and reserve. Add the coconut milk to the softened onions and garlic in the pan, strain in the tamarind juice and bring to the boil. Add the spiced beef mixture, bring back to the boil, then add salt to taste. Cook gently, uncovered, for 2½ hours or until the sauce is much reduced and the meat tender. Stir in the reserved coconut cream, then transfer to a warmed serving dish. Just before serving garnish with crisp deep-fried onions and shredded chilli.

Perkedel Jagung

Corn Fritters

There is no doubt that freshly cooked sweetcorn is better for this recipe. Do not add salt to the water as this tends to toughen the kernels. Although the spring onion and celery leaves are optional, do try to include them if possible as they provide an attractive colour contrast to the golden yellow corn.

MAKES 20

2 corn-on-the-cob, or 350 g (12 oz) can sweetcorn, drained
2 macadamia nuts
1 garlic clove, peeled
1 medium onion, peeled
1 cm (½ inch) lengkuas (laos root), peeled and sliced, or ½ teaspoon laos powder
1 teaspoon ground coriander
peanut or vegetable oil, for frying
3 eggs
2 tablespoons desiccated coconut
salt
2 spring onions, finely shredded (optional)
few celery leaves, finely shredded (optional)

Cook the corn-on-the-cob in boiling unsalted water for 7–8 minutes. Drain, leave until cool enough to handle, then strip the corn from the cob using a sharp knife. Pound the macadamia nuts, garlic, onion, lengkuas or laos powder and coriander finely in a mortar and pestle, or work in a food processor. Heat 2–3 teaspoons oil in a wok or deep, heavy-based frying pan, add the pounded mixture and fry gently without browning until it gives off a spicy aroma. Remove from the heat.

Whisk the eggs, add the fried spices, coconut, salt to taste, corn and the spring onions and celery leaves (if using). Heat more oil in a deep frying pan and shallow-fry spoonfuls of the batter until deep golden on both sides. Remove with a perforated spoon and drain well on paper towels while frying the remainder. Serve immediately.

OPPOSITE: *Clockwise from top; Spiced Beef in Coconut Milk, Prawn Crackers (page 145), Chicken with Turmeric (page 181), Eggs in Hot Spicy Sauce (page 181), Corn Fritters, Vegetable Pickle (page 151), Vegetable Broth from Bali (page 180). Centre, boiled rice.*

GLOSSARY

Abura-age/JAPAN & KOREA. Fried beancurd, available ready-prepared in packets or frozen. It is often thinly sliced and included in salads and soups, or opened to make a pouch which is then filled with sushi (vinegared rice).

Agar-agar/CHINA. A seaweed derivative, available in long white strands or powdered form. It is colourless and tasteless, and when used in very small quantities it has the ability to set large volumes of liquid. Powdered gelatine may be used as a substitute suitable for non-vegetarians; allow 4 tablespoons gelatine to 25 g/1 oz agar-agar.

Ata/INDIA. A type of wholemeal flour used to make Indian unleavened breads. It is also known as *chappati* flour. Wholemeal flour can be used as a substitute.

Bagoong/SOUTH-EAST ASIA. A thick paste made from fermented shrimps or anchovies. It is an essential item in every Philippino home and is used to add piquancy and flavour to boiled rice and other cooked dishes.

Bamboo shoots/CHINA/JAPAN & KOREA/SOUTH-EAST ASIA. The tender young shoots which appear at the base of the bamboo are gathered at the end of the rainy season, parboiled and canned. After opening, store them in cold water which is changed daily, this way they will keep for about 7 days. Canned bamboo shoots are available sliced or unsliced.

Banana leaves/SOUTH-EAST ASIA. Traditionally used for wrapping food to be cooked, banana leaves also impart a special flavour. In the Far-East they are also used as a convenient wrapping to contain foods bought from markets or roadside stalls. Aluminium foil is a suitable alternative.

Bananas, green/SOUTH-EAST ASIA. Sometimes known as *plantains*, these bananas can only be eaten cooked. They should retain their firm, starchy consistency even when fried or boiled.

Bangkwang/SOUTH-EAST ASIA. Sometimes known as *chinese turnip*, this crisp-textured vegetable is frequently used in stir-fry and spring roll recipes. If not available, used a crisp green apple or celeriac.

Bean curd/CHINA/JAPAN & KOREA/SOUTH-EAST ASIA. Known as *tofu* in Japan and Korea, bean curd is made from puréed soya beans. It is soft, white and has a cheese-like texture, which ranges from firm to 'silken'. Bean curd is high in protein and very low in fat, and is therefore highly nutritious. It has a bland flavour but blends well with other ingredients. Fresh bean curd will keep fresh for several days if stored in the refrigerator; vacuum-packed long-life bean curd is also available and will keep for several months. For *fried bean curd*, see Abura-age.

Bean paste, sweetened red/CHINA. This reddish-brown paste is made from puréed red beans and crystallized sugar. It is sold in cans and should be refrigerated after opening. If unavailable, sweetened chestnut purée can be used as a substitute.

Bean sauce/CHINA. Both black bean sauce and yellow bean sauce are widely used in China. Both are made from salted soya beans that have been ground to a paste and mixed with flour and spices. Bean sauce is sold in cans or jars and should be refrigerated after opening.

Bean-sprouts/CHINA/SOUTH-EAST ASIA. Fresh bean-sprouts, grown from mung or soya beans, are now widely available. They can be stored for up to 2 days in the refrigerator. To blanch bean-sprouts, pour boiling water over them, drain, then plunge into iced water; drain again and use as directed.

Beans, salted/CHINA/SOUTH-EAST ASIA. Both black and yellow salted beans are available, although black salted beans are more common. They are soya beans which have been steamed, spiced and preserved in salt. Sold in cans or packets, they will keep for up to 1 year.

Beefsteak leaves/JAPAN & KOREA, see Shiso leaves.

Beni-shoga/JAPAN & KOREA. Sweet pickled root ginger traditionally used to garnish *sushi* (vinegared rice) dishes.

Besan/INDIA. A very fine flour made from ground chick peas. It should be sieved before use as it tends to form hard lumps during storage.

Blachan/SOUTH-EAST ASIA. Known in Malaysia by this name, or as *balachan*, this pungent shrimp paste is used extensively throughout South-East Asia, and is called *kapi* in Thailand, *terasi* in Indonesia and *ngapi* in Burma. It is available in large blocks although very small amounts are used. Blachan should be dry-fried or gently heated before use. It will keep almost indefinitely.

Buah keras/SOUTH-EAST ASIA, see Macadamia nuts.

Burdock/JAPAN & KOREA, see Gobo.

Candlenuts/SOUTH-EAST ASIA, see Macadamia nuts.

Cellophane noodles/CHINA, see Noodles.

Channa dal/INDIA. Also known as chick peas, channa dal are one of India's most popular and versatile pulses. Channa dal are also ground into the fine flour known as *besan*.

Chappati/INDIA. A type of unleavened bread made with *ata* flour, a coarse textured wheat flour. Wholemeal flour can be used as an alternative.

Chilli bean paste/CHINA. A fermented bean paste mixed with chilli and other seasonings. Sold in jars, the sauce varies in strength according to the brand purchased.

Chilli paste/SOUTH-EAST ASIA, see Sambal ulek.

Chilli sauce/CHINA. A very hot sauce made from chillies, vinegar and salt. Usually sold in bottles, it should be used sparingly in cooking, or as a dip. Tabasco sauce can be used as a substitute.

Chinese dried mushrooms/CHINA/SOUTH-EAST ASIA, see Shiitake mushrooms

Chinese leaves/CHINA/JAPAN & KOREA/SOUTH-EAST ASIA. Now widely available in the West, Chinese leaves or *pe-tsai* are a cylinder of tightly-packed crinkly leaves. They are used in many different types of dishes, including; stir-fries, salads, casseroles and pickles.

Chinese turnip/SOUTH-EAST ASIA, see Bangkwang.

Citrus leaves/SOUTH-EAST ASIA. These dark green glossy leaves come from the kaffir lime, papeda or magrut. They should be torn before use so that they impart their distinctive citrus flavour. Grapefruit or lime zest can be used as a substitute.

Cloud ears/CHINA/SOUTH-EAST ASIA, see Wood ears.

Coconut/SOUTH-EAST ASIA/INDIA. Both the meat and milk of the coconut are used extensively. A fresh coconut should feel heavy and sound full of juice when the nut is shaken. The 'eye' should be dry and free from mould. After breaking open the shell, the coconut meat can be prised away. Coconut juice is *not* coconut milk; it is not used in cooking but does make a refreshing drink. To make 450 ml (¾ pint) *coconut milk and cream*: empty 225 g (8 oz) unsweetened desiccated coconut into a food processor or blender. Pour over 450 ml (¾ pint) boiling hot water and process for 20–30 seconds. Turn into a large bowl and add an extra 150 ml (¼ pint) hot water. Leave to cool, then strain the coconut milk through a fine sieve (lined with muslin if possible), squeezing the coconut to extract the milk. Cover and store in the refrigerator; the *coconut cream* will quickly rise to the surface and can be skimmed off for separate use if required. To *dry-fry coconut*, place the measured amount of desiccated coconut into a frying pan or wok over a low heat. Stir continuously for 5–8 minutes, or until the coconut is golden and crisp.

Daikon/JAPAN/SOUTH-EAST ASIA. Also called *Japanese radish* and known as *moolie* in South-East Asia; the daikon is a long white radish which has a crisp texture. It is used extensively as a garnish when grated, sliced and carved, and as a cooked vegetable.

Dashi/JAPAN. Made with dried bonito flakes (*Katsuo bushi*) and seaweed (*Konbu*), dashi is the basic Japanese stock and is used in many recipes. Dashi is easy to make, but sachets of instant dashi mix, which sell under the name of *dashi-no-moto*, are available for added convenience.

Fish sauce/SOUTH-EAST ASIA. Fish sauce is to South-East Asian food what soy sauce is to Chinese. It is prepared from fresh anchovies and salt which have been fermented for several months in wooden barrels. Also known as *nam pla* or *patis*, fish sauce is pale to dark brown in colour and serves to accentuate the flavour of the food, rather than add a 'fishy' flavour. There is no real substitute.

Five-spice powder/CHINA/SOUTH-EAST ASIA. An aromatic seasoning made from a selection of five ground spices; star anise, fennel, cloves, cinnamon and sichuan pepper. Use sparingly as it has an intense flavour.

Full fat milk powder/INDIA. Used in many Indian sweet recipes as a substitute for *Khoa* (milk condensed by slow boiling). Baby milk formula is suitable, but skimmed milk powder is not.

Galingale/SOUTH-EAST ASIA, see Lengkuas.

Garam masala/INDIA. A blend of ground spices used in many savoury dishes. It can be bought ready-made but tastes fresher if made at home. To make Garam Masala, dry-fry the following spices for 5–6 minutes: 1 tablespoon coriander seeds, 1 tablespoon cumin seeds, 2 teaspoons cardamom seeds, 2 teaspoons whole cloves, 2 teaspoons mace, 7 cm (3 inch) cinnamon stick, 1 tablespoon black peppercorns and 1 teaspoon grated nutmeg. Grind the spices to a fine powder in a mill or pestle and mortar and store in an airtight jar.

Ghee/INDIA. Clarified butter is used to fry ingredients for many Indian dishes. It is made by melting butter and separating the fat from the solids. Ghee can be heated to much higher temperatures than butter. A vegetable ghee substitute is also available.

Gingko nuts/JAPAN & KOREA. Gingko nuts have a delicate flavour and texture and are usually available in cans. Both the shell and inner skin should be removed before use.

Gobo/JAPAN & KOREA. More commonly known as *burdock*, gobo is a long, slender root vegetable with a crunchy texture. Both fresh and canned burdock is available.

Golden needles/SOUTH-EAST ASIA, see Lily buds.

Guava/INDIA. The skin of the guava fruit varies from yellow to purple and the flesh from pale green to pink. They are available fresh, or canned in syrup.

Hoisin sauce/CHINA/SOUTH-EAST ASIA. Also known as barbecue sauce, it is made from soya beans, sugar, flour, vinegar, salt, garlic, chilli and sesame seed oil. It is sold in cans or jars and will keep for several months after opening, if stored in the refrigerator.

Ikan bilis/SOUTH-EAST ASIA. Literally translated, means 'little fish'. They resemble tiny dried whitebait and are used in fish stocks, or deep-fried and crumbled over Malay curries.

Kalonji/INDIA. Small black tear-shaped onion seeds; used to add piquancy to vegetable curries and Indian breads.

Kanpyo/JAPAN & KOREA. Long, dried, ribbon-like strips from an edible gourd; used for tying and securing foods, or cooked with vegetables or fish. It must be salted and soaked before use.

Kapi/SOUTH-EAST ASIA, see Blachan.

Karela/INDIA. A bitter gourd often used in vegetable curries. It has an ugly, knobbly appearance and is available fresh or canned.

Katsuo-bushi/JAPAN & KOREA. The dried fillet of a bonito fish. When flaked it is one of the most essential ingredients in Japanese cooking, as it is used as the basic flavouring in *dashi*. It is also used as a garnish and is available ready-flaked.

Kecap manis/SOUTH-EAST ASIA. A sweet soy sauce used extensively in Indonesian recipes.

Kemiri/SOUTH-EAST ASIA, see Macadamia nuts.

Khoa/INDIA, see Full fat milk powder.

Konbu/JAPAN & KOREA. Dried kelp (seaweed); it is a basic ingredient used to flavour *dashi* and other dishes. It is also used as a vegetable in its own right.

Kon-nyaku/JAPAN & KOREA. A dense, gelatinous cake prepared from arum roots. Available in packets or canned.

Lai fan/SOUTH-EAST ASIA, see Noodles.

Laos powder/SOUTH-EAST ASIA, see Lengkuas.

Lemon grass/SOUTH-EAST ASIA. An aromatic herb, available as fresh stems or dried as *serai* powder. To use fresh lemon grass, chop or slice the lower part of the stem, or bruise the whole stalk. If used whole, the lemon grass should be removed before serving. If using serai powder, use 1 teaspoon of serai powder for each stem of lemon grass specified in the recipe.

Lengkuas/SOUTH-EAST ASIA. A delicately pine-flavoured root also known as *galingale* or dried as *laos powder*. If using laos powder, substitute 1 teaspoon of laos powder for each 1 cm (½ inch) piece of lengkuas specified in the recipe.

Lily buds/CHINA/SOUTH-EAST ASIA. Dried buds, golden-yellow in colour and also known as *golden needles*. They should be soaked in water before use.

Lotus roots/JAPAN & KOREA, see Renkon.

Lychees/CHINA. An oriental fruit that grows in bunches like cherries. They have a hard, knobbly shell that is peeled away to reveal delicately-flavoured white flesh.

Macadamia nuts/SOUTH-EAST ASIA. A 'waxy' nut the size of a large hazelnut. They are also known as *buah keras*, *candlenuts* or *Kemiri*. When pounded, the nuts are used as a thickening agent.

Magrut/SOUTH-EAST ASIA. An ugly-looking citrus fruit with strongly flavoured peel and leaves. Grapefruit or lime rind can be used as a substitute.

Mee/SOUTH-EAST ASIA, see Noodles.

Mien/SOUTH-EAST ASIA, see Noodles.

Mirin/JAPAN & KOREA. A sweet rice wine. It has a very low alcohol content and is used in many Japanese dishes to add a subtle sweetness. If unavailable use 1 teaspoon sugar for each tablespoon mirin.

Miso/JAPAN & KOREA. A rich, savoury paste made from fermented soya beans. It is widely used particularly for miso soup. There are several varieties available; white (or light) miso and red miso are the more common types.

Monosodium glutamate/CHINA. Also known as 'taste essence'. It is used to bring out the natural flavours in food.

Moolie/JAPAN & KOREA, see Daikon.

Nam pla/SOUTH-EAST ASIA, see Fish Sauce.

Ngapi/SOUTH-EAST ASIA, see Blachan.

Niboshi/JAPAN & KOREA. Tiny dried sardines, sometimes used to make *dashi*.

Noodles/CHINA/JAPAN & KOREA/SOUTH-EAST ASIA. Made from rice, pulses or wheat, noodles form a major part of the staple diet in the Orient. Rice vermicelli or *lai fan* should be soaked in water, then boiled for 10–15 minutes. They can also be deep-fried in small quantities straight from the packet and used as an attractive, crisp accompaniment. Cellophane noodles or *mien* are made from mung beans. They are sold in bundles that resemble skeins of wool, and should be soaked in boiling hot water for 3 minutes. Although they have little flavour they have a pleasant gelatinous texture. Egg noodles or *mee* are sometimes available fresh and like fresh pasta they cook very quickly. Dried egg noodles should be soaked for 10 minutes prior to cooking. Japanese noodles come in a variety of types and sizes: *udon* noodles are broad white ribbons made from wheat, *soba* are made from buckwheat, and *shirataki* are gelatinous noodles made from yam-flour.

Nori/JAPAN & KOREA. The dried sheet form of 'laver' seaweed. Nori is used to roll around sushi (vinegared rice) and when cut into slivers, as a garish. Nori should be lightly toasted before use.

Onions, crisp deep-fried/SOUTH-EAST ASIA. Used as an accompaniment or garnish to many dishes. To prepare: finely slice 2–3 medium sized onions. Separate the slices and deep-fry in hot oil until deep golden brown. Drain well on paper towels, then store in an airtight container in the refrigerator for up to 10 days.

Oyster sauce/CHINA. A dark brown sauce made from extract of oysters, salt and starch.

Padek/SOUTH-EAST ASIA, see Bagoong.

Patis/SOUTH-EAST ASIA, see Fish sauce.

Persimmons/JAPAN & KOREA. Also known as *sharon fruit*, they look like large, orange-coloured tomatoes. When ripe, persimmons are soft and sweet. Dried persimmons are also available; they should be soaked in water before eating.

Pe-tsai/CHINA, see Chinese leaves.

Plantains/SOUTH-EAST ASIA, see Bananas, green.

Renkon/JAPAN & KOREA. More commonly known as lotus roots. Used in savoury dishes and when cut in a cross section they form an attractive flower-like garnish. Available fresh or canned.

Rice cakes/JAPAN & KOREA. Made by pounding boiled glutinous rice and forming it into small chewy white cakes. They are grilled and eaten with soy sauce, or added to soups.

Rice flour, brown and white/SOUTH-EAST ASIA. Used as a thickening agent, rice flour can be purchased ready-ground, or made at home by grinding rice in an electric blender.

Rice paper wrappers/SOUTH-EAST ASIA. Used for wrapping diced ingredients. Before use the dried rounds should be placed on a damp teatowel and brushed with cold water so that they become soft and maliable.

Rice vinegar/JAPAN & KOREA. A light, delicately-flavoured vinegar, used particularly for making sushi (vinegared rice). If unavailable diluted cider vinegar makes an acceptable substitute.

Rice wine, Chinese/CHINA/SOUTH-EAST ASIA, see Sake.

Rice/INDIA/CHINA/JAPAN & KOREA/SOUTH-EAST ASIA. Without exception, rice is the staple food of the Orient. *Basmati* is the most expensive Indian rice, prized for its length of grain and aromatic flavour. Patna is another popular variety of Indian rice. *Glutinous rice* is used mainly in South-East Asia; when cooked, it sticks together making it easy to eat with the fingers. *Black glutinous rice* retains its outer husk and has a nutty flavour. Short grain *Japanese rice* also clings together when boiled or steamed, which makes it ideal for making sushi (vinegared rice) dishes.

Sake/JAPAN & KOREA. A rice wine, made by fermenting freshly steamed white rice. Sake is the national drink of Japan. Lower quality sake is used extensively in cooking. Rice wine is

also used in China and South-East Asia. If rice wine is unavailable, a very dry sherry can be substituted.
Sambal rojak/SOUTH-EAST ASIA. A thick treacle-like mixture which is made from fermented shrimps and soya bean paste. It is used in salads and often stirred into soups.
Sambal ulek/SOUTH-EAST ASIA. A paste made from fresh chillies and salt. It can be purchased ready-made or prepared at home: 2 fresh chillies and ½ teaspoon salt, pounded together until smooth, will make about 2 teaspoons of Sambal ulek. Cover closely and store in the refrigerator or the freezer.
Sansho powder/JAPAN & KOREA. A greenish-brown ground spice, made from the pod of the sansho tree. The powder is used in small quantities to season cooked foods.
Sausages, Chinese/CHINA/SOUTH-EAST ASIA. Long, thin salami-type sausages which should be steamed for 10–15 minutes before use.
Serai powder/SOUTH-EAST ASIA, see Lemon grass.
Sesame seeds/INDIA/CHINA/JAPAN & KOREA/SOUTH-EAST ASIA. Used as seeds to add flavour and texture, their taste is accentuated if dry-fried. *Sesame paste* or *sauce* is made by pounding the seeds and is widely available in Middle Eastern stores under the name *tahini*. *Sesame seed oil* is used for its flavour rather than for frying, as it burns very easily.

Sharon fruit/JAPAN & KOREA, see Persimmons.
Shichimi pepper/JAPAN & KOREA. A mixture of seven ingredients: chilli, black pepper, dried orange peel, sesame seeds, poppy seeds, nori seaweed and hemp seeds. They are ground to a spicy hot powder which is often used on noodles.
Shiitake mushrooms/JAPAN & KOREA. Known as *Chinese dried mushrooms* in China and South-East Asia. Usually available dried, they should be soaked for 25–30 minutes, and the tough stem discarded.

Shirataki/JAPAN & KOREA, see Noodles.
Shiso leaves/JAPAN & KOREA. Used as a garnish and in dishes such as vegetable tempura. They are sometimes called *beefsteak leaves*.
Shoya/JAPAN & KOREA, see Soy sauce.
Sichuan pepper/CHINA. Reddish-brown peppercorns which have a stronger, more fragrant flavour than black peppercorns.
Soba/JAPAN & KOREA, see Noodles.
Somen/JAPAN & KOREA, see Noodles.
Soy sauce/CHINA/JAPAN & KOREA/SOUTH-EAST ASIA. Made from fermented soya beans, soy sauce is used extensively throughout the Orient as a seasoning and condiment. Chinese *light soy sauce* has a more delicate flavour than the richer *dark soy sauce*. *Japanese soy sauce*, sometimes called *shoya*, has a completely different flavour to other soy sauces and therefore should always be used in Japanese cooking.
Straw mushrooms/CHINA. Smooth oval-shaped mushrooms, which add a distinctive flavour and texture to Chinese dishes. They are available in cans.

Tamarind/INDIA/SOUTH-EAST ASIA. An acidic fruit resembling a bean pod. Usually sold dried or pulped. It must be made into tamarind water before using: soak about 25 g (1 oz) tamarind in 300 ml (½ pint) warm water for 5–10 minutes (the longer the tamarind is left to soak, the stronger the flavour). The pulp should be squeezed and the liquid strained before use.
Terasi/SOUTH-EAST ASIA, see Blachan.
Tofu/JAPAN & KOREA, see Bean curd.
Tsukemono/JAPAN & KOREA. Japanese pickled vegetables are available ready-made in vacuum packs and jars. They are traditionally served at every Japanese meal.

Udon/JAPAN & KOREA, see Noodles.
Urhad dal/INDIA. An Indian pulse, the seeds of which are usually sold as lentils. Ground urhad dal are used to make poppadoms.

Varak/INDIA. Silver leaf, known as varak, is used as a decoration for both sweet and savoury dishes. It is safe to eat, but aluminium foil should *not* be used as a substitute.

Wakami/JAPAN & KOREA. A young seaweed with long green fronds and a smooth texture. It is used in soups and salads.
Wasabi powder/JAPAN & KOREA. Also known as *Japanese horseradish*, wasabi powder is in fact the grated root of a riverside plant. It has a powerful flavour and is traditionally served with raw fish dishes. Available in tubes or in powder form, wasabi powder should be mixed with cold water before use.

Water chestnuts/CHINA/JAPAN & KOREA/SOUTH-EAST ASIA. A walnut-sized bulb with brown skin. Inside, the flesh is white and crisp. Canned water chestnuts are ready-peeled. Once opened, and with regular changes of water, canned water chestnuts will keep in the refrigerator for up to 2 weeks.
Wonton skins/CHINA. Made from wheat flour, egg and water, these wafer-thin wrappers are sold in 7.5 cm (3 inch) squares. They can be deep-fried on their own and served with a piquant dip sauce, or filled with a savoury mixture and then steamed, deep-fried or boiled. Wonton wrappers can be stored in the freezer for up to 6 months, and thaw in 5–10 minutes.
Wood ears, dried/CHINA/SOUTH-EAST ASIA. Also known as *cloud ears* they are dried black fungi which should be soaked in water before use. When fully soaked they look gelatinous and have a crunchy texture.

INDEX